C000161996

Sex

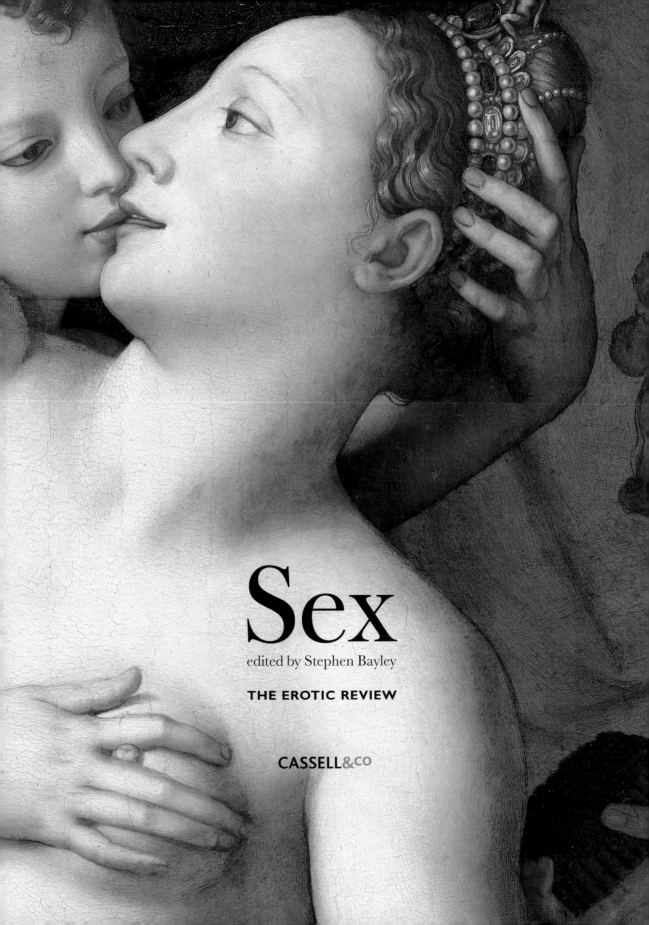

Sex

edited by Stephen Bayley

THE EROTIC REVIEW

CASSELL&CO

Contents

Introduction

'Stick your finger up my arse, old man

Thrust cazzo in a little at a time,

Lift up my leg, manoeuvre well,

Now pound with all inhibitions gone.'

SONNETTI LUSSURIOSI, Aretino

Introduction

The Nooks of Lechery
By way of introduction

Stephen Bayley

TO DISCOURAGE THE ARISTOCRATIC FASHION for sodomy, Venetian prostitutes used to pose topless on The Bridge of Tits in the Carampane district. Half a millennium later, *Moby Dick* (1851), Herman Melville's great story about man being all at sea with the forces of Nature, was banned in England not for any lewd suggestiveness in the title, but because the narrative included inflammatory words such as 'underclothes'. We are now more familiar and less uncomfortable with sexually explicit material. If Modernism is the defining influence on contemporary culture, sex helped Modernism define itself.

Frank depictions of nudity in art and film, literary descriptions of all styles of couplings, expletives becoming common currency…all these democratisations – some would say vulgarisations – of sex have been construed as a refreshing assault on the prudish claustrophobia of the past. There's no better way to demonstrate your break with convention than to make a prostitute rather than a saint the subject of your art, as Schiele, Dix, Grosz, Picasso and many others all did. A revolution in taste that began in artists' studios has found its way onto the street. It was once considered shocking in the West – as it remains in south-east Asia – for a woman to reveal her upper arm in public. Now a very high level of sexual innuendo is commonplace and an almost equally vertiginous level of explicitness is familiar. In the mid-1990s ads were run in the United States with the copyline 'This is Debbie [an impressively busty woman] she wants you to have this pair in your car.' The ads were in fact selling molybdenum and Teflon grease guns to the motor trade. By 2001, British cities were hosting forty-eight-sheet posters boldly carrying the letters FCUK; in the same year the normally demure British *Vogue* used nipples in its advertising.

OPPOSITE: *The Romanian early Modernist sculptor, Constanin Brancusi was a pioneer of abstract sculpture, with a superb sense of form. His* Princess X *(1916) was clearly inspired by a real phallus.*

LEFT: *Grosz returned from military service to Berlin in 1918 even more convinced of society's insanity. He made satirical drawings and paintings of corruption and low life, especially whores and gamblers, documenting the anticipated collapse of capitalist society.* Beauty, thee I praise *was painted in 1919.*

The only victim of this democratisation of sex has been modesty, although the boundary between agreeable titillation and sordid taboo may have shifted a little, as has the line between exciting frankness and dismaying vulgarity: a rap record popular as I write this has a chorus whose refrain is

'I want to fuck you'. But there is a firm distinction between erotica and pornography. We get the word 'erotic' from the Greek god of love, Eros, who was known to the Romans as Cupid and known to us for his bow and arrow. 'Pornography' comes from the Greek and means the description of the lives and activities of prostitutes. You might define the distinction as the difference between natural and commercial love, but there is another distinction too. Eroticism has its ancient basis in magic and religion and finds expression in art while pornography is based in cruelty and coercion and finds expression in crime.

In ancient Greece Phallophores carrying phallic images on the ends of sticks were a regular sight in religious processions. In Rome and Hindustan the gods Priapus and Siva had a specific – and indeed rather active – sexual character. To some archaeological authorities, the plan of the Christian church, itself derived from the Roman basilica, with its sequence of entrances and spaces, is an architectural symbol of the female reproductive system. In medieval times brothels were known as 'abbayes', the source of an association between the Church and sex that has stimulated erotic art and literature from Chaucer to Diderot. The sanctified state of sacerdotal celibacy was not known to all the Holy Fathers. Any amateur of Renaissance history knows that the odour attending a great many popes was not one of sanctity, rather of lubricity. Although it has a primarily forensic rather than erotic character, the existence in the Vatican of a *sedia stercoraria* is revealing of how blatant sexual matters were in the Church. This chair, somewhat like a commode, allowed properly appointed officials to feel the dangling testicles of cardinals who were candidates for the papacy, this as a check against the possibility of electing a female Pope.

Maurice Girodias, influential boulevardier and proprietor of Paris' Olympia Press, the independent publisher of many of the twentieth century's greatest writers, insisted on making literary judgements to distinguish between erotica and pornography. On the whole, as patron of Henry Miller, J.P. Donleavy, Lawrence Durrell, Vladimir Nabokov, Samuel Beckett, Jean Genet, Raymond Queneau and William S. Burroughs, he was right, although he did not entirely escape criticism for printing words that even in the 1950s and '60s were still taboo, although he insisted that four-letter words never hurt anyone.

A useful touchstone in testing for the existence of pornography was provided in the US courts by Justice Brennan who defined obscenity as that which was 'utterly without redeeming social importance'. These taboos were, however, relatively recent, products of an age of excessive delicacy eloquently described by Catherine Johns in *Sex or Symbol* (1983).

We are only now shrugging off that delicacy and this very book is evidence of the phenomenon. But it would be wrong to assume a historically specific taste for delicacy which tended to suppress sex was a universal characteristic of Western culture, still less of others. Scottish poet William Dunbar's *A Bout of Wooing* (1503) contains possibly the first printed 'fuck'. Shakespeare enjoyed erotic wordplay and made multilingual sexual puns. The lewd Pistol, to offer just one of hundreds of examples, says in *Henry IV* 'A foutra for the world and the worldling's base!' 'Foutra' being derived from the French *foutre* for 'fuck'. Nor did verbal (or indeed any other) taboos concern to the smallest degree the seventeenth-century English poet John Wilmot, Earl of Rochester, who gave us characters including 'Queen Cuntigratia', 'Fuckadilla' and 'Buggeranthos'. Jesse Sheidlower, a lexicologist, confirms in his book *The F-Word* (1995) that even in the puritanical United States, the journey away from such sanctimonious 'decency' has begun. He tells us that when a guest on *The Jerry Springer Show* used the twelve-letter word 'motherfucker' on air, only the 'u' was bleeped.

The old sex gods are now fully integrated into the modern world, but it was a fascinating process. 'To conquer Priapus', H. Cutner says in *A Short History of Sex Worship* (1940), Christianity 'had to…admit some of the Pagan rites and call them Christian ceremonies'. An edict of Charlemagne's from the ninth century is hilariously eloquent on the sexual and moral licence of the Early Church: 'We have been informed, to our great horror, that many monks are addicted to debauchery and all sorts of vile abominations, even to unnatural sins…We command our monks to stop swarming about the country, and we forbid our nuns to practice fornication and intoxication. We shall not allow them any longer to be whores, thieves, murderers &c; to spend their time in singing improper songs. Priests are herewith forbidden to haunt the taverns and marketplaces for the purpose of seducing mothers and daughters.'

BELOW: *Thomas Rowlandson was the finest satirical draughtsman of his day in Britain. The watercolour* Behind Convent Walls *(c.1800) is typical of the fantastical, bawdy scenes he painted to earn a living (after squandering an inheritance on gambling).*

In the latter Middle Ages women would go to Mass wearing a Roman *fascinum*, a phallic amulet: the British Museum's Secretum contains many astonishing examples of winged penises turned into hatpins for Christian pilgrims. These had an explicit character both erotic and religious, surviving evidence of pagan belief and, one assumes, pagan practice. Chaucer and Boccaccio, Marguerite d'Angoulême and Rabelais are the best observers of this medieval bawdy. Boccaccio said wise teachers should encourage the young to read Ovid's *Ars Amatoria* (1 BC), the Roman love manual. Renaissance erotica was more refined, less robust, but just as sexual. Sixteenth-century Italian poet Pietro Aretino has been described by the American scholar Lynne Lawner as 'the first journalist and publicist of the modern world'. It is therefore unsurprising that this pioneer of PR wrote the most notorious of all sex books. Aretino's *Sonnetti Lussuriosi* were composed as a commentary on erotic drawings made in 1524 by his friend, the architect Giulio Romano. Subsequently engraved by Marcantonio Raimondi, Romano's drawings were of sixteen variously ambitious sexual

positions, or *I Modi*, known in English as *Aretine's Postures*. Notoriously out of circulation for four hundred years, the rediscovery of *I Modi* at the beginning of the twentieth century made it a classic of erotic publishing.

A brief reading of the *Sonnetti* provides a stirring reprimand to those who feel our contemporary obsession with sex is destructive of civilised values. In Lynne Lawner's robust translation (of 1982, a different source from the

LEFT: *This early fifteenth-century manuscript by the Master of Lancelot is a treatise on health. The illustration shows coitus.*

one Evelyn Welch uses in her discussion of depictions of sexuality in her essay on the Renaissance, 'Facing Flesh') our lascivious hero says:

Let's fottere, my love, let's fottere,
Since all of us were born only to fottere.
You adore the cazzo and I adore the potta.
The world would be nothing without this act…
Don't leave out my balls –
Take them inside the potta.

Another sonnet begins with the woman memorably saying:

Stick your finger up my arse, old man
Thrust cazzo in a little at a time,
Lift up my leg, manoeuvre well,
Now pound with all inhibitions gone.
I believe this is a tastier feast
Than eating garlic bread before a fire.
If you don't like the potta, try the back way:
A real man has to be a bugger.

fottere = fuck
cazzo = prick
potta = cunt

Pope Clement VII ordered *I Modi* to be burned; the engraver, Raimondi, was imprisoned and a death sentence was threatened against anyone attempting a new edition. The severity of this papal reaction suggests that *I Modi*'s lustful, energetic and irreverent invitation to sex was a pagan challenge to the Church.

Chaucer and Aretino map the narrative and technical – even gymnastic – limits of eroticism, but nudity itself has not always been a dominant consideration in sexual transactions. Japanese lovers are often depicted fully clothed and in Hindu culture today, it is not unusual for a husband never to have seen his wife entirely naked. Sixteenth-century French essayist Michel de Montaigne found the prospect of total nakedness off-putting and warned against too close an inspection of the nooks of lechery: 'The skillfullest [*sic*] masters of amorous dalliance appoint for a remedy of venerous passions a full survey of the body.'

An opposing view came from Robert Burton. His *The Anatomy of Melancholy* (1621) contains one of the very first accounts in English of the specific role of nudity in erotica: 'The very sight of the naked parts causeth enormous concupiscences and stirs up both men and women in burning lust.'

Despite the continuous presence of eroticism in culture since a Sumerian first incised a symbolic slit in a stone found in the desert, or a magician in Willendorf fashioned an earth mother who combined in her ripe proportions the dual stimuli of fertility and sex, constraining forces – social, moral, practical, medical – have tended to keep sex stimulatingly furtive. The Elizabethan magician, Simon Forman, used Latin in his description of his sexual encounters for the purposes of discretion. For the same reason Samuel Pepys, in a diary note for 16 January 1664, disguised his embarrassment in execrable franglais when he wrote that at the cabaret with Mrs Lane, 'Je l'ay foutée sous de la chaise deux times, and the last to my great pleasure.'

In England, sexual puritanism was an active social force by the early eighteenth century. The first book to be banned for its erotic – as opposed to political or religious – content was *The Fifteen Plagues of a Maidenhead* (1707). As a result, the notorious *Fanny Hill, or the Memoirs of a Woman of Pleasure* (1749), an early masterpiece of dedicated erotica, in fact uses restrained language. Here you will find little more frank than: 'the emotion grew so violent that it almost intercepted my respiration.' Giovanni Giacomo Casanova spent so much time in the act of seduction that he had to postpone the writing of his remarkable memoirs until the very end of his life. Eventually published in twelve volumes in France between 1826 and 1838, they too are elegant and inoffensive, if undeniably erotic. As Brillat-Savarin was a philosopher in the kitchen, so Casanova was a philosopher of the bedroom, although that title was, in fact, assumed by his near contemporary, the Marquis de Sade, whose *La Philosophie dans le Boudoir* (1788) is only one volume in his massive encyclopaedia of sexual

ABOVE: *Japanese* shunga
*prints illustrated a 'floating
world' of highly aestheticised
sensuality. This woodcut
of a couple making love by a*
hibachi *is in the style of
Eisen (1790–1848).
Originally presented as one of a
series of twelve (one for each
month) the symbolism of the
kettle on hot coals would
instantly have been understood
by collectors.*

perversions, which included the astonishing *Les 120 Journées de Sodome ou l'Ecole du Libertinage* (1785). In *Justine* (1781), for instance, we find cannibalism, coprophagy, vampirism, Satanism, pederasty and other cruel practices, all of which gave the world the term Sadism. The Marquis, who spent twenty-seven years of his life in prison as a consequence of his reckless dissipation, died in the lunatic asylum of Charenton. Some say he suffered from what was called a 'libertine dementia', although the alienist Royer-Collard, then head of the asylum, declared him to be quite sane.

De Sade recognised what British sex psychologist Henry Havelock Ellis called the 'immense importance of the sexual question'. De Sade wrote:

If there are beings in the world whose acts shock all accepted prejudices, we must not preach at them or punish them…because their bizarre tastes no more depend upon themselves than it depends on you whether you are witty or stupid…What would become of

OPPOSITE: *A classic Persian erotic miniature, c.1750, entitled* A couple making love on a terrace.

OVERLEAF: *François Boucher's* The Odalisque *(1745). An 'odalisque' is a female slave, a motif which has inspired hundreds of artists to paint voluptuous nudes.*

your laws, your morality, your religion, your gallows, your Paradise, your gods, your hell, if it were shown that such and such fluids, such fibres, or a certain acridity in the blood, or in the animal spirits, alone suffice to make a man the object of your punishments or your rewards?

The era of Casanova and de Sade – not to mention Boucher, painter of one of the most blatant invitations to sex since Pompeii – was also the age of Thomas Bowdler whose ten-volume *Family Shakespeare* (1818) purged all the Swan of Avon's bawdy the better to protect British youth from vice of a sexual character. Not satisfied with unmanning literature, Bowdler went on to castrate history and censored Edward Gibbon's *Decline and Fall of the Roman Empire* (1776–88) of all its ripe descriptions of a chorus of Syrian damsels performing their lascivious dances to the sound of (barbarian) music. Bowdler was the intellectual ancestor of the Victorian prudes, or what the publisher Maurice Girodias called 'the hounds of decency'.

But Victoria's Great Britain also had its brilliant champions of erotica. Sir Richard Burton's translation of *The Thousand and One Nights* (1885–88) is a monument to intelligent liberalism, as well as to scholarship. But, even the distinguished soldier-poet Burton could not entirely escape the repressive Spirit of the Age: his wife burned his translation of the *Kama Sutra* (as well as his diaries) in order to maintain his sound reputation. The High Victorians employed the evasive euphemism 'curious and uncommon' to describe erotica. And with a thoroughness appropriate to that age of giants, High Victoriana produced one of the greatest erotomaniacs of them all, the bibliographer Henry Spencer Ashbee who, under the name Pisanus Fraxi (a smutty conflation of Fraxinus for 'ash' and Apis for 'bee'), left fifteen thousand volumes of sex books to the British Museum. This donation was something of a moral victory for Ashbee, achieved only when he made it clear to the reluctant Museum authorities that the gift of his more sober collection of illustrated copies of *Don Quixote* was conditional on acceptance of the sex books.

Ashbee's collection went blushing straight into the Secretum but by the later nineteenth century, the emerging Modernist sensibility was bolder about sex. Highly aestheticised sex and sensation were the currencies of

Swinburne, Baudelaire, Huysmans, Beardsley. At the same time, the gradual discovery of Japanese *shunga* brought the prospect of refinement to European erotica. *Shunga* (which means 'Spring Pictures') are part of the Japanese concept of *ukiyo*, or the floating world, which is to say the life of the mind. Created with the clear intention of exciting desire, but only to the highest artistic standards, *shunga* is one of the most exquisite and powerful forms of erotic art.

Some *shunga* are even today shockingly explicit: Utagawa Kunisada's woodblock print *Vaginal Inspection* (*c.*1837) is a powerfully graphic oriental *mons veneris* with each pubic hair delicately displayed above, an anus explicit below, and in between the first and second fingers of an (apparently) male hand are being inserted between labia that are gorgeously swollen and moist. But other *shunga* are more subtle: Utamaro's *Pillow of Verses* (*c.*1788) uses stacked sake cups and clams as vaginal symbols. With all the lofty refinement of Japan's unique culture, Utamaro even used the textures and orifices of a kimono sleeve to suggest sexual availability. The sexual

ABOVE: *This Japanese* shunga *print (c.1850) shows a fishergirl on a rock watching as a pair of lascivious river gods ravish her companion.*

OPPOSITE: *A Japanese gynaecological illustration of a vaginal inspection. Both clinical and erotic, it was painted on a silk scroll c.1850.*

花の事

ABOVE: *The magnificent Ford Edsel was launched in 1957, but was a commercial disaster. Research by psychoanalysts revealed that many customers unconsciously found the similarity of the almond-shaped grille to a vagina unsettling.*

frankness and graphic clarity of these Japanese prints have some equivalent in European art in the drawings of Beardsley and the paintings of Klimt and Schiele.

These artists and other twentieth-century Modernists annexed sex in the cause of radicalism. In 1913, the proto-fascistic Italian writer Emilio Marinetti coined the term 'fisicofollia' to describe this body madness, but a more general assumption equated sex with revolution. French painter Francis Picabia and American writer and painter e e cummings found further common ground between erotica and Modernism when each used the mechanics of the automobile as a metaphor for sexual congress. It says a lot about our willingness to infer sex wherever possible that a cross-section of a carburettor (discovered by Picabia in Brewer's *Motor Car Construction and Carburation in Theory and Practice*) or an account of starting an engine ('i went right to it flooded-the-carburettor cranked her') can, in the hands of an artist, appear erotic. Again, for the Surrealists, the brain-reeling rapture of sex offered easy access to imaginary life: Louis Aragon wrote of the 'decor of desires' and under the hilariously incongruous pen-name Pierre Angelique, Georges Bataille conscripted sex in the cause of metaphysical seduction. This political aspect of erotica was confirmed in 1933 when the Nazis burned down Berlin's Institut für Sexualwissenschaft (proprietor, one Dr Magnus Hirschfeld) because its twelve thousand volumes were both pornographic and Jewish.

The radicalisation of sex is, according to the critic Peter Conrad in his book *Modern Times* (1998), 'one of the twentieth century's most cherished projects'. Thus, in the late 1960s the fashionable radical Eldridge Cleaver boasted about the black penis and encouraged a female audience at Stanford University to exercise its 'pussy power'. This was, perhaps, less elegant than Balzac's comparison of the average husband's love-making skills to those of an orang-utan, but it is fully illustrative of a changed mood in society. Both sensibilities are now things of the past, but happily sex remains a pleasure. Sex makes people smile nowadays, while once they used to smirk or blush or curse. As Aristophanes knew, to all solemn and frowning men, life is a disaster. And it was Anatole France who said 'Of all sexual aberrations, chastity is the strangest.'

Sex and civilisation go together.

BELOW: Parade Amoureuse, c.*1917 by Francis Picabia, a Dadaist who used pirated illustrations of machines as erotic metaphors.*

'Man and woman are joint participants in
the sexual pleasure, and in the voluptuous
thoughts which are the cause and consequence.
Such minutes are paradise in life, are heaven
before life has left us.'

MY SECRET LIFE 'Walter' (Henry Spencer Ashbee)

Religion and
Civilisation

1

Eros and the Classical World
Graeco-Roman erotic art

Catherine Johns

GRAECO-ROMAN CULTURE has influenced and reinfluenced Western civilisation repeatedly over the centuries. From art and architecture to literature, philosophy and science, the achievements of the Classical world have helped to shape the culture of Europe and beyond, and it is easy to assume that we possess an almost instinctive understanding of that period. Yet the fundamental religious change that occurred during the later Roman Empire, the triumph of Christianity over paganism in the fourth century AD, has made one aspect of Graeco-Roman life and art especially difficult for subsequent ages to comprehend and accept: namely, its attitude towards sexuality.

The societies of ancient Greece and Imperial Rome covered a vast range of both time and place, and should not be regarded as a single entity. Yet they shared a common pagan tradition, and because attitudes to sexuality and sexual imagery and symbolism were deeply embedded in religious traditions, there was a unity over that range that set it aside from the Christian cultures that followed.

If we disregard the preconceptions of our own cultural conditioning, as we should always try to do when studying the past, two things become clear. First, the 'liberal' attitudes of the Classical world were based, not on decadence or licentiousness, but on a rational response to the importance of fertility. Secondly, sexual imagery in Graeco-Roman art may be subdivided into two broad categories; one that remained closely tied to religion and superstition, and another that was genuinely erotic, created in the expectation of stimulating some sexual response in the viewer.

The most obvious and basic visual image to evoke the idea of fertility is that of a mother, a pregnant or nursing female. Mother-goddesses remained

RIGHT: *Priapus, the son of Dionysos and Aphrodite, was the god of fertility. Appropriately, his defining attribute is an enormous penis, as this wall painting from The House of Vetii in Pompeii shows.*

PREVIOUS PAGE: Intercourse under Red Canopy. *A late eighteenth-century painting of an amorous couple, the man representing Shiva and the woman representing Shakti, practising Tantric sex. The lore of Tantra claims that sex allows transcendence through the sexual embrace, although ejaculation must be postponed.*

OPPOSITE: Sleeping Satyr *(220 BC). Satyrs were the lascivious accomplices of Bacchus, the god of drink. Here is a Roman example sleeping it off after a debauch.*

important in Graeco-Roman life and thought, however male-dominated those societies were. Whether in the form of the multi-breasted Diana of Ephesos, the Greek Demeter, the homely Celtic mother-goddesses of the northern Roman provinces or of Isis, the great, universal ancient Egyptian goddess whose worship eventually extended throughout the Roman Empire, these divine mothers were all a fundamental part of religious belief, and they were deeply venerated. Their imagery, however, contains nothing to offend even the strictest Christian, and in fact the parallels between representations of Isis nursing Horus and the Virgin Mary with the Christ-child are too obvious to require any emphasis. Mothers are noble, mothers are tender: later ages have felt perfectly comfortable with Classical mother-goddesses.

The situation has been markedly different with visual imagery alluding to the male role in reproduction. To Graeco-Roman pagans, it seemed logical that if fertility and increase were good, then the theme should also include references to the equally important male role in reproduction, ranging from scenes of sexual intercourse to the specific image of the erect penis, which, if it does not guarantee fertility, at least symbolises sexual competence.

The ancients were perfectly well aware of the darker side of sexuality, and of its funny side, too. Bawdy of the coarsest kind, both verbal and visual, was the norm in Greek comedy and its Roman counterpart. Its origin lay in the satyr plays, focused on the activities of the mythical creatures who came to symbolise the animal side of human nature. Satyrs were part human, part animal, with horses' tails or the curly horns and hairy legs of goats, and they possessed large, and therefore ugly, penises, frequently in a very noticeable state of arousal. (As a study of Greek art clearly shows, the Greeks believed that to be elegant and aesthetically pleasing, male parts should be small and unobtrusive.)

The lively and totally vulgar activities of satyrs were often shown in Greek painted pottery, and would presumably have given rise to much merriment at the male drinking-parties where the pottery was used, but the underlying religious theme was still there. Even Greek drama itself, which is the foundation of all Western theatre, was developed not primarily for entertainment but as an act of worship to the god Dionysos (Bacchus), whose own rites included drinking, dancing and music. Where there is drinking, dancing and music, sex is pretty sure to follow.

The Greek god Pan, a god of the woods and fields, had the appearance of a satyr and was one of the participants in the rites of Bacchus: his worship continued until late-Roman times, and it is surely no accident that in later mythology, the Devil has the horns and legs of a goat. Pan was a powerful and sometimes sinister deity, and was responsible for the awe and fear (panic) that can afflict humans in wild and lonely places. Sexual desire and untrammelled sexual activity may be enjoyable and even amusing, but the potential for a more threatening aspect is always there, and the Greeks and Romans recognised that fact in their acknowledgement of the power of male sexuality. While Pan was often, but by no means invariably, depicted as ithyphallic (with penis erect), another, more minor deity was only ever shown in this condition. Priapus was a spirit of the countryside and also of cultivated land and gardens. He ensured the fertility of crops and herds, and exercised a protective, territorial role. Representations of this god show him with the fruits of the earth, and with an oversized erect organ.

At the height of the Roman Empire, when its territory extended from Britain to North Africa, from Spain to Syria, we find an extensive range of mythological and everyday sexual imagery in the decorative arts, but one element is particularly noteworthy, namely the representation of the erect penis itself as a shorthand reference to all these matters. The phallus became an amulet, a good-luck charm able to attack the Evil Eye and promote health and all good things.

It is difficult at first for the modern observer to understand that bronze horse-brasses or gold necklace-pendants modelled in the form of a penis and testicles, or carvings of these organs on a wall, are not primarily about sex, but about good luck. Yet we know that a charm in the form of a shamrock does not allude to botany, nor does a horseshoe-shaped one symbolise equestrian pursuits. The principle is the same, and the shocked and embarrassed response of Victorian scholars to Roman phallic objects missed the point.

Notwithstanding the underlying serious symbolism, whimsical elements crept into this aspect of sexual (not erotic) art. One of these was the personification of the phallus as a fantasy creature, perhaps in recognition of the way in which it is a body-part that often seems to have an

OPPOSITE: *An Attic red-figure vase of the sixth century BC showing a Dionysian revel.*

OPPOSITE: *A Roman bas-relief of* Leda and the Swan *(first century AD). The swan (a bird with an impressive penis) was chosen by Zeus as one of his many feral disguises when visiting Earth.*

independent mind of its own. Bronze mobiles or wind-chimes with suspended tinkling bells were made to keep away evil influences as well as to provide a pleasant sound, and many are known in the form of a phallus-bird or phallus-beast, complete with legs, wings, tail or ears. Phallus-birds were a common artistic conceit, and some of the Latin slang terms for the penis had animal or bird connections. Even in a Roman frontier province like Britain, local potters made drinking-vessels with phallic decoration, sometimes including phallus-birds.

The gods and goddesses of Greece and Rome led active sex lives, and artists had no compunction about illustrating their affairs in graphic detail. The mythology surrounding the principal god of the Greek and Roman pantheon, Zeus or Jupiter, includes numerous tales of his liaisons with a variety of partners, human and immortal. Shape-shifting is a common magical component of ancient story-telling, in Classical and other societies, and Zeus did not always approach his paramours in human form.

One of the most famous stories was that of Leda, the wife of Tyndareus, seduced by Zeus in the form of a giant swan. The image of Leda in the embrace of this huge, masterful bird was a common one in Classical art, in everything from marble sculpture to the decoration of pottery lamps, but it is intriguing that it also remained a popular motif in Renaissance and Neo-Classical art, in contexts where a direct representation of human – or divine – copulation would have been unacceptable. Perhaps the sheer improbability of the myth made it appear less threatening than other ancient images of cross-species pairings. But, before we assume that the sexual embrace of a very large swan was an altogether less carnal experience for a human female than copulation with a mammal, human or otherwise, we should reflect on the fact that male swans possess a sexual organ very like a penis.

Sexuality was implicit in many of the myths surrounding Aphrodite and her Roman equivalent Venus, and her son Eros (Cupid); these were deities who were concerned with sexual love and desire. In both Greek and Roman society, the centrality of such themes in religious thought meant that their extension to the affairs of human beings was regarded as acceptable.

In our society, scenes of violence represented in art are handled with calm, however frightening and distasteful the reality would be; graphic sexual scenes cause shock and alarm, however pleasurable the reality would be. When we consider the truly erotic elements in the art of Greece and Rome, we must remember that in those cultures, the 'shock, horror!' response had been suppressed by the sheer familiarity of phallic and sexual elements in religious contexts. The effect is similar to that brought about in our own society by the frequent vicarious experience of violence and suffering seen in the news media. We are still horrified by the reality of violence, and ancient Greeks and Romans would still have been shocked by lewd behaviour in inappropriate contexts, but representation (even of real events removed in time and space) is not the same as reality before our eyes.

From Classical Greece in the sixth century BC to the later Roman Empire, in the fourth century AD, objects were made and used that were decorated with scenes of human lovemaking. Many of these were everyday domestic objects, such as the Greek painted pottery referred to earlier and its later Roman counterpart decorated with moulded decoration in low relief. Exquisite gems engraved and set in gold jewellery, and the elegant silver tableware that was a sign of wealth and status in the Roman world, could incorporate erotic scenes. Paintings survive only seldom, but where they do, we find some erotica, and manuscripts also included illustrations of this kind where they were appropriate to the text.

Post-Classical sensibilities have found it challenging enough to deal with candid pictures of heterosexual lovemaking, often in positions carefully chosen to make the conjunction of male and female organs very clear. That the ancients also unconcernedly depicted male homosexual activities has been an even greater problem to many imbued with Judaeo-Christian values. Both Greek and Roman attitudes to homosexuality were profoundly different from those of later ages, and it is unlikely that we can now comprehend all the nuances. One element was the belief that all sexual relationships were unequal, involving an active and a passive partner; in the male-orientated society of antiquity, the vital thing was to be the active partner. The sex of the passive one was not especially important. This, of course, is an over-simplification, but it gives some indication of the different attitudes that lay behind the art that now survives, and the objectivity required when we observe it.

RIGHT: *Detail of an Attic red-figure kylix (sixth century BC) illustrating consensual and athletic sodomy.*

Lovemaking scenes such as those on Greek red-figure cups or Roman Arretine vases may appear rough and perfunctory in some cases and tender and emotional in others. Classical civilisation represented a peak of sophistication that was not achieved again until many, many centuries later, and we still have much to learn about the beliefs and understanding of that period of human history. We may think that our comprehension of human sexuality is highly evolved, but it may be that the Greeks and Romans had already come to terms with this important aspect of life more successfully than we have.

Ancient Sex Manuals
The sexual arts of India and China

Christopher Hart

I T IS VIRTUALLY IMPOSSIBLE to talk about sex in Chinese and Indian culture without talking about religion, an incongruity, tinged even with blasphemy, to Western ears. But the sex and religion link is hardly surprising. They are the two great paths to immortality that we are offered. Sex offers us the physical immortality of the bloodline, while religion offers us the spiritual immortality of the soul. Christianity has traditionally viewed sex as a rival, a distraction, a false promise. The Eastern religions, especially Hinduism and Taoism, see sex and religion as working hand in hand.

But this hasn't made the Asian attitude to sex loftily religiose or sanctimonious. Far from it. The Asian attitude to sex is essentially pragmatic, as any visitor to Thailand will know. It lacks both the puritanism and the prurient obsession with sex that has characterised the West since the baneful evasions and repressions of Saint Paul and Saint Augustine. In the third century AD, Origen, an early Greek Christian scholar, went so far as to castrate himself, so as to concentrate his mind more fully on the kingdom that is not of this world.

To the classical Taoist, this showy act of self-mutilation would have been lopping off one of the great sources, not only of pleasure and well-being, but also of spiritual enlightenment, that was available to humanity. Whether Princess Shan-Yin of the Sung Dynasty (tenth to thirteenth century AD) had spiritual enlightenment in mind when she ordered a special bed to be made for her, so that she could enjoy the attentions of no fewer than thirty men simultaneously, is perhaps debatable. But it certainly suggests that, in early Chinese culture, sex was regarded without guilt. Like Princess Shan-Yin, the Taoists were great believers in sheer quantity. 'The more women with whom a man has intercourse,' wrote one early Taoist sage, 'the greater will

OPPOSITE: *Ancient Chinese traditions of erotic illustration continued well into the twentieth century. Many of these prints were produced for export to the West. This couple with a pillow book is a late Qing-Dynasty watercolour of c.1920.*

be the benefit.' Another advised, 'If in one night he can have intercourse with more than ten women it is best.'

The essence of Taoism has the simplicity of all great ideas. There is a life force, *ch'i*, the breath of life, and also spiritual enlightenment and progress. To increase your life force, you must balance the two opposing principles of passive *yin* and active *yang*. One of the finest perceptions of Chinese philosophy is that, against the common misapprehension that women are *yin* and men are *yang*, in fact both sexes are compounded of both, men being minor *yin* and major *yang*, and women vice versa.

The details of other people's sex lives are always difficult to ascertain, as evinced by all those useless sex surveys. (I never did understand the mathematics of this.) How much more difficult to know about the sex lives of the ancient Chinese – except that we have the Pillow Books.

The Chinese Pillow Book was a characteristically pragmatic manual on how to have good sex, intended as bedtime reading for both men and women. Admittedly, pragmatism has its downside: ancient China had absolutely no concept of romantic or sexual love, and very little, it seems, of their ever-present green-eyed handmaiden, sexual jealousy. For Western tastes, these Pillow Books can at times be just a little too pragmatic and mechanical, but one should remember that sex, especially mechanically prolonged, five-hour marathon sex, was believed to serve a higher purpose: that of an ever greater harmony of *yin* and *yang*. Without copious and regular sex, a man would quickly become deficient in *yin*, while a woman's *yin* would dry up and lose its potency.

This view of sex threw up some curious standards. Anal sex, fellatio and cunnilingus were all fine and perfectly natural, and homosexuality and lesbianism were accepted, the latter regarded as an inevitable development in the enclosed women's quarters, and only thought of as detrimental if excessively large dildoes were used. They did have their taboos, based upon a culturally specific mythology of sex, as are all taboos. One of our great popular obsessions in the West currently is the insistence that children have no sexuality whatsoever, which would come as a surprise to most other cultures. For the Taoist Chinese, one of the greatest taboos was simply male masturbation: a terrible, *yin*-less waste of precious life-force. A key point was that a man's *yang* essence, i.e. his semen, was of limited supply, and must

ABOVE: *The title of this vernacular Chinese watercolour (c.1900) translates as* Two into One Goes. *The sexual position is a variant on another oriental practice where a man enjoys two embracing women, favouring each with alternative intermittent thrusts.*

be carefully tended, while a woman's *yin* was inexhaustible; and so girls could play away to their hearts' content.

The physician Master Tung-hsuan, a kind of seventh-century Dr Alex Comfort, gives all sorts of advice in his Pillow Book on how men can delay ejaculation. In fact, he even teaches, along with other Taoist masters, that men can reach orgasm without ejaculating at all, thereby offering the tantalising possibility of multiple male as well as female orgasms. In the 1960s, Masters and Johnson supposedly added the scientific proof of this, demonstrating that, in men, orgasm and ejaculation are two separate physiological processes. One can't help wondering, however, that if this is really possible, why on earth an awful lot more men haven't become Taoists.

One of the great charms of the Chinese Pillow Book is, of course, the euphemistic style. The penis might be referred to as the 'Jade Stalk', or 'Red Bird', 'Coral Stem', 'Heavenly Dragon Pillar', 'Swelling Mushroom'. The vagina was variously the 'Open Peony Blossom', the 'Golden Lotus', the 'Receptive Vase', or the 'Cinnabar Gate'. String these together, and you have Master Tung-hsuan advising young couples that her 'Jewel Terrace' should be caressed before he introduces his 'Jade Stalk' into her moistened 'Cinnabar Gate'. A culture, by comparison, which talks of dick and shlong, minge and snatch-box, bonking and shagging, surely occupies a rather lower level of sexual sophistication. Euphemisms could be extended to acts as well as parts, my favourite being anal sex (if you see what I mean): 'bringing the Flowering Branch to the Full Moon', a rather more lyrical image than the British 'one up the Gary'.

To Chinese Taoists, the ideal woman was small, plump, and just about pubescent – rather shocking to Westerners. A man customarily married a woman one third his age, so a thirty-six-year-old marrying a girl of twelve was considered just about right. The woman to avoid had 'dishevelled hair and a coarse face, a long neck and a protruding Adam's apple, irregular teeth and a manly voice'.

For all the reams of advice on sexual technique and spiritual ecstasy, however, perhaps the wisest words come from a second-century alchemical text, the *Ts'an-t'ung-ch'i:* 'When one contemplates female and male united in sexual congress…this is not achieved by special skill, and it has not been taught to them.' In the end it is a mystery.

Later China became increasingly puritanical, with the triumph of Confucianism over Taoism, and then the advent of Christianity. But the sexual attitudes of China in its Taoist heyday have a lot to recommend them: unromantic, yes, but also worldly, optimistic, urbane and tolerant. They involved very little angst, and, so far as we can judge, an absolute absence of anything resembling S&M. Freud would have found it all dull.

The sexual sophistication of India is better known in the West than that of China, thanks to the *Kama Sutra* and the celebrated erotic temple carvings of the kind that drove poor, earnest, charmless Miss Quested quite mad in E. M. Forster's *A Passage to India* (1924). She went looking for the 'real India', you may recall, and couldn't take it when she found it.

The *Kama Sutra* was compiled between the third and fifth centuries AD, supposedly by the Hindu sage Vatsayana, several centuries after the Pillow Books of the Taoist masters of China. And given that it shares with the Pillow Books the same coolly appraising, tolerant, worldly and broadly unromantic view of sex, it is perfectly possible that it was directly influenced by them.

Hinduism, like Taoism, had an acute, forgiving sense of human reality, and only very tenuously connected sex to morality at all. The main thing was to look after one's *karma* and not pollute oneself by intercourse with social inferiors. The best way to marry an unwilling girl was to get her drunk and then sleep with her (rape her), after which you could get married to her with a priest present, and nobody could reverse it. But there are moments when the *Kama Sutra* does begin to talk about love in ways that we recognise: as a madness that can cause loss of sleep and weight, fainting and even death. If this is the fate that threatens you, advises the text, then you had better get on and sleep with her, even if she is a married woman.

The *Kama Sutra* advises prospective young wives to make themselves mistresses of the arts of singing, sewing, dancing and making artificial flowers – but also, lest we get too complacently comparative, magic and sorcery, cockfighting and how to use a sword. It is good on post-marital sex, I think, and right to classify all sexual love between two true lovers, into three kinds: 'loving congress', between lovers who have been apart for a while; 'congress of subsequent love', which is the mad passion of the early days; and 'spontaneous congress', which is what you end up with when you are both completely used to each other, but not yet bored into lovelessness.

OPPOSITE: *A Persian miniature from the mid-nineteenth century, showing two favoured sexual positions.*

PREVIOUS PAGE: *A vernacular Chinese watercolour (c.1900) of a bedroom scene. The title translates as* Unlocking the Cinnabar Gate. *Cinnabar is mercuric sulphide which, when used as a pigment, gives us vermilion. In Chinese Pillow Books, the term 'Cinnabar Gate' was often used to evoke the gorgeous redness of the female cleft.*

OPPOSITE: *A vernacular Chinese watercolour (c.1920) of a couple making love. The woman is offering her 'Open Peony Blossom' from the superior position. The older man's 'Jade Stalk' cheerfully accepts it.*

Other classifications are entertainingly absurd, from the 'Four Kinds of Mild Embrace' to the 'Nine Ways of Moving the Lingam inside the Yoni' (i.e. the penis inside the vagina). And some of its suggested remedies are not only absurd but eye-watering. Instead of Viagra, the *Kama Sutra* recommends a brisk rubdown of the male organ with 'the bristles of certain tree insects'.

Like the Chinese Pillow Books, the *Kama Sutra* also boasts some wonderful euphemisms for various positions and practices: *Utphallaka*, 'the Flower in Bloom'; *Ratisundara*, 'The Delight of Aphrodite'; the 'Jewel Case'; the 'Monkey'; the 'Crushing of Spices'; 'Sucking a Mango'… Nowadays you can even get a gay *Kama Sutra*. But since we know that in the seventeenth century, the fourth Mogul Emperor, Jahangir, kept not only three hundred royal wives and five thousand courtesans, but also one thousand young men for a little variety, we might assume that he, at least, would approve.

The best thing about the *Kama Sutra*, for us now, is that it is not about lifestyle, success, image, or about sex as product. It comprehends sex only as the indivisible give-and-take of pleasure between two people, rather than the purely take-and-take-again of the lonely pornophile or the sexual consumer. It has a lot to teach us still.

Interpretations of the functions of the erotic Hindu temple carvings vary widely. They may represent sublime spiritual states, or they may be just an early kind of advertising, stimulating passers-by to come inside and enjoy one of the many temple prostitutes who worked there. At the Rajarajesvara temple in Tanjore in the eleventh century for instance, there were more than four hundred harlots on the payroll. The elaborately carved *maithuna* figures on the outside of the temple, according to this argument, were only marginally holier versions of the secular adverts that festoon our phone boxes nowadays: 'Busty Brazilian Brunnete [*sic*], 19, new in Town. And Loves Her Work!'

Sex as a path to spiritual enlightenment was for the Hindu, as for the Taoist, a widely accepted concept. Two lovers in ecstatic and prolonged union could achieve a 'Oneness with the World Soul' matched otherwise only by the most ascetic and unworldly Brahminical practices. I like the sly fact that this 'Oneness' was much more likely to be attained if the union was not between the usual husband and wife. Participating couples would

therefore swap partners, or temple prostitutes would be brought in to help. This may all sound like a suburban wife-swapping party, but it must be remembered that in Indian life, to this day, pretty well everything that you do (including wife-swapping) is saturated with spiritual significance.

Other, more solitary Tantric devotees spent hours and even days ritually worshipping their own erect penises. Again you might imagine that this is not so uncommon in our own day among male adolescents; but we live in a secular age, and for a pustular penis-worshipping youth closeted in his bedroom, his penis is…just his penis. For the Tantric worshipper, the *lingam* was a genuine manifestation of the divine.

The impressive, mature candour with which Eastern cultures approach sex, in contradistinction to the unfortunate attitudes of the West, is especially evident in Japan. The summit of sophisticated Japanese sexual culture was the geisha: not a prostitute, as we must tirelessly be reminded, but something more like a courtesan, a highly trained singer and dancer, who might quite possibly not sleep with men at all. The geisha is the modern world's only equivalent to the ancient Greek *hetaira*, and a highly civilised institution.

Westerners were amazed when they first visited the pleasure quarters of ancient Japanese cities in the nineteenth century and found the red paper lanterns, and the scent of jasmine, the blossoming cherry trees, and the atmosphere of calm and civility and rational sensual enjoyment. When the new capital of Edo (now Tokyo) was planned in the seventeenth century, the authorities laid out a groundplan for the geishas' quarter before anything else. By the mid-eighteenth century, Edo's 'Nightless City' was a place of tea shops and theatres, with its own dialect, festivals and customs, and three thousand elegantly dressed and coiffured courtesans in embroidered silks and delicate jewellery.

Globalisation is usually a euphemism for Westernisation. If that is so, then the march of the secular will presently overwhelm the spirituality of Eastern cultures, and the lifeless secular view of sex will prevail. But it seems unlikely that cultures so ancient will be overwhelmed so easily. Globalisation might even spread the other way. Exquisitely illustrated Pillow Books in motel bedrooms, Tantric rituals instead of seedy S&M clubs, *hetairai* instead of whores… Who knows?

OPPOSITE: A Rajah in Amorous Dalliance *(possibly mid-nineteenth century). This kind of painting was produced in northern India from the thirteenth to the nineteenth centuries. They were produced by a team of artists rather than one working alone. Themes of love and seduction were popular subjects but the protagonists were not usually ordinary men and women but for the most part archetypal lovers drawn from Indian mythology.*

PREVIOUS PAGE: Lovers *from the eighteenth-century* 'Poem of the Pillow' *by Kitagawa Utamaro. In Japanese custom, the nape of the woman's neck is her most erotic aspect.*

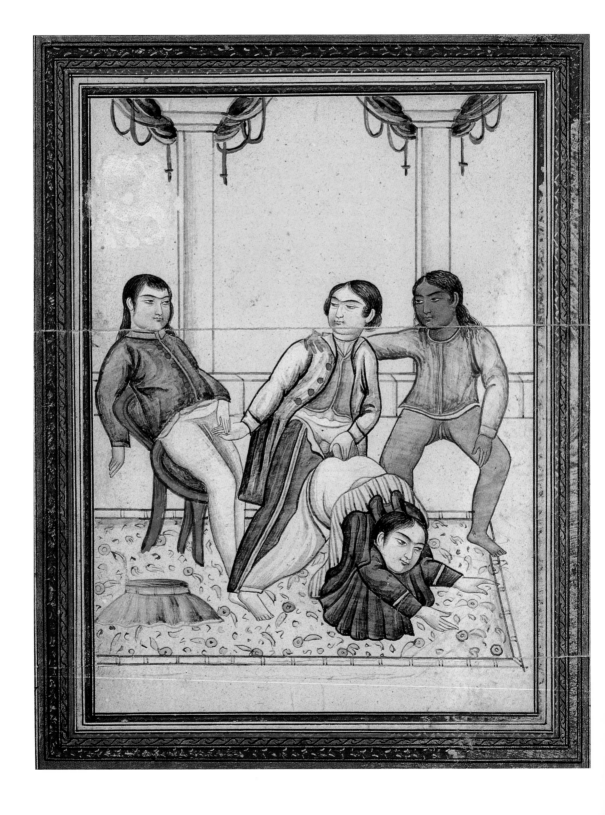

OPPOSITE AND RIGHT:
Two Persian miniatures from
the mid-nineteenth century
illustrating, opposite, a curious
foursome and, right, a more
conventional couple. It was
a Mogul convention to remove
pubic hair.

The Sin of Virginity
Sex and the Bible

Rabbi Schmuley Boteach

MANY PEOPLE BELIEVE that the act of sexual intercourse was labelled dirty and sinful from the very beginning by the Hebrew Bible. After all, the notion of 'sex as sin' has invaded every aspect of our culture. The very idea that sex can be pleasurable and enjoyable (and for women too? Gasp!) is thought to be an exclusively modern concept. Surely this was not the belief of our biblical predecessors! They were too busy self-flagellating and denying the pleasures of the flesh, right?

But the Hebrew Bible's view of sex is, in fact, widely misunderstood and misrepresented. Judaism, true to the original Hebrew Bible, did not have a denigrating nor negative view of sexuality at all. In fact, sex was believed to be the highest form of knowledge. There is no word in the Hebrew language for 'sex' other than 'knowledge'. All the 'begots' and 'begats' that take place in the Bible are preceded with a form of deep and loving knowledge.

This 'knowledge' runs far deeper than the familiarity with your partner's body terrain – the landscape of his moles, the topography of her curves. Rather, it is a knowledge of the inner being as well. In the Bible, sex is portrayed as something more than just flesh pressed against flesh, or the friction caused between skins. Judaism views sexuality as a deep unmasking of the human personality through the removal of layers – both real and metaphorical – and the quintessence of humans being exposed. So where did we go wrong?

Later, Protestant repression and the general denigration of the body, which were hybrid products of the Aristotelian and Neo-Platonic rejection of the physical in favour of the spiritual, infiltrated religion and were largely responsible for its shallow and negative view of sex and the human

RIGHT: *Eric Gill saw sexual activity and religious observation as two parts of a humane whole. He believed passionately that sexual expression should be free and uninhibited. The graphic impact of his wood engraving* Eve *(1926) is equalled only by its subtle eroticism: the erect nipple suggests sexual arousal, something the serpent appears to have noticed. This print is one of his most collectible images.*

body. This view was also a product of Zoroastrian dualism, on which many concepts of Christianity are built. Essential to Zoroastrian dualism, which found its way into Christianity via the Greek philosophers, is the idea that good and evil are always in conflict.

Dualism posits an inversely proportional thesis and antithesis as being the very stuff of existence, and therefore, G-d and Lucifer, soul and body, virtue and sin, spiritual love and physical love, are always in conflict, such that more of the latter leads to less of the former. In other words, the more we indulge the body in physical pleasures, be it eating, or having sex, or watching too much Reality Television, the less we will indulge our soul in spiritual pursuits. You can have one or the other – sexuality or spiritual goodness – but never the twain shall meet. Hence, the early fathers of Christianity always celebrated celibacy and denigrated sexuality.

Our first introduction to the human body is through Adam and Eve. In this primal state, Adam and Eve are unclothed, but they are not embarrassed. There is something lofty about the human body in its pristine condition that is only later tainted after the Sin in the Garden. Adam and Eve frolicked naked as the day they were born, the same way that children do. Having done nothing wrong, they had nothing to hide. Sexuality in the Garden is transparent. However, immediately after they dine at 'Bistro de Tree of Knowledge', they are consumed by shame and must hide themselves:

> Then the eyes of both were opened, and they knew that they were naked; and they sewed fig leaves together and made themselves aprons…the man and his wife hid themselves from the presence of the LORD God among the trees of the garden. But the LORD God called to the man, and said to him, 'Where are you?' And he said, 'I heard the sound of thee in the garden, and I was afraid, because I was naked; and I hid myself.' (Genesis 3:7–10)

Be assured, the aprons were not intended for role-playing, and the hiding was not an erotic game. The two were seeking to hide, to cover what was in fact their greatest gift: nakedness. The body and sexuality had suddenly taken on some mysterious overtone, some degrading, forbidden theme.

The ancient biblical commentators explain that at this point, the objective becomes subjective. When Adam and Eve were naked in the Garden, they related to each other as two people without pretension. When Adam looked upon Eve in his and her original pristine state, the first thought that crossed his mind was not, 'Nice hooters', but rather, 'Nice heart'. His attraction to her was based on the objective standard of Eve's actions rather than on the subjective standard of her looks. But the moment they sinned, they had something to hide. Eve suddenly felt inadequate. No longer could she relate to Adam solely in the context of her being, but rather through the lens of how strongly he felt drawn to her. She now felt self-conscious around Adam, and he was self-conscious around her. They both felt insecure and inadequate. Adam no longer related to Eve in terms of good and bad; he related to her in terms of like or dislike. He went from objective appraisal to subjective attraction.

Eve felt the need to accessorise. Insecurity pervaded her character and she ran to cover up. This is where sex began to have negative overtones. Whereas before, sex between Adam and Eve was used as the principal means by which they communicated, now it became selfish. Adam could use Eve for his own, selfish pleasure. Eve, in turn, would have to protect herself against being used by employing the cunning and manipulative techniques that have been embraced by her daughters throughout the ages. Adam and Eve replaced the easy affinity they once experienced with artifice and role-playing. Whereas before sex was about nakedness, it was now about pretence. Whereas before it was about physical intimacy, it was now about emotional awkwardness. And whereas before it was about being sewn together as one flesh, now it was about two protected bodies creating limited pleasure through friction rather than fission.

There are, in essence, three kinds of sex. First, there's sex the way it's practised today, which is 'anaesthetising sex'. Anaesthetising sex is about a hormonal build-up in the body that needs to be released. That's animal sex. It's men who use sex to fall asleep at night. It's women who will sit in a bar because they 'want to get laid'. It's not that the other person is attracted to you. Rather, it's that you have a need inside that has to be released. The essence of anaesthetising sex is pleasure caused by the release of pressure. That's why anaesthetising sex is less about foreplay

OPPOSITE: *Peter Paul Rubens',*
Adam and Eve *(seventeenth
century). With the Fall came
shame of the naked body.*

and almost entirely about orgasm. The journey is not the reward. In fact,
the journey is shunned because it just heightens the pressure. Rather, it's
about running to the finish line, to what the French call *le petit mort*, the
little death, so that peace and tranquillity are restored.

The second kind is procreative sex, which is what the Catholic Church
calls for. Again, this is sex with an agenda, the creation of a child.
But contrary to what evolutionary biologists will tell you, we know that
humans are not specifically built for procreative sex for the following
reasons:

1. In the animal kingdom the visage of the female is of no
   consequence. Human beings are the only mammals which
   make love face to face. Indeed, the disproportionately large
   male sexual appendage is designed to facilitate face-to-face
   sexual relations. Thus, human sex involves intimacy.
2. The human female has permanent breasts, while animal
   mammaries form only during pregnancy and nursing. A
   woman thereby attracts a man to her distinctive features on her
   front, rather than her rump as is common in the animal world.
3. The human female is further distinguished in being the only
   mammal to (willingly) acquiesce to intercourse during
   pregnancy or beyond the menopause. This is an impossibility
   for a female animal who will never accept a male once she has
   been impregnated, thereby demonstrating conclusively the
   capacity for humans to distinguish between pleasurable
   intimacy and procreative functionality.

So, aside from the first two functional types of sex, what else is out
there? Well, the third variety of sex is what I call relational sex – sex used
to connect. This is sex as sewing, with the male appendage representing
the needle and the female heart representing the strings of the emotions,
which when joined together leave them united as one, inseparable flesh.
This is sex exactly as G-d intended it: 'Therefore shall a man leave his
father and his mother, he shall cleave unto his wife [in other words, they
shall make love] and they shall become one flesh'. (Genesis 2:24)

The dynamic, external sexual organ of the male and its movement represents fire and passion. The static internal sexual organs of the woman represent water and intimacy. Together through the strong motions of passion, which produce even stronger emotions of the heart, man and woman become one indivisible unit – one heart, one spirit, one flesh.

Relational sex sustains a happy marriage well into five decades. It is the kind of sex that allows partners to be the only 'affair' that the other desires. That's what making love is about. You're concealed from the whole world, but there's one person whom you bring into your most private space, and who sees you with no embellishment.

Adam and Eve originally had relational sex, which they used as a deep way of understanding each other. But after eating from the Tree of Knowledge, they went from the relational to the functional, from the uniquely human capacity for intimacy, to the undistinguished animal need for hormonal release.

The biblical stories provide the best evidence of this transformation. The Bible discusses all three varieties of sex in its various narratives, lauding relational sex and condemning functional sex.

The original pristine view of sexuality was preserved in the book Song of Songs. There are twenty-four books in the Hebrew Bible, and Song of Songs is referred to by the ancient Rabbis as 'Holy of Holies', the loftiest of all Biblical books. Sex between a man and a woman was supposed to be a metaphor for the very unity of G-d. G-d also possesses characteristics of male and female. The female G-d energy is the transcendent G-d of creation, represented by an all-encompassing circle. The male G-d energy is the imminent G-d of history, represented by a line, the rod of justice, the sceptre of sovereign rule, by which G-d regulates and governs the universe. The love between man and woman was an indicator that G-d could not be divided, that G-d was really one. Thus, Song of Songs is one long erotic love poem.

So too, from the thirteenth to the sixteenth century, the Jewish mystics, the Cabbalists, always used sexual metaphors in describing the unity within the G-dhead. And that's why today, Judaism is the only religion in the world that not only rejects the virtue of virginity, but establishes virginity and being single as highly undesirable states. A man and a

ABOVE: Bathsheba *(1552) by Paris Bordone. In
the Bible, Bathsheba was the gorgeous wife of Uriah
the Hittite and had taken the fancy of King David
when he saw her bathing. G-d punished the adultery
by causing the child born of the union to die, although
Bathsheba later gave birth to Solomon.*

woman are obligated to get married, and their innocent love for each other should be manifest in the by-product of an innocent child, so that the loving process begins all over again. The person who has never married and made love to their beloved lacks insight into the human condition. And without the deep mirror of another human soul, how can we ever know ourselves?

It is interesting to note how tales in the Hebrew Bible illuminate these different 'kinds' of sex – namely, the animal, functional, anaesthetising sex versus the intimate, lofty, spiritual sex. We first see it with Noah, who sees himself as the new progenitor of mankind. He comes out of the Flood and builds a vineyard. He gets drunk. The ancient rabbis interpret the following story in Genesis to mean that Noah was sodomised by his own son:

> Noah was the first tiller of the soil. He planted a vineyard; and he drank of the wine, and became drunk, and lay uncovered in his tent. And Ham, the father of Canaan, saw the nakedness of his father, and told his two brothers outside. Then Shem and Japheth took a garment, laid it upon both their shoulders, and walked backward and covered the nakedness of their father; their faces were turned away, and they did not see their father's nakedness. When Noah awoke from his wine and knew what his youngest son had done to him, he said, 'Cursed be Canaan; a slave of slaves shall he be to his brothers.' (Genesis 9: 20–25).

Sexuality becomes associated with drunkenness, with a loss not of inhibition, but of morals. Sex is associated with our most base instincts, rather than with building relationships. And Noah's son Ham is, of course, condemned. He will be the womaniser who beds a different conquest every night, who thinks of himself as a sexual adventurer, but who is in reality nothing but a pathetic wanderer.

In contrast to this type of sexuality, the book of Genesis also tells us that the relationship between Abraham and Sarah is one of very deep love, even though they are married for ninety years without having any offspring. When they're ninety years old, Abraham says to Sarah, 'I now

THE SIN OF VIRGINITY

see what a beautiful woman you are.' He never lost his attraction to her, even when she was an elderly woman. A deep soul connection had been borne of their relationship, their lovemaking, their emotional intimacy over the years. Abraham was that rare romantic who looks upon his beloved with openness rather than judgement.

We see this again in the close relationship between Isaac and Rebecca. 'Then Isaac brought her into the tent, and took Rebecca, and she became his wife; and he loved her. So Isaac was comforted after his mother's death.' (Genesis 24:67) And this close and special bond was evidenced in their lovemaking: 'When he had been there a long time, Abimelech king of the Philistines looked out of a window and saw Isaac playing with Rebecca his wife'. (Genesis 26:9) Here the Bible uses the word 'playing' to connote their lovemaking. Their lovemaking made them into innocent children, curious about each other as if for the first time. Isaac and Rebecca are not bodily virgins, but mental virgins. Their lovemaking has a joy and freshness about it, immune to the cynicism and boredom that affects so many other couples when they have been married for many years.

BELOW: The Drunkenness of Noah *by Giovanni Bellini (1430–1516). Just when Noah thought things were getting better after the Flood, he plants a vineyard, drinks the consequences and is sodomised by his son.*

LEFT: Song of Songs
(1974) by Marc Chagall who
combined Jewish mysticism
with Modernist exuberance.

In the story of Judah and Tamar, we're introduced to a totally different
kind of sex, which is solely about bearing children. It's procreative sex
with the terrible result being that Tamar is passed from brother to brother
and eventually has to use her own father-in-law to beget seed. Their
relationship becomes aberrational because it's not about intimacy:

> And when Tamar was told, 'Your father-in-law is going up to
> Timnah to shear his sheep,' she put off her widow's garments,
> and put on a veil…and sat at the entrance to Enaim, which is on
> the road to Timnah…. When Judah saw her, he thought her to be
> a harlot, for she had covered her face. He went over to her at the
> road side, and said, 'Come, let me come in to you,' for he did not
> know that she was his daughter-in-law … About three months
> later Judah was told, 'Tamar your daughter-in-law has played the
> harlot; and moreover she is with child by harlotry.' And Judah
> said, 'Bring her out, and let her be burned.' (Genesis 38:13–24).

Later, she is of course saved. But this is not the kind of relationship that makes the heart flutter and the pulse quicken.

Yet another example of procreative sex in the Bible is the terrible story of Lot and his daughters, who fall under the impression that the whole world has been destroyed after 'the LORD rained on Sodom and Gomorrah brimstone and fire from the LORD out of heaven' (Genesis 19:24). Unfortunately, Lot's daughters don't realise that the destruction has been localised to their area, so they get their father drunk and are impregnated by him. 'The first-born said to the younger, "Our father is old, and there is not a man on earth to come in to us after the manner of all the earth. Come, let us make our father drink wine, and we will lie with him, that we may preserve offspring through our father".' (Genesis 19:31–32). On the one hand, the daughters' motives sound worthy. They are being noble by trying to ensure the continuity of mankind. But in reality, what they do is sinful because it's only procreative sex. A passionate connection is inappropriate and impossible between father and daughter. By definition, sexual intimacy involves two strangers who go beyond their distance to become one flesh. It is a fiery rather than a watery attraction, and is inappropriate to the already existing, much more calm bond, that already unites father and daughter. This error is a direct assault on their procreative view of sexuality, which is not about connection but about bearing children, not about passion and closeness, but about progeny at any cost.

The most famous of all sexual stories in the Bible is that of David and Bathsheba. This is a story seemingly about pure lust – King David saw Bathsheba bathing on the rooftop. The story started off as something animalistic, hedonistic and destructive. A man is killed, a wife is robbed. And yet David, being warned by Nathan the prophet about the terrible nature of his sin, opens his heart to complete repentance. 'Have mercy on me, O God, according to thy steadfast love; according to thy abundant mercy blot out my transgressions. Wash me thoroughly from my iniquity, and cleanse me from my sin! For I know my transgressions, and my sin is ever before me' (Psalms 51:1–3). Moreover, David's repentance is not only to G-d, whom he has wronged, but more importantly, his repentance is to Bathsheba as well. He now understands he cannot use her as a lust object.

He marries her, makes her into a wife, and promises her that her child will be the next king of Israel. Later, when Adoni'jah tries to usurp the throne, David recommits to Bathsheba:

> And the king swore, saying, 'As the LORD lives, who has redeemed my soul out of every adversity, as I swore to you by the LORD, the God of Israel, saying, "Solomon your son shall reign after me, and he shall sit upon my throne in my stead"; even so will I do this day.' Then Bathsheba bowed with her face to the ground, and did obeisance to the king, and said, 'May my lord King David live for ever!' (1 Kings 1:29–31).

David elevates the relationship to one of deep connection, of promise, of knowledge, so that the fruit of their union is the wise Solomon, a worthy son.

We can bridge the two as well. Contrast that with the actions of David's son Amnon who rapes his own sister Tamar, misleads her, uses subterfuge, pretending that he's ill so she will come and nurse him:

> Now Absalom, David's son, had a beautiful sister, whose name was Tamar; and after a time Amnon, David's son, loved her. And Amnon was so tormented that he made himself ill because of his sister Tamar; for she was a virgin, and it seemed impossible to Amnon to do anything to her… So Amnon lay down, and pretended to be ill; and when the king came to see him, Amnon said to the king, 'Pray let my sister Tamar come and make a couple of cakes in my sight, that I may eat from her hand'… So Tamar went to her brother Amnon's house, where he was lying down. And she took dough, and kneaded it, and made cakes in his sight, and baked the cakes… Then Amnon said to Tamar, 'Bring the food into the chamber, that I may eat from your hand.' And Tamar took the cakes she had made, and brought them into the chamber to Amnon her brother. But when she brought them near him to eat, he took hold of her, and said to her, 'Come, lie with me, my sister.' She answered him, 'No, my brother, do not

force me; for such a thing is not done in Israel; do not do this wanton folly…' But he would not listen to her; and being stronger than she, he forced her, and lay with her. (2 Samuel 13:1–14).

Then Amnon refuses to marry Tamar (assuming that she desires him as a husband). In fact, he suddenly detests and despises her. This is because Amnon has now satiated his desire. This is anaesthetising sex at its very worst. There was a woman that had to be had, there was a thirst that had to be quenched, there was an urge that had to be indulged. This is raw male sexuality untamed and unredeemed by any intimate, feminine influence.

The story of Amnon and Tamar is the equivalent of our modern singles scene in which sexuality is about using and being used, about not connecting and delivering all of yourself to another. It's sex as a destination, rather than a journey. It's sex as the end to an encounter rather than the beginning of a relationship. We wonder why the sexes have so much contempt for each other, but it's actually a very simple concept: a person who is nothing more than a plaything can never be respected.

The act of love, however, is an act of equalisation. A king may be a king, but if he marries a commoner, she automatically becomes a queen. If someone is only a means to an end sexually, you can never love them fully. In order to do so, he or she would have to be an end in and of themselves. Making love is not an act of usurpation, but of harmony, not a rite of passage but a place of meeting. Thus, while the Bible constantly returns to these three categories of sex – anaesthetising, procreative and relational – only the third variety, intimate sex, can lead to something truly blessed.

Asian Sensuality
Why East beats West when it comes to sex

Yasmin Alibhai-Brown

A YOUNG CITY MILLIONAIRE writes in after reading a newspaper article of mine about the ambiguous message given by the *hijab*, the head covering adopted by an increasing number of Muslim women: 'I am writing this to you with some trepidation, but I can't stop looking at the pictures which accompanied your article. I find them a real turn on. I am sick of bodies on display everywhere. Women who cover themselves have real power over our fantasies. I know I cannot ever have one of these women, and I am jealous of men who can. It must be like opening up a beautifully wrapped birthday present.' For him and a number of other men who wrote in, the chase and therefore the thrill is gone. With so much flesh proffered up for visual and actual consumption, there is nothing left to discover. I am sure traditional Muslim women will be enraged to see these confessions. They will not, however, be surprised. Many of these women are wise and knowing, and can see the world more clearly than the world is ever allowed to see or know them. In East Africa where I grew up, Zanzibari Muslim women were thought of as sophisticated, addictive lovers who could weave invisible bonds around a man and keep him intoxicated mostly by never giving him the whole of themselves. But you never saw them. They were always completely covered up in black robes, yet their eyes were animated in ways which cannot be described.

Remember the delightful ensnaring of Dr Aziz by the young woman Naseem in Salman Rushdie's *Midnight's Children* (1981). She was always ill. He was only allowed to examine her through a perforated sheet, one bit at a time. Brilliant idea. In time 'This phantasm of a partitioned woman began to haunt him, and not only in his dreams. Glued together by his imagination, she accompanied him on all his rounds, she moved into the

ABOVE: *A filmic encounter where menace mingles with eroticism from Wong Kar-Wai's* In the Mood for Love *(2000).*

front room of his mind, so that waking and sleeping he could feel in his fingertips the softness of her ticklish skin or the perfect tiny wrists or the beauty of the ankles; he could smell her scent of lavender and chambeli; he could hear her voice and her helpless laughter of a little girl; but she was headless, because he had never seen her face.'

There are lessons here. If one could step back from the ubiquity of sex in public spaces, and allow it to retreat into those small inner places where unfolding and disclosures become possible once more, we may yet discover the difference between a fuck and an experience. And it seems to me that in the midst of the Babel we inhabit that may be our last resort, the only way we will avoid the death of human passion.

These are some erotic films I love: *Pakeezah* (the name of a beautiful courtesan) 1971; *Barsat-ki-Raat* (A Rainy Night) 1960; *Guide* 1965; and latterly Wong Kar-Wai's *In the Mood for Love* 2000. You must understand, before I explain these choices that I am an Asian Muslim Briton with a complex set of attitudes towards seduction and sex, some of which are hinted at above. As a British Asian, I come from nations where the art of sexual pleasure was so central that for hundreds of years it was enshrined in religious iconography, in poetry, art and dance. Everything that the human imagination and body has ever craved or tried is represented in the ancient sculptures of India, delicate Indian miniature paintings and of course the *Kama Sutra* of Vatsayana, which was translated and published in Britain in the late nineteenth century by two members of a secret society, the orientalist Richard Burton and Forster Fitzgerald Arbuthnot, a retired Indian civil servant. Arbuthnot saw this treatise as an essential education for English men who had only ever learned 'the rough exercise of a husband's rights' without understanding the need for a wife to feel passion too and to participate as a willing part of a coupling rather than a victim of it.

According to key Islamic texts, Allah has given me the right to physical gratification which I can demand of my husband. Our clothes, male and female, are both modest, yet fluid, easily opened and accessible. The sari and shalwar khameez, it was once explained to me by an Indian Muslim cultural historian, enabled young married couples to make love in the fields during lunch breaks, without the need to undress. In the May 2001 Sotheby's catalogue on *The Arts of the Muslim World* an eighteenth-century lacquer pen-box from Persia captures this perfectly. Two apparently fully clothed lovers are shown locked in a sexual embrace on a carpet in a wood. She appears to be the more energetic and determined partner and he is obviously enjoying his good luck. Two musicians play for them and a maid plies them with wine. Even as you spy upon this private act conducted in the open, their clothes lock you out and grab back the intimacy from your inquisitive eyes. It is this play between giving and withholding, between the explicit and the implicit that creates the excitement.

Sari blouses are cut and sewn to be a thin layer over the exact shape of the breasts, but a sari keeps this delight covered. The adorned or pierced belly, so cheapened by girl pop stars, has been displayed by young Indian women for thousands of years, again with a flimsy covering so you get to see glimpses of the exposed parts. Hindi songs and Urdu poetry are obsessed with '*ishq*' (passion) and the devastation it can cause. My mother's favourite song is a tease about the red mark on the *chunni* of the bride and the way she is glowing after her first night of sex. These traditions have long influenced sexual relationships and fantasies in the Indian subcontinent and the Middle East. But there are other conventions and rules which have marched in, like unwelcome storming soldiers, through history to deny, destroy or punish physical love and lust. The forces of suppression won ground in the twentieth century, particularly in Islamic countries which responded to political powerlessness by killing all joy and earthly pleasures in their populations or by forcing them to live in a way that masks these. Hindu fundamentalism is displaying the same tendencies. Ironically the thrusting, commercialised sexuality which is sweeping across the globe is also destroying that genuine and deep sensuality which was once so carefully nurtured among these groups. Late-night sex shows on TV may work a treat for the beer-filled bloke who tumbles back at midnight and would like but can't have a shag (and many Asian men would be among them), but coarse, pretend sex cannot appeal to those with more refined tastes and traditions.

So here we are, part and yet not part of the modern sexual revolution; more knowledgeable and at ease with physical love than many Westerners (we have not until recently had to suffer any anguish about imperfect bodies), yet unable or unprepared to join in the scrum which passes for satisfying sex today.

OPPOSITE: *Contemporary Arabian wedding jewellery from Bahrain. A comfortable, erotically potent sensuality underlies the apparent chastity of many Middle Eastern and Asian cultures.*

OPPOSITE: *A Persian miniature,* Intimacy, *from the mid-nineteenth century. The freedom of oriental costume allowed considerable liberality in the manner and location of lovemaking.*

Hence my choice of films. These arousing love stories (without a single screen kiss or shared, candle-lit bath between them) should be watched in the dead of night, when the senses are most awake. They leave me flushed with restless passion which then goes on to spend itself. These are the nights that will flash before me just before I die. Most readers will not know the films. The first three are old Hindi films made in the 1950s and '60s and the last one, made in 2000, is set in Hong Kong. The films which speak to an Eastern sensibility work because they reveal nothing and still evoke the imagination, which climbs to fever pitch as a result. There are no clichés of frantic undressing, hungry love-making, long shots of active limbs and breasts and the ciggy at the end. This erotica confidently lies still in concealed chambers. Nothing is massively more. And out of this a whole way of being develops. Subtlety, the lost art of inconsequential flirting, perfumed conversations between real and imagined lovers, suggestive language and behaviour which never breaks through propriety, games of pleasure which never degenerate into crude fornication.

In *Pakeezah*, the courtesan holds back more than she will ever surrender. The customer is never satisfied. She is a singer, a dancer, a poet who can please and excite men in a thousand ways. She is always covered up, although she artfully lets some hair escape to play on her face and spends hours beautifying her feet. And it is these feet that draw a man to fall insanely in love with her, in spite of her status and inevitable social disapprobation. She is asleep, lying down on a train seat. Her feet are exposed and they grab his attention. Each foot, top and bottom, is intricately patterned with hot red henna. Flowers intertwined with ivy run up both sides (who painted this henna so painstakingly and tenderly you wonder), leading up to where he wants to be. Her eyes are made up with sooty kohl and some of this is smeared. Her open lips are red and big and slightly wet. He has to get off before she wakes up. He writes her a note and pins it gently to her wrap: 'These lovely feet, these beautiful feet. Don't let them touch the ground. They will only get soiled and violated.' How can anyone remain in control after such an incomplete moment?

Guide, made in the '60s is similarly obsessed with the feet, only in this film the heroine, played by the Muslim actress Waheeda Rehman, is an exquisite classical dancer. Most Indian classical dance is formal, controlled and with an asexual sexuality, not unlike traditional ballet. But in this film, the dancer subverts that tradition (and thereby all traditions that humiliate, destroy or neglect female sexuality) as she injects inflamed emotion, intense frustration, terrifying abandon, which in two cases erupt into a symbolic, autonomous, lonely orgasm. Her desires are drying up in her soul because she is married to a brittle, intellectual archaeologist who can only relate to women if they are carved out of stone. When this unsexed life becomes unbearable, she flouts all conventions and runs off with a man who understands these needs. Briefly ecstatic, they cannot, however, be allowed to be happy ever after. The needs of traditional morality prevail.

In the Mood for Love creates the erotic charge through understatement. Two people, a man and a woman whose partners are having an affair with each other (which they discover half-way through the film) find themselves coming together first because of the shame and misery of eating alone each night. In time, tentatively, irresistible attraction follows. They meet in hotel rooms, restaurants, their insecurity dissolving into a sweet delight. But they do not touch; they cannot touch. That would make them as bad as those who have caused them such pain. Their desire has got to be denied and contained within the confines of their lives as social beings (they live in cramped flats where all is known by all, thus adding to that sense of unattainable sex) and the end is a tragic and triumphant self-denial.

There is much to learn and emulate from the examples above. It may be necessary to mentally withdraw from the sounds and sights of sex, the detritus which has littered up life so disgracefully. There is nothing as exciting as a secret sex life. Sex loses its power and charge when it is exposed; the musky scent of sticky, intense and dark intimacy is destroyed by too much light and air and eyes staring idly on.

Sensuality is something different. It comes alive in the consciousness. You have to think about sensuality, observe it, respond to it as it unravels. It needs to be named and handled before it can exist properly. It is one of the few human qualities which, without words and images, would remain ghostly and fleeting dust.

Then there are the dances of sensuality, elegant and skilful. There are no surrenders or victories – just the delectable experience of never getting there. The rules are not known but understood. There will be no going back to his place or mine. My place is not open for business. My mind is though and in there I can manoeuvre, draw in and throw out and mystify. I learned this as a young girl, a young Asian girl whose many languages and communities have destroyed the words which would describe the sexual act or sexual pleasure. So you learn to use words that appear innocuous but which stroke the listener and linger, or provoke and withdraw. The eyes have to work hard too. No other ethnic group in the world has produced such flirtatious, captivating, live eye movements as Middle Eastern and south Asian women.

The future is bleak. The world may yet make grunting naked pigs of us all. Or we could step back and rediscover lost charms and games. It can be done. Look how Jemima Khan has metamorphosed into a culturally complex woman who is at ease in many worlds, but who seems determined to be owned by none. And see how much more desirable she has become as a result.

The Lotus Foot
The secret history of footbinding

Xiao Jiao

THE QUOTATION BELOW IS TAKEN from an early Chinese sex manual, one of many such volumes that adorn my shelves. I find it exciting that they remain indecipherable to the various people who have been carefully examining my library for clues over the years.

OPPOSITE: *A Chinese pen, ink and watercolour (c.1920). Although the foot had a potent erotic significance for the Chinese, this couple are more preoccupied with the conventional nooks of lechery.*

> Every night I smell her feet, placing the tip of my nose by the smell, which is like no identifiable aroma of perfume. I only regret that I cannot swallow down the white chestnut with one mouthful. But I can still place it in my mouth and chew the plantar. Much of it has already been 'swallowed', the use of my tongue is, naturally, subsidiary.

Here at last is a form of erotic literature that one can read without undue scrutiny from prurient neighbours on the train and there is one aspect of sex life in ancient China which I want to look at in some detail: podo-erotomania.

Reflect for a moment on your own attitude towards the foot. It is, after all, an important erogenous zone, having more nerve endings and sensorial sensitivity than almost any other part of the body. On a primary level, a well-developed, contoured arch has, since time immemorial, been regarded as erotic, especially in women. The association of ideas between small feet and a small, tight vagina is apparently not unusual, and according to Henry Havelock Ellis, 'Every prostitute of any experience knows men who merely desire to gaze at her shoes, or possibly lick them, and who are prepared to pay for this privilege.' Consider only George du Maurier's rapturous love for the foot exhibited in his novel *Trilby* (1894). Or Restif de la Bretonne's comment in *Le Pied de Fanchette* (1769): 'Women should only wear clothes that

give pleasure and ravish, however uncomfortable they may be. High heels and high hair style – that is the charm of a woman.'

The desire to render oneself sexually attractive is so deeply embedded that humankind is willing to undergo almost any form of 'unnatural' or even agonising ordeal in order to realise its erotic goals. I am not interested in discussing high heels and foot fantasies in Western civilisation, which I think are a rather run-of-the-mill affair.

The five billion inhabitants of China were, for nearly one thousand years, subject to an all-consuming fetishistic passion for the tiny 'lotus' foot. The origins of this custom are rather hazy but *pour l'histoire*, it may have started with the club-footed Empress Wu in the ninth century imposing it as a fashion dictate upon the women of the court to make herself feel better about her affliction. Or it may have been an imperial dancing girl blessed with such tiny feet that she could dance in the centre of a flower. Politically correct people suspect that lotus feet may have been part of a cunning plan by cruel men to keep the female in fetters, immobile, helpless and dependent upon them for every grain of rice. In fact, it doesn't matter a jot how it started, it just did and it did so in the middle of the eleventh century.

A typical lotus foot was rarely more than four inches long or more than a thumb across. The three most admired qualities were plumpness (signifying voluptuousness), softness (for femininity) and fineness (the mark of refinement). The golden lotus was regarded as the exclusive possession of a woman's husband. It was more private even than the genital area and permission to touch these bud-like extremities was considered an act of ultimate intimacy. Two sensual characteristics of the traditional lotus foot were the exaggerated big toe, which simulated a phallus, and the deep fleshy crevice under the arch, which was viewed, and used, as a 'second vagina'. It was furthermore believed that the willowy walk of women with bound feet resulted in an upward flow of blood that produced more voluptuous feelings in the women's genitals and buttocks, and in more extreme cases, a sexually gratifying ridging of the vaginal walls.

It required between four and six years to bring about this change to the feet – the process beginning when the girl reached the age of six or seven. A bandage, about two inches wide and ten feet long, was so wrapped as to bend the four smaller toes inward and under the foot to create an

ABOVE: *In this vernacular Chinese watercolour with gold paint,* Amorous Couple with a Spectator *(c. 1900), each woman has a 'lotus' foot.*

LEFT: The Visitor *(c.1900),
a Chinese watercolour enhanced
with gold pencil. Although a
frank explicitness is a
characteristic of classic Chinese
erotica, the notion of voyeurism
retains erotic potential. Both in
China and Japan, many young
males could afford neither
wife nor mistress so their
amatory exploits were confined
to the tantalising status of
mere witness.*

exaggeratedly high arch and instep. There were special small shoes to help hold the foot in contraction during this moulding process. Because the bound foot was little used for walking, this fascia became very soft and fleshy. For the Chinese male, this soft fleshy cleavage became the equivalent of the labia.

Howard Levy, who lived in China at the end of the nineteenth century, wrote that:

> The eye rejoiced in the tiny footstep and in the undulating motion of the buttock that it caused, the ear thrilled to the whispering walk, while the nose inhaled a fragrant aroma from the perfumed sole and delighted in smelling the bared flesh at a closer range. The ways of grasping the foot in one's palms were both profuse and varied, ascending the heights of ecstasy the lover transferred the foot from palm to mouth. Play included kissing, sucking and inserting the foot in the mouth until it filled both cheeks, either nibbling at it or chewing vigorously, and adoringly placing it against one's cheeks, chest, knees or virile member.

It was not unusual for a woman to bathe her feet in a basin of tea, then for the man to drink from it as though it were a love potion.

Moreover, the foot was commonly used for stimulation by the male in pre-coital lovemaking. This form of podo-penis arousal engendered the most intense sexual excitement in both male and female alike. (Podo-phallic manipulation is by no means restricted to the Chinese – the more discerning and sophisticated lovers in India and Japan in particular are adept at this technique of foreplay.)

Many elaborate sex manuals were sold, all dealing with the techniques of lotus lovemaking. So sophisticated did these become that special manuals were written for men, for women, for prostitutes, even for the young as preparatory sex education. For men, these manuals gave detailed instructions as to how to handle, fondle, massage and caress the lotus foot – everything from coquettish flirtation to manipulation of the penis with the feet. Some women so developed this erotic artistry that they could grasp the penis between their feet and gymnastically guide it into the vagina without manual assistance.

Women could masturbate by rubbing or stroking their own lotus feet. For others, the orgasm reached its peak of ecstasy if the lover grabbed their feet during orgasm. It was not unusual for two women (lesbians or heterosexuals) to engage in simulated intercourse by each inserting the big toe into the vagina of the other, much like a dildo. The big toe of the lotus foot was of exaggerated length and size in comparison to the rest of the foot, and could be used imaginatively as a 'mobile member'.

Levy cites the case of a woman who 'delighted in urging her female boudoir companions to use their tiny feet instead of the mobile member, and was not satisfied until she [had] changed partners seven or eight times in the course of the evening'.

Men destined from birth to become male prostitutes or the 'adopted' boys of adult homosexuals were also given the lotus foot as children. Completely heterosexual men commonly applied the act of fellatio on the big toe of their lover's lotus foot with the same skill and eagerness as the homosexual. In fact, one Chinese authority of the seventeenth century went so far as to give it his 'official' blessing, stating: 'While oral sex with the virile member of the lotus foot imitates a homosexual act, the male lotus lover need feel no more guilt about this than the woman who performs the same act upon his penis.'

Here speaks Dr Matignon, an attaché to the French diplomatic corps travelling in China in the 1890s, who saw many a lotus foot in his time:

> Touching of the genital organs by the tiny feet provokes, in the male, thrills of an indescribable voluptuousness. And the great lovers know that in order to awaken the ardour of especially their older clients, an infallible method is to take the rod between their two feet, which is worth more than all the aphrodisiacs of the Chinese pharmacopoeia and kitchen.

The bound foot was banned in China in 1902, much to many people's chagrin, I would imagine. An eighteenth-century diplomat lamented in his journal upon his return to France: 'If China were now the greatest power in the world, wouldn't every woman today be inclined to footbinding?' One could reasonably ask the same question now.

The Divine Joke
Sex and the Church

Reverend Dave Tomlinson

RELIGIOUS WRITERS have never been short of things to say about sex but not too many of them have been renowned for their humour on the subject. What a welcome surprise therefore to find C. S. Lewis subverting the Church's usual po-faced stance, talking about erotic passion as a 'divine joke'.

OPPOSITE: The Awakening Conscience *(1853)*, *William Holman Hunt.* *A kept woman is reminded of a life of virtue by a chance chord played on the piano. Ruskin said you could tell that the man is a rake because of the 'fatal newness of the furniture'.*

> For I can hardly help regarding it as one of God's jokes that a passion so soaring as Eros, should thus be linked in incongruous symbiosis with a bodily appetite which, like any other appetite, tactlessly reveals its connections with such mundane factors as weather, health, diet, circulation, and digestion. In Eros at times we seem to be flying; Venus gives us the sudden twitch that reminds us we are really captive balloons. It is a continual demonstration of the truth that we are composite creatures, rational animals, akin on one side to the angels, on the other to tom-cats. It is a bad thing not to be able to take a joke. Worse, not to take a divine joke; made, I grant you, at our expense, but also (who doubts it?) for our endless benefit.
>
> *The Four Loves* (1960)

And of course it is true: there is a delightful absurdity about two bodies writhing around in sweaty fervour, feeling, groping, stroking and caressing with ever-increasing urgency until finally collapsing in a gratified heap – laughing or at least grinning from ear to ear.

No wonder jokes about sex abound in every language and culture in the world. Some of them are funny, many of them are dull or disgusting,

OPPOSITE: *A French print of c.1830, coyly titled* No Signs of Life, *is an illustration of Voltaire's* La Pucelle d'Orléans *(1755). Voltaire's satirical poem about Joan of Arc was written as a comic burlesque containing a fair amount of licentious text. It became phenomenally popular and seventeen illustrated editions were published in the eighteenth century alone. The tone of the book encouraged an equally licentious treatment of the illustrations.*

all of them are old. Yet as Lewis observes, they do embody an attitude to sex that 'endangers the Christian life far less than a reverential gravity'. Sadly, the point is lost on many churchgoers who still adhere to what Lewis calls the 'ludicrous and portentous solemnisation of sex'. If sex really is a divine joke these people definitely don't get it – and they fully intend to wipe the grin off the face of anyone who does!

The irony in the Church having so much trouble with bodies and sexuality should not be missed. After all, Christians claim to worship the Creator of bodies. More importantly, Christianity is founded on the belief that the divine became enfleshed in a human body – complete with all the usual 'bits' and experiencing all the desires and urges felt by anyone else.

Yet, even as we move into the third millennium, the Church still can't find the grace in carnality. Most of the sticky issues that trouble the faithful revolve around some aspect of sexuality: celibacy, contraception, divorce and remarriage, homosexuality, cohabitation. Goodness knows how many people have been alienated from Christianity by the Church's stance on these subjects.

So where does all this distrust of bodiliness originate? There are certainly traces of it in the Bible. The priestly law that treats menstruating women, and men with 'a flow of semen', as unclean (Leviticus 15) hardly enhances bodily self-esteem. Yet the Bible as a whole treats sexuality as a gift of God and an essential part of being human. It also contains bits that, if translated into the vernacular, would turn many a face in the pews bright red. The Book of Ruth's account of Ruth and Boaz on the threshing floor takes a bit of explaining by even the deftest Sunday school teacher. And The Song of Songs, an erotic poem that throbs between the covers of the Bible, gloriously celebrates human sexual desire and bodiliness for its own sake. God's presence is identified in the closing section as residing in the passion of the lovers – and it is by no means clear, that they are even married.

The real source of the problem lies not in the Bible but in the dualistic ideas that contaminated the Church in the early centuries. Despite its repudiation by orthodox Christianity, Gnosticism – a system of belief that was prominent in the second century AD – with its insistence on the inherent sinfulness of the flesh percolated into the psyche of the early Church with subtle and devastating effect. From Clement of Alexandria in the second century AD and his pupil Origen through to Augustine in the sixth century and down to our own day, the dualistic exalting of spirit at the expense of matter has characterised much, if not most, of Christianity.

The Church Fathers had all kinds of problems with sexuality. A modern-day sex therapist would probably have a field day with these guys. In the fourth century AD Saint Ambrose thought that sexuality was an ugly scar on the human condition, Saint Jerome likened the body to a darkened forest filled with the roaring of wild beasts that could only be controlled by rigid diet and strict avoidance of sexual attraction, and Origen was voluntarily castrated to demonstrate how unimportant sex was!

Throughout the early centuries of the Church, marriage was treated with great suspicion, and the superiority of virginity and celibacy over marriage was taken for granted. Augustine tolerated marriage for the purpose of procreation provided the couple did not succumb to lust – 'You can do it but you mustn't enjoy it!' The essence of Adam and Eve's fall, Augustine argued, was the loss of control over the body, especially over the phallus. To think that lust can be tamed is a delusion (he had lived with a woman for thirteen years prior to being converted). So for Augustine the sex act, which is not under the control of the rational mind and will, but seems to take place on its own, is sinful and transmits original sin to every child that is born of the flesh.

But the Church Fathers were a 'small class of literary celibates'. Just how much their teachings affected the average Christian is unclear (perhaps about as much as the Vatican's stance on contraception affects most Catholics today). The stress on virginity, on the horrendous nature of any sexual sin and on the superiority of celibacy to marriage probably appeared almost as alien to many a Christian lay person as to their pagan neighbours. But gradually over the centuries, through the teaching of the clergy and the development of penitential discipline, this outlook came to shape the values and attitudes of the Christian Church as a whole.

In the sixteenth century, the Reformation certainly moved things

OPPOSITE: Learned Friends *from Voltaire's* La Pucelle d'Orléans (Joan of Arc), c.*1830. The clergymen attempt to verify La Pucelle's claims of virginity (see caption on previous page).*

OVERLEAF: *An orgiastic scene of* Lovers *(1585–89) by Paolo Fiammingo. The conventions of Classical art allowed depictions of erotica in the disguise of myth.*

OPPOSITE: Reading, *French School (c.1860). The painter in his studio is the subject of this anonymous nineteenth-century picture. The painter looks to his model to paint the body of the Magdalene. The artist painting a religious scene is portrayed in a creative endeavour to reach a higher plane. The model however has not removed her shoes nor bonnet which suggests a much more earthly body, grounded in the erotic.*

on – a little! Martin Luther's approach to marriage remained, like Augustine's, basically pragmatic: sex is a necessary evil, a way of (men) combating fornication. But he did go a little further in that he effectively defended the 'right' of priests to be as lustful as the next guy, so members of the clergy were permitted to marry in order to avoid fornication. John Calvin made a bit more headway by embracing the legitimacy of pleasure. But he could not let go of the then universal belief that too much passion amounts to lust, hence sin, even in the marriage bed. So, apparently, it was still a case of not enjoying it too much.

Surprisingly, it appears that the Puritans, generally vilified for their legalism, prudery and dowdiness, actually made most progress in rejecting medieval attitudes to sex and marriage: 'Married sex was not only legitimate in the Puritan view; it was meant to be exuberant'– as described by D. Daniel in his essay 'The Puritans, Sex and Pleasure' in *Christian Perspectives on Sexuality and Gender* (1996). Sex was good, created by God for human welfare and even pleasure. And apparently, they 'were not squeamish about it'. Yet the Puritans remained deeply uneasy about 'excessive' desire, which they thought reduced people to the level of animals, and couples were expected to pray before having intercourse. Nowadays, of course, people are more inclined to beseech the Almighty in the midst of love making.

Notwithstanding the Puritan's 'exuberant' sex lives, another three hundred years or so would need to pass before any real change of attitude toward sexuality would occur in the Church. But changes there have been – mostly over the last forty years or so of the twentieth century. Nowadays, none of the mainstream Churches make childbearing the primary end in marriage, the Vatican alone holds out on recognising the legitimacy of contraception, sexual pleasure is assumed to be the rightful expectation of both men and women, and homosexuals and cohabiting couples are widely accepted into communion in many churches.

But shifts of attitude in Church institutions do not tell the whole story. Throughout the centuries, a gulf has probably always existed between the pronouncements of the Church and the practices of ordinary Christians. Nowadays, that gap is wider than ever before, and factions proliferate across the Churches between those who desire increasingly progressive policies and those who think that things have gone too far already.

Two distinct paths of theology are emerging. The first, labelled 'a theology of (or about) sexuality', tends to argue in a one-directional way: 'What do scripture and tradition say about sexuality and how it ought to be expressed? What does the Church say? What does the Pope say?' etc. But feminist theologians, gay theologians and others are developing a 'sexual theology' that asks: 'What does our experience as human sexual beings tell us about how we read scripture, interpret the tradition, and attempt to live out the meaning of the Christian gospel?'

The contrast between the two approaches is clear: the first revolves around given authorities like scripture, tradition and papal statements, with no real voice for present-day experience; the second actually begins with present-day experience, which then becomes the basis for a whole new discussion with scripture and Church tradition. Both seek to take the Bible and the Church seriously, but they go about it in quite different ways.

Sin still rears its ugly head in the new sexual theologies. But, it is not sex that makes a person sinful. It is the person who can make sex sinful. That is the conclusion of Father Kevin Kelly, an eminent Roman Catholic theologian whose work typifies the new approach. In his challenging book, *New Directions in Sexual Ethics*, Kelly asserts that sex is not sinful. It is a gift of God. 'What is sinful is the way human persons can behave destructively towards themselves and others in the sexual field.' What is sinful is what violates the good of the human person, 'integrally and adequately considered'.

So what about something like casual sex? The quality of sex is intrinsically bound up with the quality of the relationship, Kelly argues. Casual sex sells us short as relational beings, capable of interpersonal love. In that sense, it is dehumanising since it is living below our human potential. 'It also fails to do justice to us as bodily persons since it involves two persons using each other's bodies for individual pleasure without interest in and concern for the profound body-person each of them is.'

That said, Kelly recognises the danger of the Church imposing its values on a society that does not necessarily proceed from the same moral starting point. If people are to be taken seriously as moral agents, a 'Yes, but...' or

OPPOSITE: Sweet Memories (c.1870) by Count Mihaly von Zichy from a series Leibe. C. S. Lewis claimed that erotic passion was a 'divine joke': there is a delightful absurdity in the writhing, groping and urgency of sexual intercourse. At its heart Christianity is a body-affirming faith. Some theologians have even gone so far as to argue that sexuality and sexual congress can be a way of encountering God.

Ziehn

Bons souvenirs

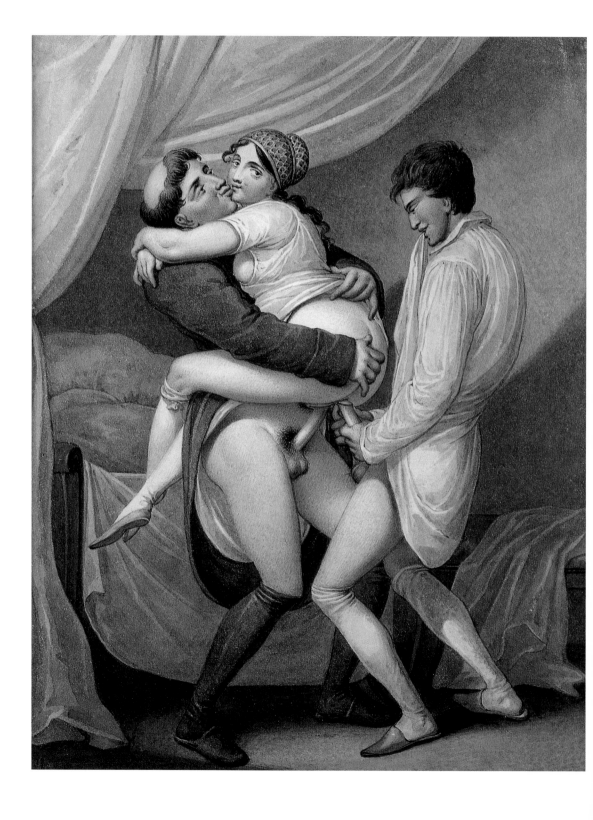

OPPOSITE: Ecclesiastical and Secular *(c.1820)*, *Georg Emmanuel Opitz. Opitz's cutely titled pen, ink and watercolour drawing plays on the fantasy the public maintains about a fabulously promiscuous clergy. Prolific in watercolour and gouache, Opitz's erotic scenes are subtle and imaginative variants of his pictures of Parisian life and the Leipzig Fair. He had a sharp eye for the absurd and self-important.*

'No, but…' response may be required to many specific questions about sexual behaviour, rather than a straightforward 'Yes' or 'No'.

Given its seemingly endless capacity to screw up people's lives, sexually, we should be thankful that the Church no longer calls the shots in society. Yet a reconfigured Christianity, committed to the crucial work of creating an appropriate ethic for today, has much to offer the wider community. The tragedy, as Richard Holloway, the former Bishop of Edinburgh points out, is that 'by exaggerating the claim to divine inspiration' the Church fails to commend some of the enduring values in the traditional Christian ethic, such as restraint. By patiently pointing to the pain and guilt created by unrestrained sexual behaviour, a strong case can be made for an 'ethic of self control'. But this needs to commend itself to people because of the benefits it offers rather than because of an imposed religious guilt-trip, as argued by Brueggemann in *The Bible and Postmodern Imagination* (1993).

At its heart, Christianity is a profoundly body-affirming faith. It not only declares God to be the creator of physical bodies, it also centres on the assertion that the divine became fully embodied in the person of Jesus Christ. There are even Christian theologians who argue that sexuality can be a sacrament – a means of encountering God. Yet this appears to have had little bearing on the guilt, shame and misery the Church has inflicted on people throughout the centuries on account of sex. If, in the twenty-first century, the Church is to offer helpful and realistic guidance to people on sex, it must climb down from the heady heights of moralism and engage in an adult conversation.

'It is hard for me to get used to these changing times. I can remember when the air was clean and sex was dirty.'

George Burns

Law and Manners

2

The Professionals
The story of prostitution

Christopher Hart

PROSTITUTION IS NOT ONLY the oldest, but one of the very few pre-human professions. Female chimpanzees have been observed in the wild, quite clearly swapping sexual favours in exchange for food (and communicating with such facial expressions as 'You'll have to give me more than half a rotten banana for that sort of thing, darling!').

Human prostitution has always been a more complex business, a ritual of some sort: once sacred, now proudly and unashamedly profane. Perhaps prostitutes always represent whatever is most significant in their culture. The first were earthly representatives of the powers of fertility and the goddess of love, available only on certain special feast-days in the religious calendar. Their modern daughters, on the other hand, represent instant gratification, available 24/7, preferably in exchange for cash (though major credit cards accepted).

Any mention of cash (or credit cards) is conspicuously absent from literature's first dealings with prostitution, in the *Epic of Gilgamesh* (2000 BC, at the latest). It seems the golden-hearted whore here is doing her thing as a favour, and/or an offering to the goddess. Gilgamesh is the local king, brave, strong and clever. Out on the steppes beyond the city lives Enkidu, a hairy, boorish brute who eats grass and frightens people. To tame Enkidu, Gilgamesh dispatches a harlot, a wanton from the temple of love, to get him off the grass, show him a really good time and convert him from his hairy, boorish ways. When she first encounters Enkidu out in the desert, she makes herself naked and welcomes his eagerness; as he lies on her murmuring love she teaches him the woman's art. For six days and seven nights they lie together, for Enkidu has forgotten his home in the hills. And after this seven-night horizontal marathon, the *Epic* adds, somewhat redundantly, Enkidu

PREVIOUS PAGE: *Popular German pornography (c.1925). The title translates as* Would you like your aperitif now, madam?

↑ UPSTAIRS ↑

PEEP SHOW

↑ UPSTAIRS ↑

PEEP SHOW

↑ UPSTAIRS ↑

PEEP SHOW

↑ UPSTAIRS ↑

PEEP SHOW

↑ UPSTAIRS ↑

PEEP SHOW

↑ UPSTAIRS ↑

PEEP SHOW

↑ UPSTAIRS ↑

PEEP SHOW

↑ UPSTAIRS ↑

PEEP SHOW

↑ UPSTAIRS ↑

has grown weak. Thus the grunting, asocial male is seduced and civilised by the sexual wiles of the female. *Plus ça change…* Far from corrupting men, the harlot in Gilgamesh is the force that saves them.

Another early example of the saving 'tart with a heart' appears in the Old Testament, in the Book of Joshua. Rahab is a harlot of Jericho, her name in Hebrew meaning large or wide, so we can guess that she was a girl built for comfort rather than speed. She appears to have worked from home while living with her mum, dad and siblings. She sheltered the Israelite spies when they came to case the joint, and when Joshua finally blew the trumpets and the walls came tumbling down, her hospitality was rewarded. The Israelites went in and slew everyone in Jericho, man and woman, young and old, because God told them to do it, in the finest Old Testament fashion, but Rahab the harlot and her family were spared.

In ancient Babylon in the fifth century BC, according to Herodotus, the Father of History (or the Father of Lies, as some sceptics maintain), every Babylonian woman had to go once in her lifetime to the temple of the goddess of love, and honour the goddess by offering herself to any passing stranger for a silver coin. Such of the women as are tall and beautiful are soon released, says Herodotus, but others who are ugly have to stay a long time before they can fulfil the law. Some have waited three or four years in the precinct.

The ancient Greeks had their *hetairai*, whose beauty and skills are so charmingly illustrated on many a Samian vase. They also had their lower-ranking streetwalkers, of whose *modi operandi* another, quite different artefact survives: a sandal whose sole is so studded that when the girl walked on an unpaved surface, it printed in the sand behind her the simple invitation, 'Follow me'.

In medieval times, libidinous Englishmen could resort to the brothels of Southwark in South London, safe, as Reay Tannahill, author of *Sex in History* (1989), dryly puts it, in the knowledge that they were under the respectable jurisdiction of the Archbishop of Canterbury and the Bishop of Winchester. The Parisians found release among the whores of the Ile de la Cité, under the very eye of Notre Dame herself. The medieval Catholic Church in general tolerated the business as a necessary evil.

OPPOSITE: *The French have continuously produced mass-market erotica. This example is from the early twentieth century. The keyhole motif enhances the erotic nature of the print by imbuing the subject with the aspect of voyeurism.*

OPPOSITE: *In French erotic photographs like these the sitters adopt poses somewhere between farce and duty. Once available in large numbers, original prints are now quite rare and expensive to collect.*

The 'Golden Age of Prostitution', however, and also the best-documented, was surely the eighteenth and nineteenth centuries: the age of the courtesan as well as the streetwalker. A bout with a prostitute did not have to be inter-class intercourse. It could involve encounters with the very highest society 'gels'. Not all young men about town liked to wallow in *nostalgie de la boue*. Many liked their women to be educated and genteel. It was common for ex-governesses to become the kept women of wealthy men, and there are even accounts of definitively upper-class girls becoming prostitutes. As late as the 1920s, there was the story of the Guards officer who was shown into a room in a brothel in London's Mayfair, only to find his own pretty little sister perched on the edge of the bed. (History does not record whether they were bold enough to eschew conventional morality on this occasion, and enjoy themselves anyway.) With wives and respectable ladies forbidden from knowing what either they or their husbands wanted in bed, technical skills flourished in the brothel. The Victorian Age – the 'Golden Age of Whoredom' – nurtured such luminaries as Theresa Berkley, the Queen of the Flagellants, in whose establishment clients could, according to the advertisements, be birched, whipped, fustigated, scourged, needle-picked, half-hung, holly-brushed, furze-brushed, butcher-brushed, stinging-nettled, curry-combed, phlebotomized. Madame Berkley always kept her whips in water to ensure maximum suppleness, and she invented a flogging machine called the Berkley horse, which made her so rich that when she died, she left a small fortune to her brother. Unfortunately, he was a missionary by profession, and when he discovered the rather murky source of the money, he felt duty-bound to refuse it. This was the age of Lola Montez, who had embarked upon her chosen career by the age of thirteen. Lola could be very choosy. She declined a night with the Viceroy of Poland because he had false teeth. She enjoyed three husbands and numerous lovers, including Franz Liszt, Alexandre Dumas *père*, and Louis I of Bavaria, whom she allegedly caused to enjoy ten orgasms in one twenty-four-hour period.

There was Laura Bell in the nineteenth century, who charged Prince Jung Badahur, the Prime Minister to the Maharajah of Nepal, £250,000 for a single night. He paid. Later in life she enjoyed a Damascene conversion and married a nephew of the Bishop of Norwich. Most celebrated of all, perhaps, the apogee of nineteenth-century courtesanship, was the inimitable Lillie Langtry. She counted among her lovers King Edward VII, Crown Prince Rudolf of Austria, a Texan rancher called Moreton Frewen, King Leopold of Bavaria, George Alexander Baird, James Todhunter Sloan from Indiana, Ernest Terah Tooley and Whitaker Wright. They were all very rich, and in time, so was she. (Advice to young ladies: Sleep with a wise man and it won't make you wise. But sleep with a rich man and just see what happens.)

Of course, the lower echelons of the trade could be abjectly miserable. Not all were Mayfair courtesans, fêted by generals, composers and kings. A bout with a prostitute could be an encounter with the grubbiest, most pitiful street tart in a soot-blackened alley. In Victorian times, different parts of the great cities represented certain aspects of prostitution. London's Regent Street was the acknowledged and accepted haunt of daytime prostitutes, while by night they hawked themselves on Haymarket. There were some 80,000 prostitutes known to be operating in London in the mid-nineteenth century, and perhaps the real figure was nearer 120,000. Stand in any London street in Victorian times and accost twelve women: one of them, statistically, would be a prostitute. But she might not even call herself a prostitute, for she might also be a seamstress, dressmaker, waitress, or laundress, who simply turned the occasional trick in addition to her usual trade when times were hard.

However, we should be wary of assuming that a prostitute's life was nothing but misery, syphilis and gin. In the words of one young working-girl, to Henry Mayhew, the great Victorian social documenter, 'I am not tired of what I am doing. I rather like it. I have all I want and my friend loves me to excess.' (This is an echo of what many female porn stars claim nowadays, rebuffing the pity/disapproval that comes at them, primarily from feminist quarters.) Mayhew, in the fourth volume of his *London Labour and the London Poor* (1862), divides prostitutes into six distinct classes: Kept Mistresses/Prima Donnas; Convives; Lodging House Women; Soldiers' and Sailors' Women; Park Women; and Thieves' Women. They could all be had, for a price. But then, so could a Victorian wife. At the lowest end of the scale were dockside whores with evocative (if not always appealing) names such as 'Black Sarah', 'Cocoa Bet', 'Bet Moses', 'the Mouth of the Nile', 'Salmony-faced Mary Anne', and 'Long Nance Taylor'. Even the lustiest

OPPOSITE: Lovers *(c.1923) by Georg Grosz. Throughout his career Grosz was upbraided for insulting contemporary moral sensitivities by painting scenes of lewdness and low-life without apparent censure.*

OPPOSITE: *A vernacular French illustration from c.1880. Contemporary etiquette did not require functional nudity.*

young man might have found it hard to get aroused by the prospect of congress with 'Salmony-faced Mary Anne'.

Aside from the lone operators, there were, of course, the brothels. These could be merely 'quickie' places of resort, advertising themselves with such codes as 'For private apartments, ladies, massage rooms, baths, foreign-language schools', or even 'rheumatism cures'. Or they could be palaces of the erotic imagination, opulent establishments like the Archery Rooms, in what is now Warren Street, London, where servant girls could be found dressed *à la Grecque*, or wearing only fig leaves, or as opera dancers whose greatest talent was the double shuffle. (Quite what this bit of Victorian slang signifies, I do not know, but it certainly fires the imagination.)

A more exact analysis of the grades of prostitution appears in Alain Corbin's magisterial tome on French prostitution, *Women for Hire* (1990). The standard designation for a legally tolerated brothel in nineteenth- and early twentieth-century France was a *maison de tolérance*, for an aristocratic and haut-bourgeois clientele, wanting discretion, luxury and virtual silence. Cheaper establishments, *maisons de quartier*, were for the middle-classes; simpler still were the *maisons d'estaminet*, usually attached to a bar, full of noise, smoke, laughter, booze and women in dressing-gowns that left bare the shoulders, arms and breasts. At the bottom of the barrel were *maisons d'abbattage*, quickies, where the woman would be lucky to get even a glass of beer, and in the event of the arrival of soldiers or sailors on leave, queues of men would form outside each miserable, bead-curtained cubicle.

But the Victorian brothel, for better or worse, is gone, along with chambermaids and serving-girls who were 'willing for a shilling', and the dusky Creole girls of New Orleans in the US, and the saucy-eyed whores coming out at dusk to line London's Haymarket and to murmur as you pass by, 'Are you good-natured, dearie?' One can't help feeling an ache of (disgusting, recidivist, male) nostalgia, at least for the Victorian brothel. London's Albert Memorial, Manchester Town Hall, the Eiffel Tower, Brooklyn Bridge, Chicago's seventeen-storey Auditorium Building, are all very well as great monuments of nineteenth-century civilisation. But why did nobody think to preserve a London or Parisian or New Orleans brothel for later generations to gawp at and admire? All those plush red velvet drapes and muslin dresses and chandeliers and cheval glasses, all that champagne and gilt, and guilt-free girlish squeals and giggles. One can't help feeling that the brothel was just as significant a cultural artefact as some of the more high-minded monuments of the Victorian spirit.

Prostitution on a lesser scale continues to exist, thanks to what Corbin calls 'The Rise of Long-Distance Procuring': brides from Thailand or call-girls from the Ukraine. There has also been 'The Rise of Long-Distance Sex': the exponential boom in pornography (literally, whore-writing). The most famous, highest-paid porn starlets are the Lillie Langtrys of our day. For most Western women, however, economic independence and parity have made plain old prostitution a very inferior career option, while the disappearance of the virginity fetish and the widespread availability of the Pill have made it acceptable nowadays for women to have sexual desires and to act on them. This is the most civilising development of all. It is not enough for a man to have money in his pocket. Now he must have kindness, courtesy, charm and clean fingernails. The female continues to civilise the male, which is just as well, for the thought of vast populations of frustrated males, chomping herds of grass-eating Enkidus, is too horrible to contemplate. We should be grateful for the civilising influence that prostitution has had in the past, and that female company and sexual availability have in the present. Or, as Cynthia Payne, the celebrated British madam, once so pithily put it, 'Men are all right as long as they're despunked regularly. If not, they're a bleeding nuisance.' Even worse, according to someone almost as wise as Madam Cynthia, Saint Thomas Aquinas, without available female partners, men are in danger of turning into sodomites.

OPPOSITE: La folle journée de Gaby d'Ombreuse (c.1940). This print is from a series of twenty-eight coloured lithographs, privately printed by 'Les Compagnons de la Belle Epoque' in a limited edition of three hundred and fifty.

A Story of Adultery
The pitfalls of illicit passion

Christopher Peachment

W<small>E HAVE ALL DONE IT.</small> Unless you are a monk or nun who has lived obedient to your vows all your life. And even then you will still have known someone who has done it. I have certainly done it, although I am not going to rehearse the details here, because the other participants are alive and litigious. And I have known many other people who have done it. Not quite everyone I know has done it. But not for want of trying.

It was especially rife in the period between the mid-1970s and the early '90s. Exactly why this should be so I am not sure, although if I were a sociologist I would no doubt point to the spread of the 1960s hippie cult of free love. And its slow decline by the 1990s? Well, AIDS was first made public knowledge in *The Times* of 1983 there was a lot of scare-mongering throughout the following decade.

Since I am not a sociologist, I can say that the above is a load of nonsense, and that getting off with your neighbour's wife first happened about one hour after conscious life evolved on this planet. The one, the main, the only truly persistent hobby of choice for humans down the ages has been adultery.

It is said that when Moses came down from the mountain for the third time, after a long and hard bargaining session, he called together his errant band of wanderers and told them that there was good news and bad news. 'Tell us the good news first,' they all cried. 'Well,' said Moses, 'it took a lot of horse-trading, but I finally got Him down to ten.' 'Good, that's good,' they all murmured, stroking their chins, 'and the bad news?' 'Adultery is still in there,' said Moses.

I had a friend once, let me call him John. We were at university together, although he was a year below me. During his last year, while I was struggling

RIGHT: Initiation Amoureuse *(c.1943) by Suzanne Ballivet. Ballivet illustrated several erotic books,* Les Chansons de Bilitis *(1943),* Les Aventures du Roi Pausole *(1947),* Gamiani *(date unknown) and* La Vénus aux Fourrures *(1954). It is without doubt* Initiation Amoureuse *which remains her most popular body of work. Twenty-five etchings with aquatint accompany this anonymous tale of a honeymoon with a deliciously delayed consummation. This hand-coloured plate of the 'wedding night' happens only in the bridegroom's imagination.*

OPPOSITE: In the Conservatory *(c.1935) Suzanne Ballivet. The story of this couple's exploits is probably one of the longest examples of sustained foreplay in erotic literature.*

RIGHT: *A vernacular English pencil drawing from the mid-1950s, entitled* Miss Betty under the Hair-dryer. *In this extensive series the pneumatic and immaculately coiffed Miss Betty makes considerable demands on the handsomely endowed Piers.*

to make my way in the world, he embarked on an affair with a married woman. He was ideally placed to do this since, as any enthusiast for the sport will tell you, the one major requirement for an adulterous liaison is that most precious of commodities, time.

As a student he put in perhaps three hours a week in the library to research and complete his essay, another hour for a tutorial, and perhaps a further hour or two of lectures, provided there was nothing more pressing, such as a smoke in the park. The rest of his time he could devote to the heart-quickening business of plotting and executing love's true end. A business which, when one's *inamorata* is married, requires patience, devotion and rat-like cunning.

True he had little of that other required commodity, money. But she was married and so she did. And it delighted her to be in a position to pamper her younger *cavalier servente* with little gifts. No woman so generous with her husband's money, as one who is deceiving him.

He did all the right things. He would hang around under her window at all hours. Not exactly strumming his lute and warbling a roundelay, but just generally mooching around in a lovelorn way, hoping to catch a glimpse of his beloved. For this was, as far as he was concerned, the real thing, and he was very moonstruck. He hardly ate for months, and slept no more than a nightingale.

But, alongside the hopeless air of the smitten which had descended on him, there was also the craftiness of the dedicated strategist that every adulterer must be. As well as biding his time beneath his lady's window, in the faint hope of catching the merest glance, he was also calculating which room in the house she might be sitting in. And, if hubby was home, where he might be too. Could he risk a phone call? Would it be she who answered? Would the bedroom extension be functioning? Should he hang up if a male voice answered? Might she come out to walk the dog? Ah, the possibilities kept him in a state of sweet agony for hours.

He took to following her. This was not what has since become fashionably known as 'stalking'. No, she had been clever enough to let slip what her rough schedule was – fetching kids from school, yoga classes in the afternoon, seeing other women for lunches and teas, all the usual round of the idle bourgoise. And so he could effect chance meetings, and both of them would bask content in the delicious secret knowledge that it was their cunning alone that had engineered this coming together.

Sex, when it was possible, was rare enough, illicit enough and snatched enough to be the most fully satisfying, the most intense, the sweetest he had ever known. An hour-long bath together was the equivalent in time of a luxury cruise in the Bahamas. A snatched knee-trembler on Hampstead Heath, the equivalent of a forty-eight-hour tantric sex session, and more stimulating to the heart rate than a handful of speed. My friend often thought that, when sex finally occurred, he was going to die of a cardiac arrest.

I am sure that you follow me so far. You will have known this state. Or you will know of someone who has known it. And you will know exactly what came of it all. It always does.

The only slight twist to the story, which elevates it to something of passing interest, was the reaction of her husband. The thing was that he had discovered the affair even before it had been consummated. He had come across a love letter from the young man, who, being young, had used words of immoderate and undying devotion. The love letter had been in his wife's handbag and so the husband was clearly no gentleman. But then, no doubt she was aware that he might take a look through her reticule, and perhaps, just perhaps, had left it there half on-purpose, and maybe a little piquant jealousy might spice up a fading marriage, and…oh the psychological ramifications of this sort of tale are endless. At any rate, the husband discovered the proposed affair and he was complaisant.

'How very grown up,' I think I hear you mutter. How very trusting, how truly liberated, how much he must have trusted and loved his wife to allow her so much latitude. What a true liberal he must have been. Which indeed he was, right down to the constantly professed opinions that all things were relative, that everyone was entitled to 'do their own thing' and that he was indeed part of the centuries-old conspiracy to oppress women, even if only sub-consciously. (Remember, this was in the late '70s, although I also heard that particular sentiment voiced as late as 1995 by a woman still in dungarees and clogs.)

Which was all fine and dandy. At least you knew where you stood with a man like that, and my friend thought that he would have access to pursue his heart's desire without recrimination, the poor fool.

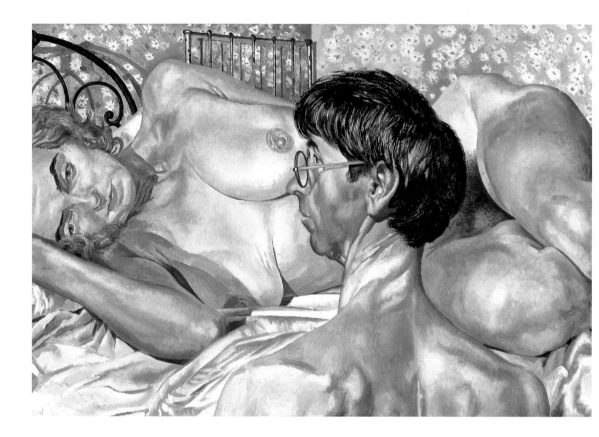

It was me who first spotted the Volvo tailing us. We were out in London's Regent's Park enjoying the sun at the rose garden, when I saw the estate car crawling around the outer circle, the sun visor lowered, and the driver obscured by deep shadow, as if that rendered him anonymous. That was just the start. What followed were the constant phone calls day and night to my friend, which responded with a lonely dialling tone when answered. This was the time before mobiles and answering machines. It was the husband trying to check on the whereabouts of the lover.

'Your lover just called,' John would say to himself, in homage to the title of that short story by Updike on this very subject. He would have done better to mutter 'Think on Madame Bovary', or 'Remember Othello', as they are rather tougher warnings when it comes to moral lessons.

Then there were the tearful calls at two in the morning from his beloved, telling of hours of bitter argument and rowing, which had just culminated in a furious storming out of the house. The threats, the lawyers, the

OPPOSITE: *Stanley Spencer, Self Portrait with Patricia Preece (1937). Spencer was divorced by his wife Hilda and he then married Preece (who was a lesbian) within the week. They honeymooned in St Ives with Preece's 'companion' Dorothy. The marriage was never consummated.*

PREVIOUS PAGE: Rolla *(the name of a novel and its heroine), 1878 by Henri Gervex. The perfect expression of post-coital tristesse.*

patchings-up, the guilt. I am so sorry about the banality of all this, but life does often proceed by cliché.

There was even the confrontation. They thought they had the evening to themselves, for hubby was abroad. Alas, he caught an early flight home. 'Words' were exchanged (actually incoherent children's taunts were exchanged), a briefcase was thrown (not very accurately), it came to blows (more like bitch-slaps from two silly girls) and then tears. Is there anything more revolting than seeing a man who can't fight trying to punch another man, and then bursting into tears?

I pointed out to John that one judicious blow, delivered coolly but hard, will resolve most fights, but John said he 'had no taste for violence'.

'Then don't commit adultery,' I said.

The whole sad story wended its way to the usual conclusion. It did not happen immediately, but then it was a year or so before the full extent of the wife's deception came out into the light of day. Lawyers were called by both parties. They duly launched themselves at top speed into their delaying tactics, and grew fat on the fees. The divorce was bloody, with each side demanding its pound of flesh. And finally, my friend met with the now-liberated love of his life, with no clear plan in view but at least the reassurance that they were now free to sport themselves as they wished, and perhaps consummate their union with a betrothal at some point in the future.

It took less than a day to realise that whatever they had had between them had died. It was not love which had fuelled their passion, it was the illicit nature of the liaison. Danger will always make the heart beat faster. And the human brain is inept at interpreting the human heart.

When watching pornography, the largest part of the pleasure lies in the witnessing of the taboo. Once past the illicit thrill, it becomes commonplace and soon palls. And, *mutatis mutandis*, in Byron's famous phrase: adultery becomes adulteration.

I believe that in the United States, nearly two out of three marriages now fail, and children expect to have anything upwards of three sets of step-parents. And for what?

It may seem strange, in a volume given over to erotica, to find a cautionary tale. Well, I would not wish to be too condemnatory. Adultery can happen in the best of families, and occasionally for the best of reasons.

But consider the damage done: the betrayal of that intimacy which you have slowly established with your partner; the loss of trust; the unleashing of that strongest, ugliest, most corrosive of emotions, jealousy. It may not end in physical violence, but the damage done to the soul is pernicious.

I find it interesting that nowhere in the Bible does Christ have anything to say about our sexuality, with the one small exception of the story about the woman taken in adultery. You will recall that his response was 'he that is without sin among you cast the first stone at her.' That is the bit that most people remember. But he then went on: 'Neither would I condemn thee; go and sin no more.' A sentiment just as wise and telling as the first one.

And if that is all just too pious for you, then remember that most cynical of poems 'The Latest Decalogue' by the Victorian Arthur Hugh Clough (1862), in which he updates the ten commandments for his times:

Do not adultery commit;
Advantage rarely comes of it.

Victorians would have gagged hard at the cynicism of that word 'advantage'. Instead of being subject to a brass-bound moral principle handed down from on high, adultery was now something to be weighed in the balance and decided upon according to whether one might gain some advantage from it. These days, adultery is so commonplace, we can read the sentiment straight.

I have never married, but the same friend asked me not long ago what I would do if I ever caught my wife being unfaithful. The answer is simple, for I am not a liberal in such matters. Kill the both of them.

'So you would never consider adultery?' my friend continued. Of course I would, I am a man.

OPPOSITE: *An illustration from* Clayton's College *(c.1950), a classic of 1950s pornography. Breasts are firm and round, nipples over-sized, penises heavy, brows low. This erotic* 'roman noir', *thought to have been penned by Marcel Valotaire, was illustrated by several artists, in this case in twelve lithographs by an anonymous hand.*

Under Lock and Key
Censorship and the secret museum

David Gaimster

S INCE THE INTRODUCTION of the printing press over five hundred
years ago, the dividing line between art and obscenity in western
Europe has been constantly changing. The political and moral dilemma
between access to sexual culture and its regulation has a long heritage in
Britain going back decades before the drafting of the first obscenity laws in
the mid-nineteenth century. If museums are a physical metaphor for the
way in which the present sees the past, then the history of their collections
has the potential to reflect the development of social and moral attitudes to
the culture of historical and contemporary civilisations. Perhaps it is here,
rather than in the literary sphere, that we can best trace the origins of public
delicacy towards the erotic and the development of the strict division
between legitimate and illegitimate culture. The 'secret cabinets' of Europe's
oldest archaeological collections in Naples and London form a unique index
to changes in public sensitivity to the sexual customs of the ancient, classical
and medieval worlds and to the new cultures being encountered through
the growth of empire. Fresh investigation of these collections has produced
a new chronology for the evolution of pornography as a distinct
cultural category.

The classification of antiquity on moral, as opposed to strictly scholarly
grounds, can be traced back to early archaeological discoveries at Pompeii
and Herculaneum, two flourishing Roman towns in the vicinity of Naples
obliterated when Vesuvius erupted in AD 79. Metres of ash buried the cities
and when excavations initiated by the Bourbon King Charles of the Two
Sicilies in the mid-eighteenth century revealed streets, houses and shops in
near-perfect preservation, they provided a snapshot of everyday life in the
Roman Empire. But almost as soon as the excavations began, the field

OPPOSITE: The Car of
Venus, *a pornographic cartoon
of the late nineteenth century.
Venus' chariot was meant to
be carried through the air by
swans, fused here with
phalluses. It was while on
a car journey that Venus
heard the dying moans of
her son, Adonis.*

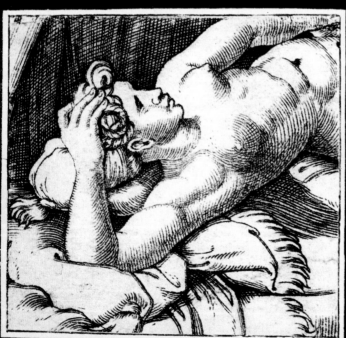

OPPOSITE: *A sheet of heavily censored engravings showing two of the sixteen* I Modi, *a sort of sixteenth-century good sex guide. Originally drawn by Giulio Romano in the early 1520s, the drawings were copied shortly afterwards as engravings by Marcantonio Raimondi. This sheet was acquired by the British Museum in 1830 and was kept in a restricted area of the Department of Prints and Drawings until the end of the twentieth century.*

notebooks recorded with ill-concealed embarrassment the discovery of more and more 'obscene items': amulets, lamps, murals and reliefs depicting sex, raw and explicit, often in the style of caricature. An immediate casualty of the new discoveries was the myth of the austere moral grandeur of the Romans. In 1795, we read for the first time of the existence in the Herculaneum Museum of a room, number XVIII, the first 'secret museum', reserved for 'obscene' antiquities, which could only be visited by those in possession of a special permit. With its star exhibit, a marble statue of Pan making love to a she-goat, the room represented a new taxonomy for the study of antiquity, that of the 'archaeological obscenity', one that was to be perpetuated across Europe for almost two hundred years.

In February 1819, the heir to the Neapolitan throne, the future King Francesco I, visited the museum accompanied by his wife and daughter. He suggested that 'it would be a good idea to withdraw all the obscene objects, of whatever material they may be made, to a private room.' To this room, at first crudely labelled the 'Cabinet of Obscene Objects' and in 1823 more coyly the 'Reserved Cabinet', only those people of 'mature years and sound morals' would be admitted. According to a contemporary guidebook, when the collection was first installed it contained two hundred and two 'abominable monuments to human licentiousness'. Libertarian zeal, however, drove the publication in 1866 of a catalogue of the 'Pornographic Collection', as it was significantly called, compiled by Guiseppe Fiorelli. Despite obvious discomfort in the vocabulary used to describe the artefacts, with its over-reliance on obfuscatory Latin terms, its arrangement forms the first nineteenth-century attempt at scientific classification of sexual culture and formalised the 'secret museum' as a curatorial concept for the first time. The word 'pornography' leaped in to English usage as a direct result: the 1864 edition of *Webster's Dictionary* defined it as 'licentious painting employed to decorate the walls of rooms sacred to bacchanalian orgies, examples of which exist in Pompeii'.

Although the nineteenth century invented pornography, it did not invent the obscene. If sex was to be regarded as something separate from the rest of human experience, then it was Christianity which effected that divorce. From its foundation the Church sought to police sex by private confession and public censure. From the early sixteenth century, sex and the print medium proved to be a powerful combination, and in the atmosphere of Reformation Europe, a potentially subversive medium. The Roman Catholic Church embarked on a policy of actively destroying prints with erotic scenes, including a set of sixteen drawings of couples in various sexual positions created by the young Italian master Giulio Romano in the early 1520s. Known as *I Modi* ('the positions'), the drawings – a kind of early good-sex guide – were first circulated privately and then made into engravings by Marcantonio Raimondi for public distribution. Today, however, only nine fragments of the sixteen original engravings are preserved in the Department of Prints and Drawings at the British Museum. Acquired in 1830, the single sheet mounted with the heavily doctored fragments can be traced back to a private English sale of 1812. Looking closely it is possible to observe that the censor has cut out the genitals leaving only heads and flailing limbs, enough to indicate vigorous sexual coupling. Despite their disembodiment, the fragments were considered too vulgar by the Museum for cataloguing along with the general collection and were kept until recently in a separate folio in the Departmental Keeper's office. The degree of explicitness made possible by the detail of the copperplate engraving helps to explain the reasons for their suppression.

The sensibilities involved in the suppression of the *I Modi* engravings prefigure those behind the creation of a Secretum or 'secret museum' of artefacts in the British Museum during the early nineteenth century. Examination of the Secretum register indicates that some antiquities from the ancient Egyptian, Near Eastern and Classical civilisations were segregated from the run of the collections on the basis of their obscene nature as early as the late 1830s, with many more joining them during the 1840s and '50s. Some of these derive from collections donated by the foremost antiquaries of the day including Sir William Hamilton (husband of Nelson's Lady Hamilton), formerly Envoy Extraordinary to the Court of Naples, who donated votive phalluses made of wax from churches in Isernia, and Richard Payne Knight, author of *A Discourse on the Worship of Priapus and its Connection with the Mystic Theology of the Ancients* (1786). The book, a study of customs and artefacts relating to the Roman fertility god, Priapus, was privately reprinted in London in 1865 by John Camden Hotton, a publisher of pornography. Artefacts were soon being segregated

BELOW AND OPPOSITE:
A group of medieval pewter badges with an emphatic expression of genitalia, excavated in London in the early nineteenth century. Usually depicting saints, such badges were sold at pilgrim shrines, although these explicitly profane examples may have been made for more secular fairs and markets. The bronze pipe-tampers (opposite) are early nineteenth century.

on account of their peculiar subject matter in the manner of the 'secret collection' in the Naples Museum. Chief among them was Joseph Nollekens' small-scale terracotta version of Pan copulating with a goat after the marble original from Herculaneum, seen by the sculptor in the Naples Museum whilst on the Grand Tour in the 1760s. The same divisive approach to erotic culture was being applied simultaneously to printed matter. By the early 1840s the first published pornography was being assembled into the Private Case of the British Museum Library, now the British Library.

In 1865 the British Museum Secretum took on its official status with the donation of four hundred and thirty-four diverse objects described as 'Symbols of the Early Worship of Mankind' by Dr George Witt. It is this collection of antiquities from ancient, Classical, medieval European, Oriental and contemporary cultures which illustrates more than any other the growing anxieties of Victorian curators in relation to artefacts of an erotic nature. George Witt was born in Norfolk in 1804 and graduated in medicine from Leiden University in 1830. Returning immediately to England as a qualified doctor, he resumed his appointment at the Bedford General Infirmary, soon afterwards becoming Physician to that institution. In 1834 he was elected a Fellow of the Royal Society and Mayor of Bedford. In 1849 Witt emigrated to Australia and practised in Sydney for several years before dropping medicine altogether to become a banker. Having amassed a considerable fortune he returned to England in 1854 to take up residence at Prince's Terrace, off London's Hyde Park. His wealth enabled him to indulge in his taste for collecting antiquities, and it is said that he used to hold Sunday morning lectures, presumably for a select audience, on his collection of phallic artefacts.

The artefacts were of sufficient archaeological merit and scope for the British Museum Trustees to approve the acquisition of the Witt collection as it covered all the principal ancient and classical cultures as well as the medieval and Renaissance worlds and contemporary cultures from the colonial sphere. Witt's interest in the antique was almost entirely phallocentric, his thesis being that all pre-Christian cultures across the globe shared a common religious heritage in their worship of fertility gods and goddesses. His obsession with phallicism is reflected in the composition of the library which accompanied the collection. Personally monogrammed books include *Des Divinités Génératrices ou du Culte du Phallus*, published in Paris in 1805, and the 1865 edition of Payne Knight's *Discourse*. Key objects include Greek figure vases, Egyptian sculpture, Roman terracottas and bronzes, Indian temple reliefs, medieval profane badges, the insignia of eighteenth-century secret societies as well as watercolours and prints of early discoveries from the ancient and contemporary worlds. Of particular interest are a series of leather-bound and gold-embossed scrapbooks arranged loosely by culture: Grecian, Etruscan, Roman; Persian, Egyptian; Indian, Tibetan, Chinese, Japanese; two volumes of Japanese prints; Indian drawings; aboriginal America; and Modern. Compiled over many years they contain sketches, watercolours, pioneer photographs and descriptions of objects held in both public and private collections. Most intriguing is the dense correspondence preserved with fellow collectors of phallic objects from Britain and Europe who sent him illustrations and descriptions of their

BELOW: *The chastity belt was probably an invention of the Victorian imagination. (There is still no hard evidence.) This prized example, possibly a fake, was a favourite of the Victorian collector, George Witt, and was part of his 1865 gift of erotic artefacts to the British Museum.*

finds. Witt was clearly the centre of an international nexus of collectors indulging in antique erotica. Like him they were all gentlemen of education and means who would have considered themselves capable of responding in a detached, scholarly way to the subject matter. Looking through the scrapbooks, however, one can sense a certain tension in the taxonomy which is more difficult to interpret. Amongst the engravings of Roman bronzes and pottery lamps are eighteenth-century sketches of copulating couples by Henry Fuseli, nineteenth-century Japanese hand-tinted porn cards, a Victorian 'reproduction' of a medieval chastity belt, early French photographs of female nudes in classical poses and a series of Victorian pornographic cartoons showing the 'Car of Venus' and a version of the 'Ages of Man' which would today qualify as truly paedophile in character. These explicit images go far beyond an interest in early fertility cults and call into question the professed rigour of Witt's scholarship and his motivation for collecting.

The Witt collection reveals the degree of trauma experienced by Victorians in their encounter with the antique and the further reaches of the British Empire. The classical world was regarded as a model for nineteenth-century European civilisation, its architecture and art a blueprint of decency, taste and cultural aspiration. What then of the discovery beneath the Vesuvian ruins that private life in the Roman world was also a very public experience? The visitor to Pompeii today is acutely aware that its citizens were surrounded by images of sex, on tavern signs, street corners and on the dining-room walls of private homes. Revealing their own prejudices, the early excavators reasoned that the erotic murals and artefacts could only derive from brothels. The finds confirmed the realisation that the antique world was characterised by a quite different social and moral code from that of nineteenth-century Europe with its increasing onus on delicacy and manners. Similar tensions afflicted imperial Britain's encounter with the indigenous cultures of its colonies in India and the Far East. Here, in monumental religious art, particularly temple reliefs, heaven was depicted as a highly sexualised place, whereas the Victorian celestial vision was entirely chaste in character. The only strategy, therefore, was to suppress the past and hide away the artefacts which might be misunderstood by all but the most educated and robust of mind, who could be trusted to respond

OPPOSITE: *One of the plates illustrating an erotic mural found at Pompeii, from the catalogue of the Naples Secret Museum, published in Paris, 1857. These are not precise archaeological records, but highly mannered illustrations showing nineteenth-century-style figures which do not convey the graphic strengths of the originals.*

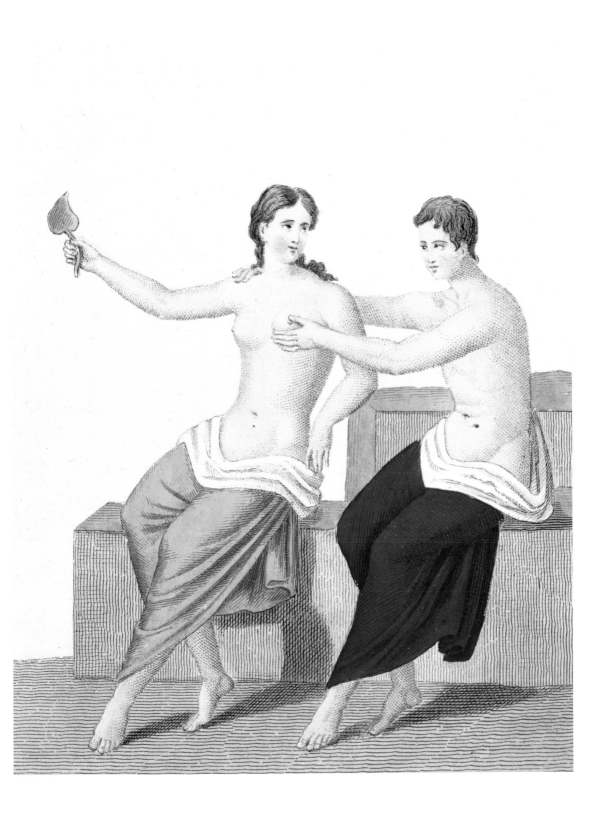

appropriately. This was, essentially, the rationale for the secret museum.

Following the line of the Obscene Publications Act, passed in Britain only in 1857, the creation of the secret museum enshrined a new code for cultural consumption: that what gentlemen chose to look at was a matter of taste, but that there must be regulations to control the circulation of images or erotic objects among the more 'vulnerable' sections of society. The division along gender lines in particular belies deep-seated fears held by the British establishment, namely the quasi-Darwinian view that if women or children were exposed to the erotic, even if antique, it might provoke a breakdown in the social order. Female sexual pleasure threatened not only

OPPOSITE: *A pornographic version of* The Ages of Man *from the 1865 gift of George Witt which made its way straight into the British Museum's Secretum.*

the stability of marriage but also the position of men themselves and their own sense of identity. Victorian Britain, it must be remembered, read Edward Gibbon's *Decline and Fall of the Roman Empire* (1776–88) as a cautionary tale. It warned that sexual excess (as illustrated by the objects found in the Bay of Naples or assembled in Witt's collection) led directly to moral degeneracy and, as a result, collapse of the economic and social order. The perceived undeveloped nature of the female mind and immaturity of youth in such situations posed a dark threat to the stability of the British Empire. In addition, class prejudice formed a further layer of anxiety. The first obscenity laws were part inspired by fear of the reaction of the working masses to cheap printed pornography. The 'casual' nature of the sex lives of the poor was already the object of a moral crusade by the Victorian reformist establishment. The paternalistic approach to erotic culture, whereby archaeological discoveries were preserved but hidden from view to all but the most suitable, represents a typically Victorian solution to contemporary social neuroses. It involved removing artefacts from their original contexts and grouping them under the new and artificial heading of the pornographic.

It was not until the inter-War period that attitudes in the British Museum relaxed, and in 1939, the Trustees were informed that part of George Witt's 'phallic and allied antiquities and works relating to primitive mysteries' had recently been redistributed to appropriate departments. After further phases of dispersal of the Secretum in subsequent decades, the challenge today is to explain the context in which these objects were made and appreciated in the past. This educational concern is reflected in the British Museum's decision in 1999 to purchase the Warren Cup (so-called after its former owner), a Roman silver drinking vessel decorated with scenes of homosexual lovemaking, probably made during the reign of Nero (AD 54–68). The cup is decorated with two scenes, each set indoors with two males sharing a mattress, one showing the *erastes* (the older, active lover), the other the *eromenos* (the younger, passive lover). Their ages and status are carefully delineated, indicating that the young people were members of the elite class. Had the British Museum purchased the cup when it came up for sale in the 1950s, it would almost certainly not have been put on display. Homosexuality was still illegal in Britain and depictions of young boys being penetrated would

ABOVE: *A drawing and reconstruction of an erotic Indian temple relief from one of George Witt's scrapbooks which he had copied from Richard Payne Knight's* Discourse on the Worship of Priapus *(1865). The actual relief comes from a temple in the area of Bombay, brought to Britain by the captain of* HMS Cumberland *in 1734, and subsequently acquired by the British Museum.*

OPPOSITE: *A reconstruction of a fragment of cameo glass illustrating a homosexual liaison (c.50–75 AD), found near Rome in the early nineteenth century. This drawing was part of a set made in 1826 for the collector Edward Dodwell. The drawing first went to the Department of Manuscripts but the authorities' censorship moved them to the Secretum by the end of the century.*

have caused public outcry. Today, in contrast, the new acquisition sits in the centre of the Wolfson Gallery of Roman Antiquities. The display challenges the modern museum visitor against interpreting the scenes through early twenty-first-century eyes and enables us to see the drama of sexual conventions and transgressions in the Classical world. For the Victorians this was not an option. The Secretum was a product of its time, place and culture. It is a historical artefact in its own right and deserves greater sympathy and study. Its tensions and contradictions serve as a warning to future generations against imposing their own contemporary prejudices on the erotic culture of the past.

A Good Lay
What do we really want?

Kate Copstick

AND IT WAS ALL GOING SO WELL. By dint of restricting my focus group to heterosexual male friends, I had a unanimous definition of 'the good lay'. OK, not exactly scientific, but satisfying. And what more could you ask of a good lay ? Not only unanimous but succinct, almost purist in its simplicity, if just a little sad. And enduring, as it echoed precisely the very first definition I ever heard. It was, I remember, after one summer dinner with an assortment of fellow undergraduates, tumbling gently over a sunset into comfortable inebriation and ending at the, then, seemingly inevitable game of 'Truth, Dare or Double Dare'. The pink-faced King Crimson fan on my left was pressured to admit to the best sex he had ever had. I remember my surprise, thrill and self-satisfied smirk when he said that I was. Two disgusting dares, one double dare involving a foreskin and a satsuma and one confession of fantasies about sex with an alsatian – dog not Riesling producer – later, we were back at the boy with the George Washington complex. Showing minimal ability to learn from his mistakes, he opted for 'truth' again and was asked by an unnatural blonde in undisguisedly disbelieving tones, why. Easy, it has to be admitted, sprang to my mind. Always a virtue for those of us whom age cannot wither because we pretty much started withered. But he thought. He smiled. I may have blushed. 'She…she's so enthusiastic!' he announced. He definitely blushed.

And enthusiasm it was that, all these years later, was still, unanimously held to be the *sine qua non* of the good lay. By a cross-section…or, to be honest, a mildly inebriated and actually rather benign section of heterosexual masculinity. Imagination came up – if you will pardon the expression – close behind. A willingness to experiment came a close third.

OPPOSITE: *Kitsch pornography from Germany (c.1925). This series portrays many poses of bourgeois women exploiting their menservants. The title translates as* Absolutely nothing is too much trouble. *In an unusual order of events, the paintings of these illustrations were done after the original prints.*

OPPOSITE: *Above and below left: kitsch pornography from Germany (c.1925),* The Art of Choosing Good Servants. *Below right:* In Classical Mode, *some antique sodomy. Above right: French School (c.1825),* The Reading Lesson. *Interfering with (lubricious and compliant) chambermaids has been a consistent motif in erotic literature.*

One young man on a late night wrote 'must give good brain as well as good head' on my arm, but he works in television, so one assumes he was going for style over substance. And there has been, over the weeks, talk of wanting it to be 'relaxed', of men not wanting the pressure of being required to deliver the kind of performance that would, elsewhere, garner Olympic Gold. But genuine enthusiasm was of the essence. And why should I have been surprised? Ask any cook who their favourite dinner guests are and they will name, not the beautiful and the aesthetic, the trendy and the smart but those who love to eat. Those who enter the room and sniff appreciatively, whose pupils dilate at the sight of devourable deliciousness, who close their eyes and breathe deeply the hot perfumed air, who use fingers and tongue to tease a bird apart and lips to suck the juices from ripe fruit, who do not count calories or cavil at a little lipslicking fattiness. Those who are always ready for a little more. And it is an equal joy to make the two-backed beast with someone whose favourite animal that is.

One of the most memorable – if not lyrical – odes to sexual enthusiasm came from that marvellous old enthusiast himself, John Wilmot, Earl of Rochester. His 'Lines Written Under Nelly's Picture' read…

She was so exquisite a whore
That in the belly of her mother
She placed her cunt so right before
Her father fucked them both together

Shudder at the imperfect rhyme if you must but it has a smack-you-in-the-face quality of gut-felt admiration that all talk of 'Walking in beauty, like the night' lacks, even though one knows Byron enjoyed a good walk-in beauty with the best of them.

Sex is treated less well by literature than the run-up to and fall-out from it. The nuts and bolts of what exactly a great lay does with his nuts and bolt are not the stuff of great literature. Great writers have an unfortunate tendency to talk of love, passion, desire. Which is all very well but, when looking to find a pointer to the classically good lay, a little like reading a recipe for chocolate fudge cake that simply says 'it must be delicious…rich and sensuous, sweet and moreish'. D. H. Lawrence's sex is always an event of cosmic proportions. I suspect he would have no concept of a 'good lay'.

Since sexual specificity became acceptable in mainstream literature, few writers have used the licence particularly well. One only has to look at the Bad Sex Award each year to appreciate how hard it is to communicate with the pen that which is, of its essence, not about words.

Henry Miller has a lot of sex in his novels, but doesn't spend much time enthusing about it. John Updike writes good chap's sex but Martin Amis makes it sound as nihilistic as he does everything else. Annie Rice gives great sexual pen. She describes cocksuckers almost better than she describes bloodsuckers. Her *Beauty* trilogy is full of full-on sex. Sex that is satisfying because of the abandon, the wholeheartedness, the athleticism and the sheer …enthusiasm of the participants.

Enthusiasm. The sexual Rosetta Stone that decoded the great lay. But something of a searing indictment of the British heterosexual female that those males of the species to whom I spoke seemed so thrilled just to find one that enjoys bullying off for a game of horizontal hockey.

Of course a good lay cannot, fully, be so easily defined. Even semantically it throws up problems. For consider…is a good lay the same thing as a good fuck? Can someone be a good lover and yet not a good lay? Or vice versa.

Personally, the good lays of my life have been ongoing, the good fucks I have fucked only once. For my money…which it never was…that is the difference. The term in English has a definite whiff of disrespect, possibly the legacy of English middle-class morality, but, all the same, palpably bound up with those definitions of its essence: men say it is about enthusiasm – but just as the gourmand is undoubtedly more fun than the gourmet, he does not attract the same respect; women, about technique and 'knowing what you want' – yet is not the artist always lauded above the technician?

When waxing lyrical on the subject of 'the soft-top roaring up the happy highway' we tend to say things like 'he was a fabulous lover'…'we had a very passionate affair'. But 'a good lay' is not about love…or necessarily passion. Indeed if my focus group is representative, passion is the stuff of which dreams are made when mere enthusiasm is so highly prized.

OPPOSITE: Pan and Syrinx (c.1920). There is no tradition of cunnilingus – the stimulation of the woman's genitals by the man's lips and tongue – in fine art, although it is a familiar element in the pornographer's repertoire.

And then I talked to a Frenchman and my 'enthusiasm' thesis was undone. Without a moment's thought he answered 'time'. And, without so much as dipping a toe in the quagmire of the sexual divide I knew to be there, I was given an antithesis. That he specified 'time' assumed the enthusiasm was already there. A quantum leap of sexual faith that no heterosexual Englishman is psychologically equipped to make! I spent time in Venice…and in southern Spain. And again 'time' – that one word that takes so much for granted – was the defining factor of the good lay.

Oh, a Euro-equivalent of 'enthusiasm' was there somewhere down the 'lay line', but it was higher than ordinary enthusiasm…'a woman who will truly give herself to me', 'a woman who will abandon herself to me'…my Rosetta Stone was looking more like a fragment than a whole.

I should have known. You only have to finger your way through the 'Memoirs' of Casanova who constantly 'increased my attentions until she became submissive as a lamb' or was 'enchanted to find her submissive to my caresses'. One, reportedly 'blissful' deflowering began with 'a little scream' and then 'several sighs announced the completion of the sacrifice'. So much for enthusiasm on her part. The Latin Layer wants a woman melting like ripe mozzarella on the pizza of their passion, the French Fucker a delicious dame liquefying like garlic butter on his uncurling escargot.

But here, unexpectedly, lay (ah, the joy of the naturally arising pun) a way to increase the sexual happiness of two groups of people exponentially. For when, repressing my feelings of dread, I asked a group of women (well, women and girls) the same question, I – having recovered from the writer's cramp induced by transcribing more demands than hit the table in Israeli–Arab peace negotiations – realised that there was, too, a kind of hideous homogeneity in what they wanted. They wanted everything.

Where are the daughters of Erica Jong whose ideal of 'the zipless fuck' should have had more practical effect than it did? Where are the equality generation? When did Eve Ensler's whining Vagina Worshippers take over?

The most recent research tells us that 43 per cent of women claim pathological lack of satisfaction with their sex lives from lack of arousal to inability to orgasm. Medics have now come up with everything from spinal implants that give orgasms by remote control and clip-on clitoral stimulators that mimic cunnilingus through genital stimulants such as 'Dream Cream' to female-variant Viagra. All, incidentally, invented by men (while the most famous female inventions are the bullet-proof vest, the windscreen wiper, fire escapes and laser printers…hmmm). My gut tells me it's about time they came up with a reality check.

I know Helen Gurley Brown wasn't talking sexual specifics when she said 'you can have it all', but boy does she have something to answer for! Women, if my girls are representative, don't want a lay. They, if anything, want to be laid. A little like an S&M relationship, they want to be the Bottom, but they want to be in control. That 'great technique' or 'knowing all the moves' and 'being able to do exactly what I want without my having to say anything' (my grammar, not hers) figured so highly on the heterosexual woman's wish list for a great lay must send a chill through the average chap's cherished

OPPOSITE: *Chinese School, (c.1920)*, Foreplay. *Nakedness was not considered a prerequisite in Qing-Dynasty lovemaking. This kind of silk painting was produced in fairly large numbers to satisfy the export market that hungered after exotic erotica.*

OPPOSITE: Earth Inviting *(1926). The graphic simplicity of Eric Gill's amorous couple makes the sexual intention deliciously explicit. Gill linked sexuality and religious expression throughout his career but towards the end of his life he began to wonder why he had not separated his erotic from the sacred. Gill himself did not have what many would consider to be a 'normal' sex drive, having incestuous relationships with two of his sisters and two of his daughters.*

parts. That that has to be combined with 'sensitivity', 'imagination', 'an ability to surprise and delight' and 'not being as selfish as I am' has to make Felicity Five Fingers an increasingly attractive option.

But…enter the French and Italian males (let me rephrase that)…this is where the Italian and French male comes in (not much better). Whatever, they are much more suited in approach and desire to giving the English female her ideal lay. It does present a depressingly passive/aggressive image of female sexuality. But maybe that's the way it goes. There is a wonderful passage from Henry Miller's *Nexus* (1960), which paints a graphic picture of mutually satisfying sex between a 'fucker' and what Miller's character John Stymer calls 'a fuckaree': 'The young girl I spoke of – she thinks I'm a grand fucker. I'm not. But she is. She's a real fuckaree. The more I fuck the more I concentrate on myself. Now and then I sort of come to and ask myself who is on the other end. Must be a hangover from the masturbating business… the girl of course, has a great time.'

It doesn't sound like a great lay. But it gives each the lay he or she wants. And what lay is better than that? Oddly enough I spent an hour or so with one of my favourite 'fuckers' just last night. I had reluctantly returned from Venice that morning and was sunk in gloom. He called. He asked if I fancied a fuck because he really did. And I really did too. He pretty well hits most points on my personal 'great lay list'. He is doing it for himself and that, I suppose, is the pre-eminent element of my definition. When he goes down on me he does it because he loves it. When I go down on him he knows I'm doing it for my enjoyment as much as his. When we fuck we are, each of us, on our own little sensory stairway to heaven. We don't talk (another part of my definition) and when we finish fucking we have to go because I am having dinner with someone else. We have never been romantically inclined towards each other: our relationship is (another part of my definition) about sex. He doesn't love me. He loves sex with me. All the great lays of my life have had that as the bottom line. My *sine qua non* is that a great lay must simply be about the lay without adding layers.

A great lay is a fragile thing, easily destroyed by a whispered 'I love you.' A great lay is a selfish thing, compromised by 'tell me what you want me to do.' A great lay is a chemical reaction, not reproduceable by numbers. If you love sex then you're probably a great lay. And I'm still enthusiastic.

'Cinq à Sept'
Liaisons and affairs

Christopher Hart

T HE PHRASE *CINQ À SEPT* denotes not just a trysting hour or two, but a whole philosophy of marriage and life. It signifies both that relaxed, twilight time of day, from five till seven in the evening when the usual constraints are put aside and lovers can enjoy each other; and also the triumph of French rationalism over a more romantic, less realistic ideal of lifelong monogamy and fidelity. Five till seven is the time for both a sun-downer and a knee-trembler. It is two particular hours for two particular people, and – apologies for the vulgar pun – two and two make phwoarr.

Cinq à sept are hours of leisure, pleasure and licensed indulgence for the weary married man and his young cocotte. A very French idea, but one which, unlike some other French ideas we could mention – the deconstructionist theories of Jacques Derrida, for instance, or dunking your bread in hot chocolate at breakfast – travels rather well.

Paris remains the spiritual home of the *cinq à sept*, however. A man who knows about these things told me that during a recent stay in the city, the institution seemed to be alive and in rude good health. How on earth did he know this? Did he himself… ? He shook his head and explained. As he was changing in his room at around quarter to seven, ready to go out for the night, he heard the unmistakable chorus of hot-water pipes springing into life and showers coming on. These might have been the showers of happily married couples, sprucing up in preparation for a night out on the town – except that married couples have no need to stay in hotels. Nor was this the kind of establishment, with its discreet offer of special 'day-rates', that would be frequented by casual tourists. And so, with powers of observation and deduction worthy of S. Holmes himself, he surmised that this was a hotel that still played host to an admirable range of *cinq à sept* rendezvous.

OPPOSITE AND FOLLOWING PAGES 152–163: *Feodor Rojanowski, (known as Rojan) active 1930,* Idylle Printanière *– a classic twentieth-century French limited-edition series of erotic prints. The delicate technique of these seductive, hand-coloured lithographs is an ideal complement to their subject matter. The couple meet in the metro, indulge in foreplay in the taxi on their way to a* hôtel de passe *and, in one of the most wonderful pieces of sustained stimulation, do not achieve penetration until plate twenty-seven (of a set of thirty prints). Indeed the couple's amorous dalliance would have filled the whole* cinq à sept *with few moments to spare. We reproduce fourteen images from the series here.*

The *cinq à sept* is a quintessentially bourgeois institution. It is the lazy, languid, magical time between the end of work and the return home to the more conventional, domestic pleasures of family life. For the weary businessman, office worker or bank clerk, knocking off at five, the next two hours are a little fragrant zone of vice and pleasure. One hopes that this latitude is extended to the wife, naturally, taking the two precious hours to receive the attentions, perhaps, of some impoverished but ardent-hearted art student with whom she recently struck up conversation at a gallery.

For the nineteenth-century aristocrat, the time for dalliance and gallantry was more like *cinq à cinq*, followed by a ride home to bed at dawn, a good day's sleep, and up again at about three in the afternoon for a champagne breakfast and a recommencing of the merry round. Awfully bad for you, but the kind of pattern followed by the many admirers of Nana in Zola's eponymous (and impeccably researched) novel of 1880. Here, in the Paris of the dying days of the Second Empire, young Nana doesn't even start to receive gentlemen callers until around midnight. Her clients are wealthy, titled, bored, unemployed and no doubt unemployable. Having no work to come from or go to means that there is no need for them to squeeze the occasion for love into an urgent two hours, although what this gains in time it might lose in intensity. There must be a certain fervour generated by the keen consciousness that you and your lover have only two hours to play with (each other).

It is a nebulous time of day without strict appointments or divisions. One should of course be home by early evening to greet one's dear spouse and bright-eyed children – but 'early evening' is an elastic term, allowing quite enough leeway to squeeze in a little something extra beforehand. And besides – this is what the French are very good at, despite all the prejudiced Anglo-American talk that the Euros are way behind in equality for women – the deal cuts both ways. The husband has his mistress and the wife her lover, and so long as the twain never meet, the marriage will have a longer shelf-life than most.

And all thanks to the civilised invention of the *cinq à sept*. It is a time of day that is neither quite one thing nor another, neither day nor night but an alluring blur of the two: twilight, dusk. In magical rituals, one performs one's spells at midnight – neither one day nor another – and at crossroads – neither one road nor another – because it is in such uncertain and ill-defined times and places, such interstices in nature, that supernature can leak in from beyond. Similarly, in the highly structured bourgeois day, its every daylight hour so grimly accounted for and watched over by the all-seeing eye of the 'Work Ethic', there is a time when this controlling presence suddenly evaporates and is replaced by a sense of liberation, possibility and exhilarating uncertainty. What do we do now?

Here we have a charming sequence of illustrations to help us. First of all, we see the man approach an attractive-looking young *fille* on a railway platform. This is perhaps a somewhat fantasy version of the *cinq à sept* rather than the norm. For what these two trysting hours are more usually about is the meeting up of two established lovers in a hotel bedroom where they have probably been, on a special 'day-rate,' many times before. In the illustrations, on the other hand, we have the moment of first encounter and seduction, headily erotic certainly, but perhaps not so realistic. But it is important to realise that no exchange of money is made. This young lady is not a prostitute. She has been chatted up by the man, and, liking what she sees (unaccountably, I have to say, since he seems a rather complacent, pudgy-faced individual to me), she agrees to go with him a little way. And then a little further. And then a little further…She is not being paid to do so, although to be sure, if they meet up again for a second bout, she might welcome a gift from him of a necklace, or some new silk stockings.

After the train comes a cab ride, and here things begin to get steamy. That position she finds herself in, sprawled on the floor with her legs up in the air, offering herself to her new partner's probing finger, might look athletically appealing, but I do hope he doesn't excite her so much that she kicks out in tense-muscled ecstasy and he ends up with a French heel in his left nostril. Then they arrive at the hotel and the gentleman very chivalrously pays the cab fare. (You always pay in the end. Even marriage is, as Shelley so rightly pointed out, only a form of licensed prostitution – notes to *Queen Mab*, 1819.) I like the rather more subtle picture of the girl sitting on the edge of the bed, revealing just a tantalising peek of her stocking-tops and taking off her earrings. There is a brisk pragmatism to this gesture that chimes realistically with the whole institution of *cinq à sept*. There follows the love-making proper, the man tupping her from behind while still in his shirt, suggesting the quickie nature of the whole enterprise. And then the final scene, again with that endearing note of pragmatism, the walk over to the all-important bidet, to wash the various scents and secretions of your lover from your still-tingling flesh, before your return home to the bosom of your family. Mind you, the bidet can apparently be fraught with its own kind of difficulties, if the reminiscences of Ava Gardner, regarding her absurdly tempestuous affair with Frank Sinatra, are anything to go by. 'The problems were never in the bedroom. We were always great in bed. The trouble usually started on the way to the bidet.' So be warned.

The *cinq à sept* provides for a certain space and time, a short-term separation of habitual lives which means that things can rub along without excessive friction. Separation of lovers is the key, however. Inviting your lover back to the marital home can only invite disaster. Lord Nelson once made the mistake of asking Lady Hamilton home to meet the wife for dinner whilst they

were in the midst of their torrid affair. Halfway through dinner, Lady Hamilton had to flee the room to throw up in a handbasin. Her queasiness was brought on partly by nerves, and partly by the fact that she was pregnant with Nelson's child at the time. It is a golden rule never to mix mistresses and wives. Like Churchill and Hitler, they will know of each other's existence but they should never actually meet – unless you are a king, in which case you can get away with pretty well anything. Charles II was once in mid-session in his chamber, exercising his royal prerogative with a lady of the court, when Queen Catherine strolled into the room. Spotting an unfamiliar silk slipper on the floor, she simply looked across at her husband and the suspicious bump under the sheets beside him, laughed, and left him to it without another word. This degree of tolerance is, however, unusual.

A more unfortunate attempt at *cinq à sept* was that of Edward VIII, then the Prince of Wales, when he first aimed to seduce Freda Dudley Ward, long before he had even met Mrs Simpson. After a dizzy night of dancing with Freda – like Wallis, a married woman at the time he fell for her – Edward went straight home and sent her a message saying that he would be round for tea the next day at 5pm: the traditional trysting hour. He addressed the letter to 'Mrs Dudley Ward'. Unfortunately for Edward, Freda lived with her mother-in-law, also Mrs Dudley Ward, who opened the letter, got terribly excited and was there breathlessly waiting for the handsome prince when he turned up. A bolder man – Casanova, for instance, or Victor Hugo – might have made the best of a bad job and seduced the mother-in-law, saving Freda for later. But the faithful Edward somehow grinned his way through the ordeal, and arranged a more successful meeting with his intended another day. He got his way, and the affair lasted for a remarkable sixteen years, until Mrs Wallis Simpson appeared on the scene.

The institution of *cinq à sept* may not be strictly in accordance with the Judaeo-Christian tradition of monogamy, it is true. It is an approach to marriage, love and libido that is realistic rather than idealistic. Marriages may last, it says; but they are more likely to do so if each partner's longing for something extra, for excitement on the side, after the initial thrill with the spouse has begun to fade, can be met quietly and discreetly, without fuss and without moralising. Judging from the sound of the showers of Paris at around 7pm, the arrangement still works.

Taboo
Moving the boundaries

Stephen Bayley

'TABOO', ARCHIBALD LYALL SAYS in his book *The Future of Taboo in these Islands* (1936), 'shades off on the one hand into superstition and on the other into good manners.' Good manners have their basis in a moral principle. Sex taboos might be defined as activities based on immoral principles, but their frontiers shift as often and inevitably as hemlines.

The word taboo comes from the South Seas, a happy discovery of Captain Cook's voyage to the Pacific (1785). The navigator was made taboo when the natives of the Sandwich Islands thought he was violating sacred territory by trying to establish an observatory there. Although the actual word is Polynesian, the concept of taboo, which is to say the prohibition of a person or activity on account of impurity or the violation of conventions, was familiar to ancient Egyptians and Jews. Since the institutionalised ostracism of Biblical times, the meaning has drifted so that today a taboo is an activity that the majority finds reprehensible. In the purple language of the bodice-ripper, it is 'forbidden love', although what is forbidden is a matter of taste and tends to change with time. Of course, it need hardly be emphasised that prohibition has a strong aphrodisiac quality. Hunger, Cervantes said, is the best sauce. Sexual appetites are greatly stimulated by hunger's metaphorical equivalent.

A century ago, masturbation was a taboo, although Cynical philosophers of ancient Greece encouraged it as a defining act of self-sufficiency. One imagines Diogenes rocking slowly from side to side in his barrel, although Plutarch tells us that he used to pleasure himself in the marketplace, thereby providing a memorable image of the cynic's hostility to the world and his love of self. While it was a taboo, masturbation was rarely discussed explicitly although, appropriately enough for an act which – Diogenes apart

OPPOSITE: *Choisy Le Conin was the pen-name of Franz, Marquis von Bayros, a prolific Austrian erotic artist. This sexual fantasy in line block,* Erotic Paroxysm, *could be an illustration of a passage – possibly about inversion – from his countryman and contemporary, Freud. It is part of a series called* Erzahlungen am Toiletentische *published in a limited edition of 510 in Munich in 1911. This series caused von Bayros to be subject to prosecution and he fled Germany to Vienna where he found more conducive society.*

OPPOSITE: Lesbian Couple c.*1930*. *Lesbianism has been tolerated longer than male homosexuality. This kind of erotica was more widely available and cheaper than illustration or handcoloured prints and therefore was sold to a much broader audience.*

– usually takes place in private, it is often a covert theme in literature. Great men, Havelock Ellis, fuelled by liberating Freudian insights, boomed in his *Studies in the Psychology of Sex* (1897–1928), were often given to masturbation. Rousseau, in his *Confessions* (1782–89), describes how it became his chief sexual pleasure: 'I learned that dangerous supplement which deceives Nature.'

The solitary calling of the writer is both a sympathetic symptom and, just possibly, a cause of masturbation. The melancholy in the stories of Nikolai Gogol has been attributed to a solipsistic post-masturbatory *tristesse*. Goethe and Kierkegaard both masturbated with gusto and with evident literary reverberations at different stages of their careers. The US Naval Academy at Annapolis disapproves, however. A Navy Department ordinance of 1940 said that recruits 'shall be rejected by the examining surgeon for…evidence of masturbation' although it did not specify what this evidence might have been: RSI to the wrist, friction burns or a dopy grin and a faraway look in the eye?

Lesbianism, while for a long time a taboo subject in polite conversation, has been tolerated far longer than male homosexuality. The Biblical taboo against masturbation goes back to Genesis 38:8–9 and the unfortunate Onan with his spilt seed. Since then the Church has condemned the waste of semen, a charge of which even the most energetic lesbian is innocent. From Diderot's *La Religieuse* (1796) about pent-up emotions in a nunnery to Pierre Louÿs' prose poems *Les Chansons de Bilitis* (1894) full of ripe *fin-de-siècle* literary heavy petting in an atmosphere of steamy exoticism, female homosexuality has had, as it were, an easier ride than the male form of inversion.

Sodomy is now desensitised, however, although that is perhaps an inappropriate term given the nature of the exercise. To the ancient Greeks, as students of Attic red-figure vases know, male homosexuality was commonplace. Yet *Paedicatio* was later considered so grave a threat to Nature that Justinian, who ruled the East Roman Empire from 527, believed it to be the cause of earthquakes, a theory not yet unproven. It was only as recently as 1895 during the Oscar Wilde trial that the public was introduced to 'the love that dare not speak its name'. During the twentieth century, it began to speak its name more frequently, often employing the elegant and eloquent voices of writers of the calibre of Gore Vidal, James Baldwin and Jean Cocteau. As a result, a century after

Wilde went to Reading Gaol for buggery, heterosexual counsellers at Cornell University are required to watch hardcore gay movies as part of sensitivity training lest an unconscious flinch or shifting of buttock reveals a lurking homophobia.

Oral sex has been another taboo. It took until 1972 for 'fellatio' to enter *The Oxford English Dictionary*. There is an interesting, if small, gastronomic sub-history here. An Anglo-Saxon woman unwilling to perform this most gratifyingly selfless act is known in US slang as a vegetarian, or a wife. The Marquis de Sade believed in the stimulating properties of a mouth full of sperm, although it must be said that de Sade believed a lot of very odd things indeed. The nineteenth-century sexual anthropologist, John Hunter, in his *Essays and Observations*, said that semen 'when held for some time in the mouth produces a warmth similar to spices'.

Homosexuality and auto-eroticism are accommodated into daily life. Bill Clinton made fellatio, hitherto on the boundaries of respectability, a subject of breakfast-time news debate in a radio context usually reserved for farmers and polite rabbis. Nowadays, the true amateur of taboo must search the tributaries not the mainstream. Archaeologists of motivation, forensic medicine specialists, the Vice Squad, brave web-surfers, criminal courts and psychiatrists are familiar with the encyclopaedia of modern taboo. Besides the tragi-comic theatre of auto-erotic asphyxiation, there is necrophilia, a taste made almost respectable in the poems of Christina Rossetti and the dollar-a-page erotica of Anaïs Nin. Its existence was helpfully explained by Richard von Krafft-Ebbing in *Psychopathia Sexualis* as appealing to the socially insecure since it did away with the risk of rejection.

The science of deviation knows a multitude of other taboo areas. Indeed, there is a range of transgressed prohibitions that is richly evocative of the nearly infinite variety of man's imagination and erotic impulses. The *American Journal of Psychiatry* is a fertile source:

Mysophilia: sexual dependency on soiled material
Apotemnophilia: sexual excitement from amputation
Kleptolangia: sexual gratification from theft
Klismaphilia: sexual gratification from enemas
Pyrolangia: sexual arson

ABOVE: *Achille Devéria and Henri Grévedon. This picture of masturbation is an illustration from Alfred de Musset's* Gamiani, ou Deux Nuits d'Excès *(1833). This particular version is a typical work of nineteenth-century erotic illustration. The story recounts the tale of the corruption of a young innocent girl by an older sophisticated lesbian, the Countess Gamiani (supposedly based upon George Sand). They are soon joined by a man – a situation which became a powerful prototype for subsequent erotic publications.*

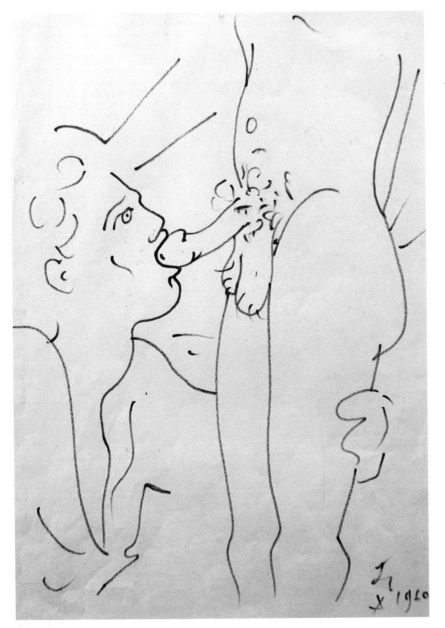

LEFT: *Jean Cocteau,* Fellatio, *1960. Cocteau was one of the greatest homo-erotic artists. The French expression for blow job is 'faire le pompier', perhaps an oblique reference to a hose.*

RIGHT: *Tom Poulton, from* The Biking Series. *It is persistent male fantasy that women achieve gratification from the friction between bicycle saddle and human seat.*

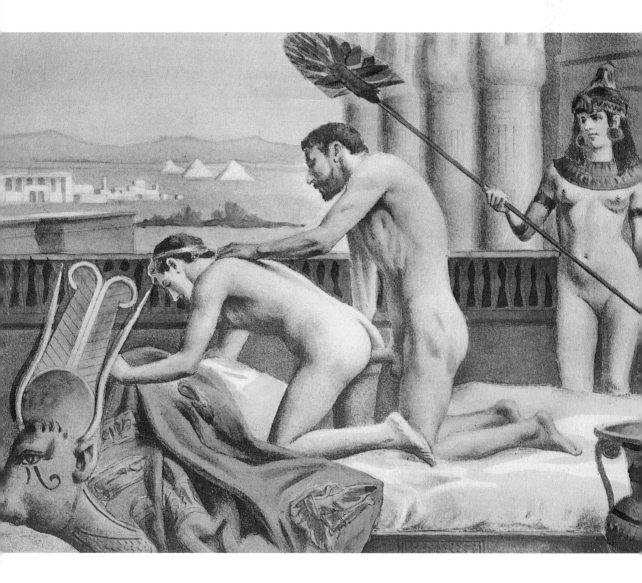

But there are four classic taboos that retain the sense of horror that defines the subject. While incest, adultery, rape and zoophilia were known (and condemned) in biblical times – The Book of Leviticus uncompromisingly suggests a death sentence for a man who 'lies with a beast' – these taboos have animated myth, literature and the folk tradition of jokes ever since. Their sheer consistency and staying-power tempt the suggestion that they may even have an instinctive character. Somewhere in the primitive backbrain we want to make love to our sister, our neighbour's wife, his ass …with or without their consent. Incest had no meaning, at least no

OPPOSITE: *Paul Avril. This
illustration of Antinous,
an exemplar of male beauty
and companion to the Emperor
Hadrian, is from F. K. Forberg's*
De Figuris Veneris.

OVERLEAF: *Nicolas François
Regnault,* La Nuit *(eighteenth
century). A coloured stipple
engraving typical of the
titilatory prints that would
have been collected by certain
members of the upper middle
class and the aristocracy or the
Ancien Régime. This kind of
image would have been
elaborately framed and hung
in the collector's private
apartments.*

forbidden meaning, for the Egyptians: Cleopatra married not one, but two, of her brothers. And the Bible's Song of Songs says:

I am come to my garden
My sister, my spouse

In *The Holy Sinner* (1951), Thomas Mann caught the perhaps inevitable frisson of brother–sister sexual relations. The cultural sanction against mother–son incest – etymologically from the Latin for 'soiled' – has been transmitted in the West as the Oedipus myth, gleefully exploited by Freud in an elaborate campaign of batty hypothesising, nicely discussed and dismissed by Richard Webster in *Why Freud Was Wrong* (1995). Yet, despite the near universal abomination, incest has only been a subject of law in the twentieth century. The physiological basis of the incest taboo is the assumption that reproduction between consanguineous individuals leads to a shallow gene pool from which emerge mutants and idiots, although there is by no means a scientific consensus on this since experiments with animal breeding do not wholly support the retrograde argument.

Instead, the real basis of the taboo may be social: the anthropologist Claude Levi-Strauss said that the prohibition of incest was a defining part of man's journey from 'nature to culture'. Which is to say the more cultured we become, the more likely we are to want sophisticated variety – rather than the embrace of an easy-going relative – in our sexual diet. In this context it may be relevant to say that, for instance, the Mbuti – a pygmy tribe from Central Africa – do not have a word for incest. Nor do they manufacture microwaves.

Sex without consent is as familiar as it is ugly, although as recently as 1981, J.M.V. Browner could write in *Vive la Différence* that rape is a 'perfectly natural function'. Forensic definitions of consent vary. There is, indeed, a form of moral ambiguity about rape, expressed with more delicacy by Anthony Storr in his book *Sexual Deviation* (1964): 'The idea of being forcibly overpowered by a male must have occurred to every woman at some time, although not all women recognise that the apprehension to which such thoughts give rise is not unmixed with pleasure. The situation of being overpowered by a male is also one in which permission is given to be erotic,

since the victim is forced to comply. Thus "she cannot help it", and can enjoy the thrill without incurring either blame or responsibility.'

In a speech at UCLA in 1972, Norman Mailer pugnaciously declared 'A little bit of rape is good for man's soul', unconsciously confirming the selfish primacy of phallocentric culture which has done so much to stimulate the anaphrodisiac hordes of militant feminism. Melanesian Vakuta women, on the other hand, rape males as a matter of custom.

For some unhappy couples, adultery offers the only reliable prospect of sex after marriage. It is so familiar that it is scarcely a taboo, even if its ability to shock and destabilise make adultery the chief inspiration of the novel from Flaubert's *Madame Bovary* (1857) to Tom Wolfe's *The Bonfire of the Vanities* (1988). Even the Talmud allows extra-marital intercourse in exceptional circumstances, although these are surely rare: namely, if a man falls off a parapet and lands on a woman, accidentally causing a 'genital union', then this unlawful coupling may not be sinful.

Zoophilia, or bestiality, is sex between humans and animals. Throughout classical myth, Zeus' visits to earth in the form of a bull with designs on ravishment, reveal the central part zoophilia plays in the erotic imagination. His frequency suggests his visits were not unwelcome. Zoophilia involves fantasies of power, control, abandon, primitivism, feral sex: all powerful erotic stimuli. Yet when a couple were found *in flagrante* in medieval England, it was the custom to hang both the person and the animal, irrespective of the genus of the perpetrator. It is true that in some American states the severest punishments remain on the statute books for men contemplating making love to a cow, while the law offers no sanction – or even criticism – if you murder a cow and eat it, a practice institutionalised by McDonalds.

A variation of bestiality, offering admirable spectacles for the depraved, is mixoscopic zoophilia, or the pleasures of watching animals copulate. Catherine the Great of Russia – whose extraordinary collection of erotic furniture was destroyed in the fire of the Palace of Govitchna in 1944 – entertained her guests with displays of rutting animals. There is even a myth about her own demise being caused by an improvident offer of *venus aversa* to an excited stallion. Alas, Herman Goering did not succumb to a stallion, although he shared the Empress' tastes in animal husbandry and wifery.

Coupling with animals may be a consistent masochistic fantasy in

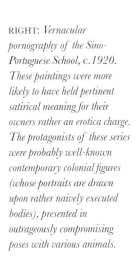

RIGHT: *Vernacular pornography of the Sino-Portuguese School, c.1920. These paintings were more likely to have held pertinent satirical meaning for their owners rather an erotica charge. The protagonists of these series were probably well-known contemporary colonial figures (whose portraits are drawn upon rather naively executed bodies), presented in outrageously compromising poses with various animals.*

pornography, although A.C. Kinsey's *Sexual Behaviour in the Human Male* (1948) actually found that eight per cent of men and three per cent of women claimed sexual experience with animals.

Taboo is a dark, if sometimes ridiculous subject. It is unimaginable that some transgressions will ever be condoned, although the cautious might concede that Queen Victoria would be surprised to walk into a Stockholm hotel bedroom, turn on the TV and find an image of a woman wearing no clothes with one gentleman's penis pumping up her bottom and another gentleman's penis discharging itself generously into her mouth as she winks cheerfully to camera while giving a happy-looking attendant an energetic hand job. As the playwright Richard Brinsley Sheridan has a character say in *The Critic* (1779), 'Nothing is unnatural that is not physically impossible.' So, there is still some way for the editorial board of the *American Journal of Psychiatry* to go. Maybe the next erotic frontier will be…the return of taboo.

Orgies
Girl power rules ok?

James Maclean

OH THE ORGY! What a veritable Cheshire Cat of an event! Shimmering miasmically on the borders of the collective consciousness, a feral mirage beckoning to the civilised mind, convulsive, dangerous, always a temptation.

OPPOSITE: *Jacques-Philippe Caresme*. A Satyric Orgy before a Herm *(c.1780)*. *In turn, the herm shows its appreciation of the spectacle.*

Picture this: unruly pine trees scent the air with resin, giving shade from the hot Aegean sun, their scattered needles providing a soft and inviting carpet to the little glade's floor. In its centre stands a herm of Bacchus. A goat's bleating announces the arrival of a strange group of men, beasts and women; the latter lead the way, a throng of men follow, stumbling, already a little drunk, and like the women, half-dressed in animal skins or naked and crowned with a wreath of vine leaves. While some make a clumsy sort of music on their rustic instruments, the animals are tethered; from baskets appear figs, bunches of black, bursting grapes, leaf-wrapped cheeses, succulent roasted meats and honeyed cakes; a feast begins, with dark, heady wine poured from goatskins and gourds. Prayers are intoned, incantations muttered, but the wine is already working its own magic, a more potent catalyst still, charging the atmosphere with raw lust. To lively music, a round dance begins, becoming faster and more lewd as the company flings itself into a wild, gambolling rout. Whoever is still clothed becomes naked, whoever is naked becomes aroused: hands stray over a warm brown breast and its dark bud of a nipple, they clutch at tumescent genitalia. The dance ends and now the orgy proper begins: men and women copulate freely, immoderately, sharing partners, the smells and sounds of sex floating on the warm air. They only pause to eat and drink in order to revive their flagging energies; now the sounds become more urgent: the slap of flesh against

flesh, the murmur of wine gushing carelessly over bodies, the sharp little ecstatic cries. As the afternoon's blue shadows lengthen and the sprawled orgiasts fall into a fitful slumber, the soft, haunting notes of reed pipes are heard. The satyr, spirit of the woods, with the ears, tail, legs and budding horns of a goat, flickers in and out of their consciousness, dancing on the periphery of their vision.

Renaissance artists such as Botticelli created a pastoral, bowdlerised vision of the Bacchanalia that was palatable to their classically minded patrons; it was a vision that artists attempted to refine and improve upon down the centuries. The true Bacchanalia, or Dionysia (take your pick, Bacchus or Dionysos, both names for the Greek god of wine, fruiting vegetation and ecstasy) were probably not quite so Arcadian. Dionysos represented the rising sap of nature; elaborate secret rites (*orgia*) were held in his honour. In post-Mycenaean times these rites became increasingly popular with women, and in an early expression of female empowerment, they thought nothing of abandoning their families, forming into groups (*thyas*) and taking to the hills, dressed in animal skins and ivy crowns with a cry of 'Euoi!' upon their lips – a sort of spontaneous girls' night out, if you will. Waving fennel wands bound with vine leaves and tipped with ivy (*thyrsoi*) they danced by flickering torchlight to the strongly rhythmical music of flute and kettledrum (*tympanon*). Inspired by their god, the bacchantes became possessed of occult powers, they could suckle animals

ABOVE: *Johann Heinrich Ramberg*, Three Nymphs in a Landscape; *Thomas Rowlandson*, Don Quixote and Sancho Panza; *Ramberg*, Garlanded Swains with a Nymph; *Ramberg*, Swain with Two Nymphs; *Rowlandson*, The Inspector; *Ramberg*, Inspecting the Hearth while Stoking the Fire.

and charm snakes; they also acquired a superhuman strength which they used to tear living victims to pieces before indulging in a ritual feast (*omophagia*). The men were harder to convince, not least because of a rumour that Pentheus, the King of Thebes, had been just such a living victim, ripped to pieces by the (female) bacchantes when he was discovered indulging in a little voyeurism at their expense. Exactly when men joined the party is unclear, but already in 186 BC, Bacchanalia were banned by Roman senatorial edict as they had become notorious for their 'gross immoralities' – presumably between both sexes. Poor young Orpheus was another, still more mythic, victim of this monstrous regiment of bacchantes and maenads. After the splendidly romantic gesture of rescuing Persephone from the Underworld, he was foolish enough to get involved in a Bacchic orgy, where the women of Thrace tore him to pieces, spurred on by Dionysian zeal. Foolish, because he was trying to convince them that Apollo, Bacchus' rival, was the better god. In Aeschylus' version, after dismemberment, the songster's head was unceremoniously tossed into the sea where it floated off, still singing, until it was washed up on the shores of Lesbos to rather conveniently become an oracle.

But these were temporary triumphs for female dominance: two different types of orgy were taking shape, one at least, a very male event. The first was the unorganised, spontaneous intimacy between strangers that has its roots in a type of behaviour that only crowds can generate: one

LEFT: *Thomas Rowlandson,*
Rustic Pleasures. *For the
urban erotic artist, the lusty
pursuits of the country folk,
freed from the constraining
etiquette of city life, were a
continuous inspiration.*

of emotional expression: dancing, orgiastic behaviour, even religious ecstasy (the scenes in Paris and London at the end of World War II were fine examples of this). The second came from a leader (or leaders) of society who, having absolute power, might introduce the orgy as a manifestation of this power, or simply because it was in this area that his (or their) sexual preferences lay. These institutional orgies could be enacted by the state for the people: the elaborate sexual marathons organised for the crowds of Rome's Colosseum tended to involve a form of group sex that was more orchestrated than extemporaneous. Today we might view them more as a hybrid of mass rape and a circus spectacular. Of all the Roman imperial orgy-givers (and there were quite a few), the teenage Emperor Elagabalus outshone them all for pure decadence. This Syrian boy had plenty of fun in the four years of his reign before his demise. In AD 222 his grandmother had his treacherous Praetorian Guards hack the eighteen-year-old to pieces and throw the remains into the sewers. Most famous was his unpleasant trick of smothering fellow orgiasts to death with rose petals – several cartloads full.

An earlier contender for the state decadence prize, and also an inspiration for Byron, Delacroix and Berlioz, was the last Assyrian king, Sardanapalus. If he existed at all, he was said to have ended his reign in the seventh century BC with a final, spectacular banquet and orgy, slaughtering his favourite concubines and taking his own life before the besieging hordes that were sacking Nineveh could enter his palace. Later, in the fourth century BC, came Alexander the Great, a dedicated follower of Bacchus who made sure he found time for full-scale orgies between and during his conquests. Men were firmly back in the driving seat. But whether male- or female-dominated, violence and orgies have always been linked. Even in today's metaphoric use of the word, we tend to say 'an orgy of destruction' or 'an orgy of murder and terror'. Is this because of an atavistic fear of a reversion to some wild human condition that would inspire satyriasis in men and nymphomania in women and bring about the destruction of civilisation as we know it? Indeed, Pan – satyr-son of Hermes and the god who chased nymphs and terrorised travellers – inspired panic. In the popular imagination the orgy has become the bogeyman of conventional morality, a Rubicon of decadence.

Unless you count the rape and pillage of the sort the Norsemen indulged in as an orgy, not much group sexual revelry took place over the next few centuries. The Dark Ages no doubt had their moments, but the heavy hand of Judaeo-Christian morality was descending. These were centuries of war and survival, the painfully slow genesis of modern Western culture. Perhaps courtly love and the chivalrous ideal of the Middle Ages as evoked by the legendary Arthur and his knights have a darker, more carnal side. After all, from illuminated manuscripts of the time there are glimpses of bawdiness. And there were also the bathhouses or 'stewes' where the medieval urban sophisticates indulged in all manner of sexual shenanigans. But in fact, it was the Renaissance and its new thinking and re-evaluation of classical culture and values that awoke the orgy from its long sleep; against this background there was a slackening of rigid Christian morality – amongst the ruling classes, at least. There were pioneers: as daughter of Pope Alexander VI and a member of the most important family in Renaissance Italy, Lucrezia Borgia was well-placed to conduct her private life in any way

RIGHT: *Thomas Rowlandson,* The Pasha. *Rowlandson never actually left Covent Garden in his entire career, but the luxurious erotic imagery of the Orient and Middle East nonetheless inspired him. Byron caught the same mood of sublime excess in his poem* Sardanapalus. *Islam allows four wives, in addition to any number of pleasure girls acquired from the slave market.*

LEFT: *Thomas Rowlandson,* An English Bacchanalia *(c.1780). Dancing revellers take pleasure in the coming together of verdure, drink and sex.*

she cared; indeed, rumours of secret, incestuous orgies at the Vatican were rife and, given the complexity of her sexual liaisons, entirely plausible.

Although Lucrezia may have been a bad girl in a clandestine sort of way, it wasn't until Philippe, Duc d'Orléans, the regent for the future King Louis XV, set up his court in 1715 that sexual dissipation began to take place on an altogether grander and more public scale; while it's true that at first, private parties were held by members of the French court in the relatively discreet setting of the luxurious *petites maisons*, soon orgiastic secret societies began to proliferate, such as *Les Aphrodites*. These were the hallmark of eighteenth-century depravity, and were often no more than parties of prostitutes organised for the collective pleasure of the aristos. It was a mood picked up by Watteau and his imitators, although paintings such as *The Embarkation for Cythera* (1717) were merely innocent allegories compared with the full-scale licentiousness that took place for the amusement of the jaded Regent. Even in stodgy, Hanoverian old England, Sir Francis Dashwood's Hellfire Club may have inspired Hogarth's series of paintings *A Rake's Progress* (1733–35), which contains a splendid scene of incipient orgy set in a brothel. The rustle of silk taffeta, the thrust and parry of boudoir wit: ah! the elegance of these sexual minuets. But was the substance of the eighteenth-century debauchery less pleasant than the theory? Unwashed (but heavily scented) bodies, lice crawling under powdered wigs, rouge concealing the ravages of age, carious teeth, the disaster of pregnancy and the uncertainty of sexually transmitted disease. De Sade bused (well, coached) his girls, carefully selected by his gentleman's gentleman, from the centre of Paris to his *petite maison* in the suburbs. Casanova was meticulous in his use of prophylactics.

The orgy's etiquette has always been difficult to transcend: how many people to ask? Should you allow servants or 'professionals' to participate? Who will take care of the catering and the laundry? Do you insist upon ablutions beforehand? An entry fee? A doctor's certificate? Such banal considerations might be ignored by the spontaneous orgiast, but the latter-day orgy-giver no longer accepts that a well-planned orgy must inevitably be a cross between *après-sport* communal bath and a village fête. France, always in the vanguard of sensual delight, after banning its brothels in the mid-twentieth century, cast around for a more democratic solution to

OPPOSITE: *An orgiastic scene in the style of Hokusai. There are three arguments for the perceived uses of this type of print. The first suggests that they were produced for samurai who could not afford to visit a courtesan; the second posits the idea that they were kept as talismans by samurai; and the third explains that they could have been used as instructions in the sexual arts for young girls before their marriage.*

OVERLEAF: *An orgiastic scene, possibly Persian, c.1880. Another quiet day in the harem: experienced slaves whose purpose was to give the Shah every pleasure.*

appease the national libido. The *partouze* club (from the French *partouzer*, meaning to take part in an orgy) was born. Discreet at first, Paris now boasts several of these fine institutions. More sophisticated and smaller than its New York cousin, Plato's Retreat, here is the democratic orgy in its finest form: pay an entry fee, abide by the quaint and rather formal Gallic etiquette and a good time is had by all.

At the end of the day, the orgy's prerequisites are simple, but perhaps misleadingly so: a group of five or more people of both sexes, a comfortable, private environment, food and drink, and no shortage of time. The orgy is not for the sexually faint-hearted nor the emotionally fragile. Moreover, anonymity is never really guaranteed. And the massed flavours, smells and emotions of group sex are strong meat for the uninitiated – in the heat of the moment, might not he or she stop to consider the source of a leaking orifice? Exudate or ejaculate? But overriding this reluctance is the primordial male's desire to cover as many females as he can and the female's delicious ache to be penetrated on an equal basis, to experience satiety (an

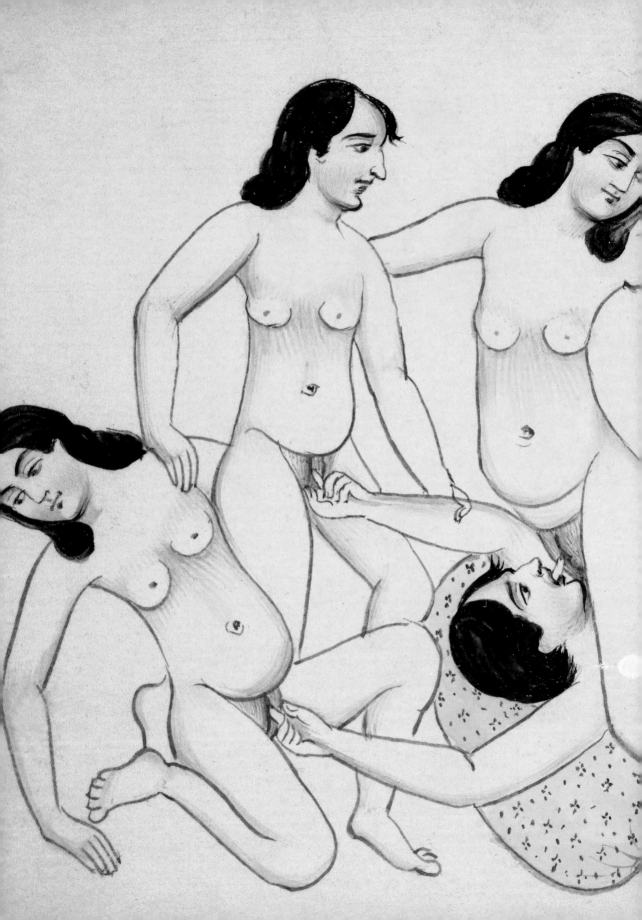

endless parade of erect phalluses) and sample the thrill of sexual comparison in a multiplicity of partners. True, there have always existed those rural fairs and holy days (as depicted by Breughel), a sort of *faux*-bucolic orgy just waiting to happen: an excess of beer, wine or local firewater; and, of course, dancing – the perpendicular expression of a horizontal desire, in particular, group dancing; visitors from neighbouring villages; more tolerance on the part of the elders; all these ensured a heady mix of pheromones, excitement and lowered inhibitions.

It is entirely reasonable to take the prosaic view that orgies have more to

BELOW: *Peter Paul Rubens,* Diana and Her Nymphs Surprised by Fauns. *Diana was the Roman goddess of fertility. Rubens' style is gloriously orgiastic even when he is not depicting an orgy.*

do with the eternal search for Mr or Miss Right than merely untrammelled sexual anarchy. More anthropologically complex is the idea that they are the antidote to a rigid moral code that could inhibit the important natural process of a good gene mix and, in the rural context, cause inbreeding. Or is the orgy merely Nature in all her seismic glory, with the sort of smirk on her face that terrifies our civilised institutions, saying, 'Look – you humans are blessed (or cursed) with sex organs as disproportionately large as your brains – so why not give the latter a rest and let the former take over for a while?'

'…then he asked me would I yes to say yes my mountain flower and first I put my arms around him yes and drew him down to me so he could feel my breasts all perfume yes and his heart was going like mad and yes I said yes I will Yes.'

ULYSSES, James Joyce

Sex and the Arts

3

The Geisha
Icon of the 'floating world'

Lesley Downer

O N A KYOTO BACK STREET one sultry evening, I caught a glimpse of a geisha. She came flitting towards me with a faint tinkling of bells, like an apparition from another age. Swathed in a richly patterned blue-and-gold kimono, she pattered by on high wooden clogs. She was a vision made for darkness, for an era when geishas used to float through the gloom of unlit teahouses, glimpsed only by flickering candlelight. Her painted face glimmered white, transmuting her into a shamaness who could transport men into another world, a world of dreams.

She passed with a rustle of silk, revealing a breathtaking expanse of exquisitely painted white back. At the nape of the neck, the part of the body which Japanese men find most sexy, was a lick of naked, unpainted skin, forked like a serpent's tongue. It was the most mesmerising of all, a reminder that behind the alabaster mask, beneath the layers of silk and brocade, there was a real flesh-and-blood woman. Not only that: this subtle flash of naked skin was a potent reminder of her womanhood. For the shape evokes and depicts the female private parts.

Geishas are the ultimate feminine icons. Every part of their being and their costume is designed to hint at possible delights. Literal-minded Westerners often assume that geishas are high-class courtesans. But they are far more mysterious than that. They are actresses, players of an eternal game. Were sex to be freely on offer, the eroticism would lose its edge. Everything is in the promise, the fantasy which the geishas weave for their customers. To spend time in the floating world of the geishas is *asobi* – 'play'. The 'floating world' is a fantasy created by women for men, where they can forget themselves in the pursuit of pleasure, utterly different from the real-life world of work and family. And the game that they play there is love.

OPPOSITE: *Kitagawa Utamaro,* A Beauty Applying Her Makeup. *Eighteenth-century* shunga *traditionally depicted images of geishas, courtesans and actresses. Here, a geisha is shown mid-ritual, applying her white makeup. Geishas leave a swathe of skin naked at the nape of the neck – said to symbolise the* mons veneris.

PREVIOUS PAGE: *Pablo Picasso,* Seated Nude with Arms Crossed above her Head, *1972. Picasso executed many erotic images throughout his career. During his late period his riotous nudes seemed to explode with life. They became resplendent symbols of burgeoning life as he realised his was nearing the end.*

ABOVE: *A* shin-hanga *image (meaning 'new woodblock') of* A Beauty Combing her Hair *(1920). This kind of image moved away from the* shunga *tradition of highly stylised images of courtesans and actresses. The influence of the West encouraged more intimate, domestic depictions – note that the girl is not wearing makeup.*

The only Western equivalent to geishas were the hetaerai of ancient Greece. They were far from prostitutes; there were plenty of those available to satisfy a man's desires. The hetaerai, conversely, were trained to be the brilliant companions of powerful men. Geishas too are 'flowers in a high place', beyond the reach of all but the most wealthy and powerful, for whom they may be mistresses and companions.

Ask a geisha what she does and she will say she is an artiste: the *gei* of geisha means 'arts' and *sha* means 'person'. Her accomplishments are Japanese classical music and dance, which come from as long a tradition as Western opera and ballet. But her chief work of art is herself.

In Kyoto I watched a young geisha preparing for the evening's work of entertaining men at teahouse parties. Kneeling on the *tatami* floor with her shoulders bared she seemed an ordinary young woman, though extraordinarily lovely. She had the face of a classic Japanese beauty, such as one sees in woodblock prints: shaped like a melon seed, with large eyes, a dainty nose and a mouth like a bow. Only her hair, teased and lacquered into a gleaming medieval coiffure, gave away her profession.

Wielding her brush like an artist, she covered her face in a layer of thick white make-up to form a perfect oval. She was transformed, as if she had put on a mask. At the hairline, as if to enhance the illusion, there was an edge of skin left unpainted. Japanese men say that to see this line of bare flesh is like seeing a tiny glimpse of the naked woman behind the mask.

Then she whitened her back, carefully leaving bare the forked tongue at the nape of the neck. She etched her eyes in black and shaped her eyebrows into two feathery brown moth wings.

Next she began to dress, wrapping herself in layers of silken kimono underwear. Finally she put on the heavy brocade kimono, tying it in place with ribbons. Then she took the *obi*, a wide stiff embroidered cummerbund, and wound it around her waist with the help of a fellow geisha, who pulled it tight like a corset. It covered her from armpit to hips, concealing all hint of a female shape.

At the front the kimono was wrapped primly to the throat. But at the back it dipped low, drawing attention to that focal point for desire – the tantalising serpent's tongue of unpainted flesh. It was an eroticism of concealment and mystery. It left almost everything to the imagination, making every tiny glimpse of the flesh beneath all the more piquant. Lastly she painted in a tiny rosebud mouth. The artifice was complete. She was woman embodied, a compilation of markers of femininity.

Geishas were not always prim and proper. They appeared at the beginning of the eighteenth century as part of the hedonistic culture of the 'floating world'. In Japan in those days, marriage was a joyless affair. Men and women married partners chosen for them by their parents. Marital sex was a grim duty, performed for the express purpose of producing progeny. Unlikely though it sounds, it was considered highly inappropriate to take any pleasure in having sex with one's spouse.

For sexual heaven, men went to the professionals of the pleasure quarters. From the customer's point of view, the quarters were a haven for all imaginable delights. Known as the 'bad places', they were licensed by the government and located a good distance from town so as not to pollute decent folk. In this 'floating world' men could drift, living only for the moment and spending all their money in the pursuit of pleasure. It was with the courtesans of the pleasure quarters that men enjoyed love, passion and maybe lifelong commitment – certainly not with the 'honourable interior', the homebound wife.

Far from being separated from culture, sex became the heart of it. In their heyday, the brothels that lined the streets of the pleasure quarters were like salons. They were glamorous centres of sophisticated entertainment where men lounged in candlelit halls, enjoying witty conversation, exquisite food and drink and brilliant performances of music and dancing, in which they also participated. Everything had an edge. There was always flirtation, laughter and the promise of sex.

If a man was lucky, well-connected and wealthy enough, he might even be able to enjoy the favours of one of the top-ranking courtesans. They were hugely desired, all the more so because they had the right of refusal. Men bankrupted themselves trying to win their favours and still might never succeed.

There were, however, plenty of *yujo* – 'women of pleasure' – who knew very well what their job really was. As young girls they used a dildo to practise the arts of pleasing a man. They learned how to make a client climax quickly and how to fake an orgasm convincingly so as to conserve their energy for the next man. The *yujo* kept their pubic hair neatly clipped

ABOVE: *A sophisticated Japanese could assess a woman's sexual skill by the artistry used in grooming her pubic hair.*

ABOVE: *A* shunga *image from a book attributed to Eisen (1790–1848). The 'floating world' was occupied by pleasure-seeking men for the stimulation of both mind and body. Here, sex was skilfully practised with passion and art.*

with a jaunty little wisp adorning the top of the *mons veneris*. A sophisticated man about town prided himself on being able to assess a woman's sexual skill by the artistry with which she trimmed the 'Lute Strings' surrounding the 'Jade Gate'.

Yujo learned how to fit a dried ring of sea slug over the penis like a French tickler. They were adept at brewing up aphrodisiacs, for which they used charred newts, eels and lotus root. Among the esoteric sexual techniques which they practised was the erotic touching of mouths; for kissing was considered far too incendiary to be practised outside of the bedchamber.

Connoisseurs among the customers studied ancient Chinese Pillow Books, which taught them how to conserve their *yang* energy by refraining from ejaculation. They eagerly lapped up a woman's vital *yin* juices which they believed would ensure long life. The manuals detailed the different ways – some sources say thirty, others forty-eight – in which the 'Jade Stalk' might penetrate the 'Cinnabar Cleft' and move within it. This was a society that embraced sexual delights. As far as sex was concerned there was no guilt and no holds barred. No orifice, no practice and no person was out of bounds.

For samurai, sex with beautiful boys was the purest form of love and the only acceptable one; love with women was considered polluting. Similarly for monks who had abjured the company of women, there was ample opportunity for keeping one's vows and enjoying oneself. And no one thought twice about buying the favours of the beautiful kabuki boy actors.

By the eighteenth century, life in the pleasure quarters became more and more complex and sophisticated. While courtesans and prostitutes continued the role of sexual partner, a new profession arose, that of entertainer or 'arts person'. The first geishas, as it happens, were men. They were jesters, like Shakespeare's fools, who danced and played music to entertain customers waiting to see the courtesans. They also sold sexual favours.

The male geishas have largely died out. There are just six left, who perform in Asakusa, the oldest part of Tokyo. At a teahouse there, I watched a couple going through their repertoire. They climaxed their floor show with a hilarious and extremely explicit mime of gay sex, complete with tissues to swab up afterwards.

Male geishas were followed by females, who soon came to predominate. From the earliest appearance of the geisha, around 1750, there was a strict

LEFT: *A hand-tinted print from an album of nineteenth-century pornographic cards in the British Library Secretum. The scene depicts courtesans with their customers in a tea-house – more accessible for carnal pleasures than the more established, and more expensive, geisha houses. A woman of pleasure was trained to make a man climax quickly and fake her own orgasm so as to conserve her energy for the next customer.*

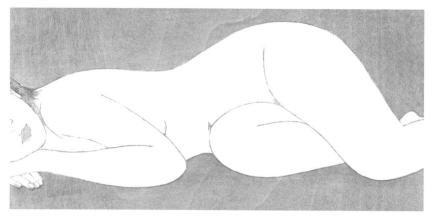

LEFT: *Tsuzen Nakajima,* Dozing, *1999.* RIGHT: *Tsuzen Nakajima,* Wading, *1999. Nakajima is a contemporary Japanese printmaker working in the tradition of ukiyo-e (images of the 'floating world'). These woodblock prints evoke physical sensations such as warm summer sun on the skin or the cool water of a stream on a bare foot, adding another sensual dimension to his prints.*

demarcation between prostitutes and female geishas. Within the pleasure quarters the courtesans and prostitutes had a monopoly on sex. Geishas were strictly forbidden to steal their customers. Their job was to entertain. Outside the pleasure quarters, however, in the towns, geishas were free to do as they pleased and often supplemented their incomes by selling their bodies – though that was never their official job. The geishas' trademark was their instrument, the banjo-like *shamisen*. The drum of the *shamisen* is of beautiful white cat skin, taken from a virgin kitten, which has never been mounted by a tomcat and is therefore pristine and unscratched.

As the decades passed, courtesans came to seem overdressed, overblown and old-fashioned. Geishas became chic trend-setters. They were celebrities, the most sought-after women about town. Every young rake wanted to be seen with a geisha on his arm.

Unlike courtesans, geishas often – in fact, usually – became the concubines of rich and powerful men. Until the coming of modern times, as marked by World War II, if a man wanted a geisha mistress, he might begin by requesting a young virgin to deflower. This happened when the girl was about thirteen. Sometimes the man might spend several nights with the girl before he finally performed the act. Each night he would lie with her, massaging her thighs with egg white and working his way higher and higher so that when the moment finally came it was not such a shock.

If a girl had had no offers by the time she was fourteen, the 'mother' or owner of the geisha house where she lived would suggest to a professional 'deflowerer', invariably rich and usually elderly, that he do the honours. The

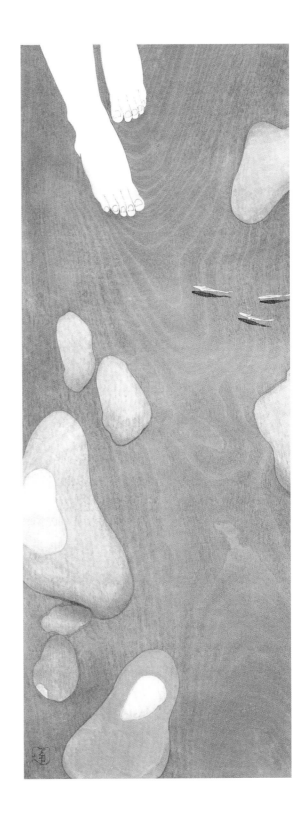

The night is black
And I am excited about you.
My love climbs in me, and you ask
That I should climb to the higher room.
Things are hidden in a black night.
Even the dream is black
On the black-lacquered pillow,
Even our talk is hidden.

Geisha song taken from *Comrade Loves of the*
Samurai and Songs of the Geishas (1928),
translated by E. Powys Mathers

ABOVE: *A Japanese gouache, c.1750, shows a couple making love. The Japanese learned from ancient Chinese Pillow Books that sex should be guilt-free and practised with a frank lack of embarrassment.*

cost for the privilege was about the same as buying a small house. It went towards paying off the girl's debt. For in those days, children were sold into geishadom; the largest part of the debt was the money that had been paid to her parents to buy her.

Up until the end of World War II, when the US occupation of Japan enforced Western ways, it was a status symbol, a mark of a man's wealth and power, to have a geisha. The wife of a successful man would have feared his career was in trouble if he did not support at least one. Once a man had chosen the geisha whom he wished to take as his concubine, he would set her up in her own house. He would also pay for all her daily needs – her huge wardrobe of luxurious kimonos and *obis*, her dance and music classes – and would provide her with a good-sized annual income. In exchange she would be his, available to entertain his guests when he had parties and to sleep with him when required. Japan's most powerful men still often entertain at teahouse parties and geishas may still be their confidantes and lovers – though these days the relationship is a discreet one.

So what makes a geisha so delectable? In conversation and in sex, their great skill is not so much their prowess as their ineffable femininity, their ability to make a man feel that he is masterful and brilliant, the handsomest, most sexy man alive.

At teahouse parties they fill men's sake cups, tease, flirt and engage in risqué repartee. Their dances, like their subtle but provocative make-up, transform the dancer into someone forbidden yet irresistibly erotic. Having spent the evening telling each man how handsome he is and how much in love with him they are, they will almost certainly say 'Goodbye' with a chaste peck on the cheek. To make themselves any more accessible would be to decrease their own high value. Yet that 'almost' remains, offering the promise of something more, as suggested in this geisha song from *Comrade Loves of the Samurai and Songs of the Geishas* (1928) translated by E. Powys Mathers:

> *I have waited all night.*
> *It is midnight and I burn for love.*
> *Towards dawn I pillow my head on my folded arms*
> *In case I may see him in dream.*
> *I hate these blustering birds.*

Facing Flesh
Art and erotica in the Italian Renaissance

Evelyn Welch

ONE OF THE MOST REPRODUCED IMAGES in western European art is an oil painting of a naked woman, one possibly in her late teens or early twenties. She is reclining against the fine linen of an expensive bed while her maidservants go through the valuable cloth and clothing in her chest in the adjacent room. As she waits, either to dress or for an expectant lover, she touches herself. Her fingers nestle amongst the hair between her legs, the tendrils curling around her fingers. Her lips are shut; she looks directly at us. She is inviting her viewer to imagine her fantasies and to anticipate her sensual satisfaction. Is she capable of pleasure, even without a male partner? Or is she merely readying herself for the job at hand?

This picture, *Venus of Urbino* (1538) by Titian, once hung in a private space, probably the bedroom of the Duke of Urbino for whom it was originally painted in the sixteenth century. Now it hangs in a public gallery and we look at it in the company of strangers. Can we assume that our exposure to naked flesh renders us immune to the original eroticism of Titian's *Venus*? Can we assume that sixteenth-century viewers, mainly male, would have responded in the same ways that we do now? Is this an artistic masterpiece, Renaissance erotica, or both?

Sexuality and sensuality were not equated in sixteenth-century Catholic Europe. Here, all bodily functions were potentially base and damning. Lustful thoughts and deeds keep humanity from spiritual redemption; only the celibacy enjoyed by the clergy, monks, nuns and friars would bring men and women to heaven. Yet even clerics and moralists agreed that sex was necessary – but only the right sort. Sex for procreation was acceptable; sex for pleasure was not. While some writers encouraged men and women to gaze at attractive pictures in order to conceive healthy children, most

OPPOSITE: Venus in Front of the Mirror, *1555, by Titian. Titian based his nudes on poses of Venus found in antique sculpture; however his paintings are imbued with a sensuousness and contemporaneity which was purely of his own making and contributed to his reputation in sixteenth-century Venice as the greatest living master. Here the way in which Venus pulls her wrap around her only serves to make her flesh seem more soft and inviting. Despite her half-hearted attempts to cover herself, this picture is more about revelation than concealment. The mirror was often used in the Renaissance as a device symbolising that the artist yearned to take its place – adding a piquant element of voyeurism to the scene.*

ABOVE: *Giorgione,* The Sleeping Venus,
*1508–10. Titian and Giorgione worked together in
1508 and Giorgione's influence became marked in
Titian's work after that (see pages 214–15).*

OVERLEAF: Venus of Urbino *by Titian (1538).
This astonishing picture of a courtesan pleasuring
herself was probably painted for the bedroom of the
Duke of Urbino. In this composition Titian revised
the peaceful idyll of Giorgione's* Sleeping Venus
*(see above) and imbued the scene with a blatant
sensuality. The direct gaze of Venus challenges the
viewer to play a complicit role.*

condemned lascivious behaviour and immoral images. Sex, like everything else, had its rules. The Church Fathers, such as Saint Thomas Aquinas, argued that the 'natural' position for sexual intercourse was the man on top; it was only just acceptable for the couple to face one another from the side. But sitting or standing while having sex was unacceptable; the man taking the woman from the rear was even worse; a woman on top was the most sinful act of all, one only matched by the crime of sodomy.

But when we find Lorenzo dei Medici, known as 'The Magnificent', the much-admired late-fifteenth-century Florentine patron of the arts, writing a sonnet entitled, 'Talking about Sodom', where he has a wife lamenting the fact that her husband only takes her from behind, we have to re-examine the social and cultural tensions that such regulations created. For most Italians, the problem of sensuality was not heterosexual sex, whatever the posture might have been, but homosexuality. In a society where elite men rarely married before their thirtieth birthday, sodomy was an important part of male sociability. As in Athens, adult men were expected to play the active role; younger boys were passive. An important moment of transition was the shift from one position to the other and eventually, when men reached true maturity, the shift into matrimonial heterosexuality. If two adult men continued to engage in sodomy with each other, they threatened the entire social order, suggesting that such affections could be permanent rather than transient. Thus the admiration expressed for the evocative young form of an adolescent, such as that of Donatello's bronze statue of *David* (*c*.1433), which once stood in the courtyard of the Medici palace, may have come from this appreciation of the young male form. Only young boys could be admired; once they matured, they were off-limits.

One scholar has estimated that up to one-third of Florence's adult male population was under accusation of sodomy at any point in the second half of the fifteenth century. Leonardo da Vinci faced such charges; Michelangelo courted them in his poetic and artistic outpourings to his young male admirer, Tomaso Cavalieri. To combat this threat of male–male sexuality, major towns such as Florence, Venice and Milan actively encouraged female prostitution as an alternative outlet. From an early period beginning in the thirteenth century, they established civic bordellos near the market centres to ensure a taste for women and practice for

marriage. Displaying one's desire for female flesh was, in many ways, a civic duty, indicating an intention to reproduce and repopulate the city.

Prostitutes, under the careful eyes of a male pimp or a madam, were there to provide a service, not to achieve their own satisfaction. At the end of their careers they were expected, like the New Testament saint, Mary Magdalene, to repent, to enter convents and to spend their final years in penitence. Their children were placed in foundling hospitals where they were raised alongside the illegitimate offspring of nuns and household slaves. But in sixteenth-century Venice or Rome, the courtesan, a more accomplished woman with social graces and pretensions, could expect to earn a large income and even achieve political prominence. They did not all die unhappily or impoverished. One Venetian courtesan, Julia Lombarda, died in the mid-sixteenth century leaving behind considerable wealth and luxurious possessions. She, like Titian's *Venus*, used male companionship in ways that were potentially problematic for contemporary society. She profited from sin yet still died in God's grace.

Is Titian's *Venus* a courtesan? Certainly the most shocking thing about her is the way she looks directly out at the viewer. Unlike other contemporary nudes who either shut their eyes or look to one side, this woman dares us to challenge her behaviour. She was undoubtedly modelled on a Venetian woman. Another image by Titian, *A Lady in Blue* (c.1536), shows her fully dressed – indeed it has been suggested that having seen her clothed, someone may have asked to see her naked. We know that the painting was created for the ruler of Urbino, Guidobaldo della Rovere, in 1538, when his wife (to whom he had been married for four years) was a nubile fourteen-year-old. The picture was always referred to as a 'naked lady' a '*donna nuda*', never by the name 'Venus'. But it is unlikely that she was considered outrageously shocking, as Guidobaldo asked his mother to help him pay for the painting. Guidobaldo's nude, like an earlier picture painted by both Titian and the Venetian artist, Giorgione, may have been designed to stimulate the right sort of sexual activity in the bedroom, heterosexual sex between a husband and wife.

Nonetheless, it was certainly thought of as a fairly steamy image in its own time. A few years later, when Cardinal Alessandro Farnese ordered one of Titian's celebrated mythological paintings, he was told of the picture being created for him, the 'nude on Titian's easel makes that of the Duke of Urbino seem like a nun'. With legs open to receive a literal shower of coins, this painting shows a mortal woman, Danae, being impregnated by the god Zeus who disguised himself as a stream of coins. That the painted woman was supposed to have the features of the Cardinal's mistress, the courtesan Camilla Pisana, made this an oddly self-referential affair.

Despite the Church's condemnation of sensuality, it seems that clerics like Cardinal Farnese were very happy to enjoy sexual pleasures in full. In 1501, the German master of ceremonies at the papal court, Johannis Burchard, wrote *Liber Notarum* (first published 1907–13). In this manuscript he describes in lugubrious terms the way in which the Pope, Alexander VI and his children, Cesare and Lucrezia Borgia, had enjoyed the Feast of All Souls: 'In the evening a supper was given in the Duke of Valentine [Cesare Borgia]'s apartment in the Apostolic Palace [in the Vatican], with fifty respectable prostitutes called courtesans in attendance. After supper they dined with the servants and others present, at first in their clothes and then naked. Later candelabras with lighted candles were taken from the tables and put on the floor and chestnuts were scattered around them. The prostitutes crawled naked on their hands and knees between the candelabra picking up the chestnuts. The Pope, the Duke, his sister, Donna Lucrezia were all present to watch. Finally, prizes of silver doublets, shoes, hats, and other clothes were offered to the men who copulated with the greatest number of prostitutes.'

Burchard was a censorious man, willing to believe the worst of his papal overlord. Nonetheless, the fact that the Pope was living openly with his mistress and placing his children in prominent political and military positions was clearly at odds with a Catholic belief in the hatefulness of sexuality.

But how many people actually knew of this? It may be that the enjoyment of sensual images and licentious behaviour was condoned as long as it was done by the elite. When this descended down to the popular level, it became problematic. If everyone could sleep with a woman, she was a prostitute; if only one wealthy man enjoyed her, then she was a courtesan or even a wife. If only a small group of men could feast on the image of an attractive nude, it was art. If it was widely available, it was corrupting and ungodly.

The first serious Renaissance erotica began to circulate around the same

ABOVE: *An early twentieth-century French School version of* Pietro
Aretino's Sonetti Lussuriosi, *copied from Marcantonio Raimondi
after the originals by Giulio Romano. Known as* I Modi, *this was a
catalogue of sexual positions.*

RIGHT: I Modi *became so popular throughout the four centuries following their first appearance in print in 1524 that the pastiches they spawned made up a good deal of erotic composition. Here, an eighteenth-century French engraving in the style of* I Modi *illustrates the sexual position known as 'soixante-neuf'.*

time that Giorgione painted his *Venus*. In the early 1520s, a member of Raphael's workshop, the painter Giulio Romano, produced a series of drawings of sexual positions. He seems to have deliberately explored those that were the most forbidden, showing women on top and men penetrating their women from behind. These undoubtedly circulated amongst a private circle of friends. But in 1524, the printer who had worked most closely with Raphael, Marcantonio Raimondi, made a series of sixteen engravings after these drawings known as *I Modi* or 'The Positions'. They were rapid bestsellers, and caused an immediate reaction from the authorities. Giulio escaped but Raimondi was jailed. The drawings weren't the problem, the fact that they were widely circulated was. Under papal orders, all copies of *I Modi* were confiscated and destroyed. But this wasn't the end. Pietro Aretino, a poet and writer based in Venice (a city with no love for the pope), was outraged by the hypocrisy surrounding *I Modi* and intervened to have the engraver Raimondi freed. Yet, a few years later, despite knowing the risks, Aretino with Raimondi went to the market again, this time with a set of Italian sonnets to accompany the plates. Aretino's conjunction of word and image was even more salacious and focused primarily on the delights of taking a woman from the front or from behind. Dedicated to all 'hypocrites…[whose] bad judgement and damnable habits forbid the eyes what delights them most', his second sonnet, in this translation by the American scholar Bette Talvacchia, gives some sense of how he hoped to be understood:

> *Put a finger up my behind, dear old man, and push your cock in, little by little.*
> *Lift this leg up high and do a good job, then churn away without giving it*
> *thought. This, upon my honour is a tastier morsel than eating pizza by the fire.*
> *And if it displeases you in my snatch, change the location: for there isn't a man*
> *who isn't a bugger.*

> *This time I will do it in your pussy and in your rear another: both in your pussy and*
> *your behind my cock will make me happy, and you happy and blissful. And whoever*
> *wants to be a great leader is crazy; whoever gets amusement from other than*
> *screwing is a good-for-nothing prick. And may Signor courtier and he may wait for*
> *someone to die; but as for myself, I think only about satisfying my lust.*

OPPOSITE: *An eighteenth-century British satirical print of* Colonel Charteris contemplating the Venus of Titian *reveals the sexual potency that Titian's image still held for the viewer two hundred years after it was first executed.*

Here in Aretino's words and Giulio's pictures, there were no allegories to hide behind, no classical references or poetic licence. Aretino highlighted and ridiculed clerics who banned sexually explicit material for the masses while enjoying images of a naked Mary Magdalene in the desert. Today, only a very small number of these prints survive, testifying to the Church's success in having them banned and destroyed. Aretino had succeeded in shaking the confidence of the elite in their distinction from the lust of mere peasants. Like the viewer in the British satirical print *Colonel Charteris Contemplating the Venus of Urbino* (c.1700), watching Venus, now an older woman with sagging breasts and a rotund belly, we are reminded that behind all the artistic connoisseurship, the enjoyment is still in the flesh.

SXE
The world's sexiest adverts

Trevor Beattie and Stephen Bayley

ADVERTISING NO LONGER MERELY REFLECTS the whims and desires of the marketplace, but tends to direct feeling, mood and behaviour. Media commentator Marshall McLuhan called it 'the main channel of intellectual and artistic effort in the modern world'. Self-preservation apart, there are no feelings, moods or behaviours more dominant than the erotic ones.

The psycho-biology of *Homo sapiens* gives the male a very distinct reproductive strategy, a genetic requirement to spread the DNA through as many healthy young females as possible. And the invitation for this is a fine body. Hence, the sexually explicit character of much advertising.

Sometimes it is innuendo, as in Clairol's famous 1950s campaign, which used a 'Does She or Doesn't She?' copyline. Apparently concerned with hair coloration, the issue was made more sexually ambiguous by the additional line 'Only her hairdresser knows for sure.' *Life* magazine turned it down as too sexually explicit, but changed its mind when research showed that most of its women staff had not noticed the innuendo. Clairol sales went up over four hundred per cent.

In Britain, the Advertising Standards Authority informally polices standards of taste and decency in advertising. Clause 5.1 of its *Code of Practice* says 'Advertising should contain nothing that is likely to cause serious or widespread offence.' Since Oliviero Toscani's campaigns showing blood-splattered newborns and death-row inmates for Benetton, no one has caused more systematically serious and widespread offence than Trevor Beattie, creative director of TBWA London. Beattie turned the initials of his client, French Connection United Kingdom, into an ineradicably visible campaign where the client was rebranded as…FCUK. Or sex writ large.

Here is Beattie's choice of the sexiest ads of all time.

OPPOSITE: *The stiletto heels and black stockings in this Sergio Rossi advertising campaign are fundamentals in the iconography of erotica, now commonplace in press ads.*

OVERLEAF: *This ad for Häagen-Dazs appeared in both the UK and the US, proving that tastes for ice cream and sex easily cross borders.*

ergio rossi

Ripe Oregon strawberries are

especially selected as we

feel

it

best complements the rich cream

flavour of Häagen-Dazs.

FRESH CREAM ICE CREAM

Dedicated to Pleasure

ABOVE: *Trevor Beattie's Wonderbra campaign,
fetishising the breasts of Czech model Eva
Herzigova, rapidly became a popular classic.*

OR ARE YOU JUST PLEASED TO SEE ME?

THE ONE AND ONLY
Wonderbra

THE PUSH-UP BALCONETTE BRA. AVAILABLE IN SIZES 32-36A AND 32-38BC.

PULL YOURSELF TOGETHER.

THE ONE AND ONLY
Wonderbra

THE ORIGINAL PUSH-UP PLUNGE BRA, NOW AVAILABLE IN COOL COTTON.

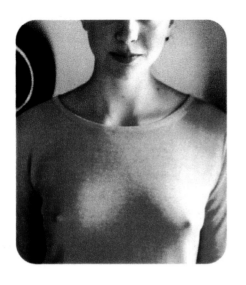

s
adve
ex

S

bliminal

ising

eriment

fcuk®

x e

fcuk®

RIGHT: *Nipples are used to eroticise computer games in this advertisement for Sony PlayStation.*

PREVIOUS PAGE: *In the 1990s a quasi-dyslexic doodle gave rise to one of the most extraordinary ad campaigns seen in Britain: French Connection UK, a fashion business, now became FCUK.*

PlayStation is a registered trademark of Sony Computer Entertainment Inc.

Sexual Spaces
Architecture and erotic power

John Pawson and Stephen Bayley

ARCHITECTURE IS AN EXPRESSION OF POWER, and power is almost always erotic. But there is more: since Vitruvius, the first-century Roman architect, the classical orders of architecture have had a sexual character. The tough, solidly proportioned Doric order has been masculine; the more delicate Ionic has been feminine. Biological and cognitive differences between men and women make buildings designed by male and female architects often different in character. Equally, there can be little doubt that the size of a building is also somewhat erotic. In the days before Sigmund Freud's insights into our sexual motivation made such an enquiry fatuous, Queen Victoria said a 'monolith five hundred feet tall' was the only way adequately to record the stature of her late husband.

OPPOSITE: *The Obelisk of Thutmos I, Karnak. There is a great difference between the erotic and the merely phallic.*

The Neo-Classical French architect of the eighteenth century, Claude-Nicolas Ledoux, certainly included in his ideal city a house of pleasure whose ground plan was based on the diagram of a penis, but sex in architecture is more subtle, as it is with food. Oysters are aphrodisiac only insofar as they give sensuous pleasure through taste and texture and it is the same with buildings. Never mind that the orifices and projections of various building types might lend themselves to crude erotic metaphors, sex in architecture is about the sense of calm and well-being provided by great building design. It is these senses that are erotic by suggestion, rather than the brute and literal bricks and mortar.

No one understands this better than John Pawson. For twenty years Pawson has been crafting an exquisite form of interior design – for private houses, department stores, monasteries and galleries – that is misleadingly described as minimalism by lazy journalists. Instead, what Pawson does in, say, the Calvin Klein store on New York's Madison Avenue or a private house

in Majorca, is refine certain finishes and effects and lighting conditions to create spaces of subtle, but intense, beauty. An inspiration to Pawson has been Adolf Loos, the Viennese architect who wrote a polemical tract called *Kunst und Verbrechen* (Ornament and Crime) in 1908. Loos said only people with criminal tendencies enjoy superficial decoration. Pawson's architecture is about the fundamentals, not ornament: as Loos said 'All art is erotic'.

Here is John Pawson's choice of architectural images from around the world that harbour an erotic charge.

LEFT: *John Pawson's Canelle Patisserie, London. The power of the latent over the blatant…*

RIGHT: *…although there are exceptions. A dovetail joint is like a diagram of sex.*

Mies van der Rohe, The Farnsworth House, Plano, Illinois, 1950.
Here is the powerful eroticism of empty space: there can be something
stimulatingly transgressional about being alone in this building.

Food and Sex
Appetites and aphrodisiacs

Rowley Leigh

MARCO PIERRE WHITE'S OYSTERS REPLACE SEX. A cold oyster, on a bed of ice is good but not good enough for Marco. He serves the oysters warm – that requires a degree of skill. The tender bivalves are perched on some slippery tagliatelle (slurp, slurp), annointed with beurre blanc, acting like gastronomic vaseline, and then topped with caviar. It's sexy: it is not, however, sex.

Aphrodisiacs never aroused anybody. Think back to Norman Douglas' *Venus in the Kitchen* (1952), the only interesting book on the subject and one written, as the embarrassing expression – given the writer's somewhat salacious proclivities – has it, firmly with tongue in cheek, and one finds an extraordinary catalogue of foods. Snails, stuffed pig's heads, brains of sparrow, calf and lamb, lamb's testicles and ears, *vulvae steriles* and marrow of leopard (!) stand alongside oysters, caviar and other more conventional dishes. These are not foods for seduction. They are the sort of viands that rheumy-eyed old men may eat, waited on by nurses whilst they dribble down their fronts and dream of sex.

For Lotharios such as these, Marco's oysters are the perfect recipe. Oysters are considered aphrodisiac because they are soft and yielding and yet hidden in a rock-hard shell. Prised open, they seem terribly vulnerable: they positively shiver and retract when exposed. And they are salty. When we surrender at our most intimate and intense moment, we do not excrete honey but salt. Marco's oysters are combined with caviar, just to underscore the point. There is an old kitchen joke: 'What is the saltiest thing in the world?' Answer: 'an anchovy's pussy'. Part of the joke is that anchovies are not sexy. Nor is most salty food. Think of bacon, ham and salt cod and you realise that salted food is peasant food and that salting is an essential act of

OPPOSITE: *The fragile connective tissue of the oyster, its subtle but unforgettable aroma and the sense it offers of a precious, revealed secret, inevitably leads to gynaecological comparisons.*

preservation whereby poor families survive winters. This is not the stuff of aphrodisiacs, not because poor people do not have sex but because food and sex may be interchangeable, are clearly metaphorically related, but they do not happen at the same time. You cannot assuage both hungers simultaneously, nor have your cake and eat it too. That, after all, is the point of metaphors, or sublimation, if we are to page Dr Freud.

Sublimation, of course, implies a taboo. Theoretically, we put food in our mouths because we are forbidden other forms of oral gratification. Freudians would say this indicates mother fixation and, I daresay, those of us who eat too much simply suffer from arrested development and wish to return to our mother's breast. Sandor Ferenczi, one of Freud's most brilliant disciples, came to believe that we all had a more primal urge and that our death wish (all sex requires a little dying, after all) represented a desire to return to the sea. The sea he alluded to was not just in the amniotic fluid of the womb, but the sea proper. The implication is that there is an instinct anterior to eating or fucking and the hinge of the oyster is the key.

Opening an oyster – or a scallop, come to that – certainly seems like an invasion of privacy. However tenderly the operation is performed, it is undeniably a rape. It may be the aliveness of shellfish that stimulates such strong intimations of sexuality. It would be wrong to think they represent the purely female and vulnerable, however. Crustacea can be extremely aggressive and threatening and I do not think this is a case of *vagina dentata* although the spectre of the preying mantis haunts many discussions of food and sex. Shellfish are strangely bisexual and interchange roles rather alarmingly. My kitchen-hands take huge, naughty pleasure in teasing razor clams. They sprinkle rock salt on the clams standing in a bucket and then laugh as the extraordinary, priapic-looking muscles jump up alarmingly out of their shells in a strange, very masculine dance. Razor clams arouse strong feelings. Once cooked, the muscles lying suggestively in their long shells, I find it difficult to suppress a giggle as they are sent out into the restaurant.

Food can often be embarrassing. I can remember a customer being served an *andouillette* (a sausage made with the intestines not just as casing but as contents too). To me, they have always suggested a coprophiliac interest and one with which I have found difficulty in identifying. This man looked slightly askance at the waitress who had deposited this thing in front of him and merely murmured 'screens, please, nurse'. I was reminded of the scene from Buñuel's *The Exterminating Angel* (1962). A bourgeois dinner party takes place. The guests sit on lavatories and chat. Occasionally they politely and discreetly absent themselves and retire to a little room where they may consume a little food in privacy before wiping their lips and returning to the party.

There is no question that the taboos are changing. Death and incest are still on the agenda but sexuality *per se* seems utterly commonplace. No one is shocked. Food has become the new taboo. Regard the variety of modern proscriptions. The general retreat from meat was signposted some years ago and now the gourmand is besieged. The great cholesterol scare attacked the emollients, the marblings of fat and emulsions of cream and butter that made North European food so extraordinarily luscious and comforting. Then the great scares, lysteria, salmonella, BSE and even poor old foot-and-mouth disease have all laid waste to the notion of taking pleasure in food. We now must eat, not to assuage hunger and take comfort from the privations of this world, but to select the correct fuel for the machines that we call our bodies.

If the assault of health fascism was not enough, body fascism has really done for good living. We fatties are ashamed. We dare not go on the beach. The obsession with leanness has wrought new havoc. As we are dragged deeper and deeper into celebrity culture we all become fashion victims. And fashion hates food. Fashion goes to restaurants in order to drink champagne, smoke cigarettes and take drugs in the lavatory. Fashion orders an egg-white omelette and a green salad with no dressing. Even if we are not obsessed with celebrity culture, it is not on to be interested in food. As food culture goes progressively downmarket, it is quite clear that our temporary infatuation with foodism is on the wane. It is not sexy. Food makes you fat and fat does not make you sexy.

Anorexia nervosa is not so new. If Wallace Simpson told her sex they could never be too thin, or too rich, she was not revealing some new and modern truth. Whatever the proclivities of the Turks, it has not been sexy for women to be fat for some time. Nor has it been sexy for them to eat. Joan

LEFT: *Edouard Manet,* Le Déjeuner sur l'Herbe, *1863. This extraordinary picture established the exact relationship of the pleasures of the flesh and the pleasures of the picnic. When it was first exhibited it caused great offence because the nude seemed to have been painted purely for the pleasure of the viewer – and her companions. The artist's friend, Emile Zola wrote, 'It simply burst the walls of the Salon.'*

Smith in *Hungry for You* (1996), somewhat reverting to the old *vagina dentata* chestnut, quotes Lord Byron, who recorded with disgust that his new mistress ate 'chicken wings, sweetbreads, custards, peaches and port wine' and gave the opinion that 'a woman should only be seen eating and drinking lobster salad and champagne, the only truly feminine and becoming viands.'

There is not a diet in the universe that forbids oysters. They are almost like not eating at all. And they are like sex, which makes them alright and kind of acceptable. The best way to eat an oyster is to lift the shell of a plump native (oh please) between finger and thumb and simply slip the quivering muscle from shell to mouth.

If you want oysters to help your sex life, eat them cold. There is an element of shock when the cold saline hits the palate. It is what golfers call a 'tit kisser' (a shot that reveals the hole, stupid). Even better, go for the *plateau de fruits de mer*. Deliciously saline, the *plateau* also contains the real secret of erotic eating. It is not what you eat but the way that you eat it. A *plateau de fruits de mer* demands a full-on approach. You have to put away the knife and fork and use your fingers. You have to suck and coax the food out of its shell. It may be no good to Lord Byron but it is my idea of a good time.

LEFT: *A modern Bacchus by Richard Sandon Smith.*

OPPOSITE: Forbidden fruit. *Ian Sanderson.*

Rhythm is a Dancer
A vertical expression of a horizontal activity

Philip Hensher

WHAT IS DANCE FOR, EXACTLY? Like many universal human practices, it has so little immediately apparent function that it tempts bigger theories. Marx, Foucault, Freud and Darwin do little to explain. Why does everybody from China to Peru at some point stand up, wriggle their bodies and go into a series of repeated, back-and-forth, unnatural rearrangements of their members for the benefit of an audience, for a partner similarly engaged, or for nobody at all? It serves no obvious purpose, but man is a dancing animal, and born so; everyone has seen with delight the moment when a toddler, making his purposeful way across the parquet, stops dead and starts to flail his limbs, as if dancing is easier or more fundamental than walking. To my four-year-old niece, it is easier to dance than sit still; her kindergarten choreographic representation of Mahler's seventh symphony has to be seen to be believed. But why?

There is, of course, a standard explanation that it is partly to do with sex, and partly to do with display. Dance, as they say, is a vertical expression of a horizontal activity; a confident dancer is wooing the urges of evolution in his immediate desire to impress, to seduce, to pull. That is not the whole of it, I think. The difference between an animal display and dancing is marked; it might make more sense to regard dancing as an expression of music, rather than sex. Hardly any dancing occurs in silence. There are various avant-garde attempts at music-less ballets; I treasure the memory of the famous night at Trade, the ultimately debauched London nightclub, where the music stopped for two minutes to mark the death of its founder, the great DJ Tony De Vit, and the ripped-to-the-tits crowd carried on dancing regardless. But dance and music go together much more indissolubly than dance and sex, and much more mysteriously.

As Wittgenstein says, however, what we cannot speak about, we must remain silent over. Dance as sex is something we can speak about; something we all instinctively feel. Even solitary dance is not isolated from sex; the teenage boy dancing in his bedroom to his heavy-metal favourite is practising for the wooing ritual. Dance can be other things; it can be art, and the balletomane works hard to subdue his inappropriate lechery (an attitude the nineteenth century would certainly have found rather strange). It can be an expression of community in which sex plays no part, and many dancers have found that sense of community much stronger than anything else; the habitués of the rave often find that sense of mass togetherness the most rewarding aspect of the occasion, and although English folk dances are often rooted in fertility rituals, I doubt that sex is uppermost in the minds of many pub-carpark Morris dancers in Britain.

But a further possibility of the dance, of spiritual transcendence, is mysteriously linked to the sexual motif. Dance makes most sense as an opening into an ecstatic world of thoughtless delight, where no one speaks of Wittgenstein and the passing of time is replaced by the measured, abstract divisions of the beat. Most non-Western religions have recognised the significance of dance – Christianity is a distinct oddity in this regard. Anatolian dervishes use the movements of the body as a means of contemplation and removal from the self. The sacred dances of the East are often misinterpreted by Western observers as dramatic statements of the faith, rather than, as in reality, an exercise of it. In the West, this spiritual dimension of dance is neglected and even denounced; there is no place in the contemplative life for the temple dancer. But the powers of dance to abolish the self, to raise spirits to a point of ecstasy, are so powerful that they must be exercised in some context. The urge to dance is as powerful as sex, and as promptly obeyed. I think, rather than as an expression of sex, I prefer to see dance as a metaphor or parallel to it. The ecstasy of dance and the ecstasy of sex become conflated, naturally. Sex is a periodic, insistent presence in dance, as dance is in sex. And sometimes it goes, and no longer seems necessary; and sometimes it seems the whole point of the exercise.

Some case studies, then. In 1977, I was twelve. That summer, my year left junior school to go to 'the big school', and the authorities, as a treat, mounted a disco. Twelve-year-olds are sometimes interested in sex, but – at

ABOVE: *Thomas Rowlandson*, A Morning
Probe. *The ecstasy of dance and the ecstasy of sex
become naturally conflated.*

LEFT: *Peter Fendi,*
Headstand, *1835. Fendi's
oeuvre is little known because
his subjects were mainly erotic
and therefore confined to private
collections all over the world.
This print is one of forty 'love
scenes' executed for a wealthy
patron friend. A set of six
hundred colour lithographs were
published posthumously in
Leipzig in 1910.*

OPPOSITE: *Ignacio Zuloaga y
Zabaleta,* La Oterita in her
dressing room. *More than
any other dance form, flamenco
is charged with sexual energy.
The immodest, but elegant,
presentation of the celebrated
dancer's magnificent breasts is
strikingly erotic.*

that period, anyway – probably more interested in exercising their own shyness. The disco began at four in the afternoon; it was certainly the first I had been to. The year was ushered into the school gymnasium, artificially darkened. For half an hour, the girls stood against one wall, the boys against another; not wooing, or eyeing each other, but just giggling in their uniforms. Some of the girls had thought to bring clothes to change into, and applied eyeshadow after the end of lessons, and it was these who first ventured onto the floor, to dance with their friends. Slowly, the others followed them, moving backwards and forwards self-consciously; then one of the boys went over, and started to dance with one of the girls; then, the whole year saw with amazed fascination, the class hero was kissing the class heroine. The girls were dancing in chorus lines, and their dances were not far from playground rituals; and suddenly, the girl at the end turned, and everyone in a long chain, like a train, chuffed out of the gym and into the playground. 'Hey! Where are you going?' the DJ called, but the giggling line circled the asphalt before returning. It was just a game; it was just a statement of a group, of belonging somewhere in this conga. The song of that summer, incidentally, was *I Feel Love* by Donna Summer.

Nearly twenty-five years later, it is eight o'clock in the morning in a club in Clerkenwell in London. What were people doing, twenty-five years ago, at eight o'clock on a Sunday morning? Waking up, turning over, lying in; getting up to make a cup of tea, going out to do a bit of weeding or to wash the car. Well, I know what people do in 2001 in Clerkenwell, they stand in the middle of a dance floor, almost naked, sweating furiously, hardly knowing where they are or who they are. Who knows how many drugs have been taken, how much oblivion has settled over these two thousand or so people? They are dancing, to and fro, aggressively, their fists punching up and down to the fastest music anyone has ever seriously tried to dance to. This disco, too, starts at four: four in the morning. Sex ought to be everywhere; these, probably, are some of the most perfectly pumped-up bodies in London and as you walk to the bar and back for your bottle of water, your naked chest with its coating of sweat slides against other chests, backs, bodies. But it is nowhere: desire is quite gone, and, though you want this place to be so full that you can barely move, you want only to dance, on and on, as you have been doing since midnight. Perhaps here, too, what you want is for dance to make you feel that you are a person in a crowd, and loving that crowd, and nothing else.

Dance, however, has always evoked sex; probably no new mode of dancing has arrived without calling up a denunciation from puritan elders. To contemporaries, the jitterbug, the twist, the waltz all seemed startlingly lewd displays. No doubt, a suitably serious historian could find denunciations of the bransle and the sarabande. These objections are very much to the point: the attraction of the dance was in the lewdness. Dance has always pushed at the boundaries of acceptable sexual display. Once, it was the one moment when men and women, unmarried, were licensed to touch each other; the ecstasy of that is recorded in Tolstoy's *Anna Karenina* (1874–76). Other dances have explored more extravagant possibilities of ecstasy: the jitterbug, that strange revival of the saltarello dances of the sixteenth century, rediscovered the delight of being lifted in the air by a man.

Is there anything left to explore? How far has dance gone? Now, I wonder. Sexual licence in the nightclubs of Europe has, by now, proceeded to such a point that one almost envies those previous ages when the touch of a hand on the waist was enough to provide the material for weeks of daydreams. In London clubs, one has seen men dancing in nothing but their boots, quite nonchalantly; towards closing time, it is not unknown for dancers to move from flirtation to snogging to the exchange of bodily fluids without troubling to leave the dancefloor. Oddly, there is some evidence to suggest that the public lewdness of the rave culture may not be accompanied by much successful sex: the ubiquitous dance drugs may have the primary effect of enhancing sensual desire, but also a secondary one of inducing male impotence.

So what is left? Well, perhaps this. One never knows, but one day, in the long night of the dance floor, perhaps you become aware of someone, dancing close to you: aware of his body starting to mirror your movements, moving closer. He meets your eyes, and smiles, and in a moment, somehow, you are dancing together, and his mouth, somehow, closes on yours. Your mouths, together, are still, and your bodies still moving to the dance. Perhaps there is only one certainty: the feeling that when you leave, together, and go to place your bodies together between sheets, those acts will be a continuation of the dance, as much as the dance has been a prologue, an invitation to sex.

LEFT: *The word lambada refers both to the rhythm, which fuses* carimbó *and merengue, and to the dance, which incorporates elements of* forró, *samba, merengue and* maxixe *(the nineteenth-century Brazilian dance). It is fast, graceful and can be very very dirty.*

OPPOSITE: *Flamenco originated among the gypsies of Andalucía. The passion of the voice, the guitar and the dancer's body creates an explicit sexual charge.*

Dirty Pictures
Sex and the cinema

Stephen Bayley

SITTING IN THE DARK WITH STRANGERS is an activity of evident erotic potential, regardless of what is being watched. But when the spectacle includes Jean Harlow saying 'Excuse me while I slip into something more comfortable' or Marilyn Monroe radiating exuberant sexual energy and strongly implied sexual availability or Marlon Brando sodomising Maria Schneider with the aid of a tub of polyunsaturated fat, or maybe it was butter, as he did in Bernardo Bertolucci's *Last Tango in Paris* (1972), then the erotic potential is amply realised. Add factors including sensuousness and emotional charge and the cinema becomes perhaps the most powerful erotic medium of all. But not least a factor is size. The nooks of lechery are, in practical fact, small, intimate and obscure. The projected magnification of cinema technology tends to monumentalise the erotic details, sometimes to sensational effect. A primitive 1896 film called *The Kiss* had this effect on Chicago publisher Herbert S. Stone: 'The prolonged pasturing on each other's lips was hard to bear…magnified to Gargantuan proportions and repeated three times over it is absolutely disgusting.'

Another erotic ingredient in the cinema is the implied voyeurism. It's been said that the cinema offers the passive spectator the indulgent direct pleasure of seeing something erotic without the implied intrusion or embarrassment of having to go about searching for it.

And this power has led to censorship, often self-imposed. In 1902 a National Board of Censorship was established in New York. This was reinforced by the self-regulation of the 1930 Hays Code established by the Motion Picture Producers' Association. A memorable guideline of this thoughtful body was that 'No inside thigh of a female may be shown between the garter and the knickers.' Another insistence of the Hays Code

OPPOSITE: *Marilyn Monroe. Perhaps the cinema's most successful erotic icon, Monroe's appeal was based on a strange mixture of innocence and availability.*

OPPOSITE: *Sharon Stone in Paul Verhoeven's* Basic Instinct *(1992). The sequence of which this image forms a part is a prized part of many video collections: connoisseurs of Hollywood's cautious journey towards the erotic freeze-frame the moment when the actress opens her legs briefly to reveal a tantalising delta of Venus.*

was that, if two people happened to be shown on a bed, then each of them must have a foot on the floor, an absolutely ingenious means, when you come to think about it, of proscribing conventional sexual intercourse.

In Britain the Cinematograph Act of 1909 was followed by the establishment of the British Board of Film Censors in 1913. A general fear was that cinema might debauch the morals of a susceptible public: providing a curious insight into the architecture of the late Imperial mind, the British Board was as concerned about blasphemy as about sex. There were to be no depictions of Christ and no nudity in British cinema.

Cinematic sex was driven underground, into a genre known as 'stag' or 'blue' movies. Typical was *The Virgin with Hot Pants* (*c.*1923). A crudely typewritten caption invites the audience, before an explicit groin shot of a woman, to 'spread the lips apart' and then we see it obligingly happen. Sex was penetration and that was that. Underground erotic cinema was artless, misogynistic; it was based on and exploited the meanest conception of the wham-bang masculine universe. Thrusting gratification at the expense of art. Happily, the disciplines of the mass market forced a certain sophistication on the treatment of sex in mainstream movies.

Hedy Lamarr appeared nude as early as 1933 in *Extase* (a film which featured a close-up of her face during orgasm), but it was only as late as 1945, in *The Wicked Lady*, that extramarital sex was explicitly discussed. By 1962, Stanley Kubrick was able to make a film of Vladimir Nabokov's nymphette-meets-paedophile story, *Lolita*. Only in 1968 was a mass British audience allowed to see a full frontal female nude, in Lindsay Anderson's *If*. More specialist audiences had, however, been given the treat of hearing a convincing female orgasm in Roman Polanski's *Repulsion* (1965). Yet as late as 1967 Vilgot Sjoman's *I am Curious Yellow*, which featured grainily frank sex, was still exciting English critics to declare it 'a danger to every human being'.

But this was before the video recorder democratised pornography. This tended towards a crossover between dirty pictures for private consumption and public cinema. While an erect penis is still not allowed, the thresholds of acceptance are continuously on the move. By 1972 Gerard Damiano's *Deep Throat* had a heroine whose clitoris was in her throat…with inevitable results. Since Yves Rouset-Rouard's *Emmanuelle* (1974) a certain level of sexual frankness – which is to say, nipples – has become commonplace.

OPPOSITE: *Catherine Deneuve in Luis Buñuel's* Belle de Jour *(1967). A classic myth of a respectable, but bored housewife amusing herself as a prostitute during dull afternoons.*

FROM TOP TO BOTTOM: *Marlon Brando and Maria Schneider in Bernardo Bertolucci's* Last Tango in Paris *(1972). The film broke new boundaries with its powerful depiction of urgent, anonymous, animal sex. The climactic scene is a sequence of sodomy, facilitated with butter.*

Krysztof Kieslowski's The Double Life of Veronique *(1991). An urban fable about ambition.*

Yves Roset-Rouard's Emmanuelle *(1974). This was the film that brought (soft focus) pornography into the mainstream of the cinema.*

OVERLEAF: *Deborah Kerr and Burt Lancaster in the beach lovemaking scene from Fred Zinnemann's* From Here To Eternity *(1953). The James Jones novel, with its raw sex and strong language, had to be heavily bowdlerised for Hollywood.*

LEFT: *Andrew Bergman's* Striptease *(1996). An erotic and artistic flop, in spite of Demi Moore's personally trained figure.*

OPPOSITE: *Stanley Kubrick's* Lolita *(1962), starred James Mason and Shelley Winters. Vladimir Nabokov's jailbait nymphet introduced Hollywood to the taboo territory of paedophilia.*

So much so that there is a risk of desensitisation. Erotic cinema is not necessarily the one where most erectile tissue or mucous membrane is on display. The implied sexuality of Scarlett on the stairs in *Gone with the Wind* (1939), or the glitz of Jean-Jacques Beneix's *Betty Blue* (1986) or the tension of Paul Verhoeven's *Basic Instinct* (1992) are all powerfully erotic, even when the actors are fully clothed. A subliminal impression of Sharon Stone's pubic hair was memorable, but not specially erotic.

How did they ever make a movie of LOLITA ?

ABOVE: *Clark Gable and Vivien Leigh in* Gone With the Wind
*(1939). Although in complete conformity with the puritanical Hay's
Code, this most famous movie of them all was charged with erotic
power and sexual symbolism.*

OPPOSITE: *Jean-Jacques Beineix's* Betty Blue *(1986), a high-
gloss film about* amour fou. *Critics hailed it as an 'overheated
masterpiece of excess' – which was also an allusion to the first,
wordless three-minute sex scene with which the film opens.*

Sex in the cinema, like sex in the world at large, happens as much in the head as it does in the groin. Luis Buñuel's *Belle de Jour* (1967) certainly has an explicitly sexual character, but the most erotic scene is not the sado-masochistic whipping and raping, or lubricated thrusting, it is instead a wistful portrait of the ineffably beautiful Catherine Deneuve looking over her shoulder: delicate, ambiguous and infinitely tempting.

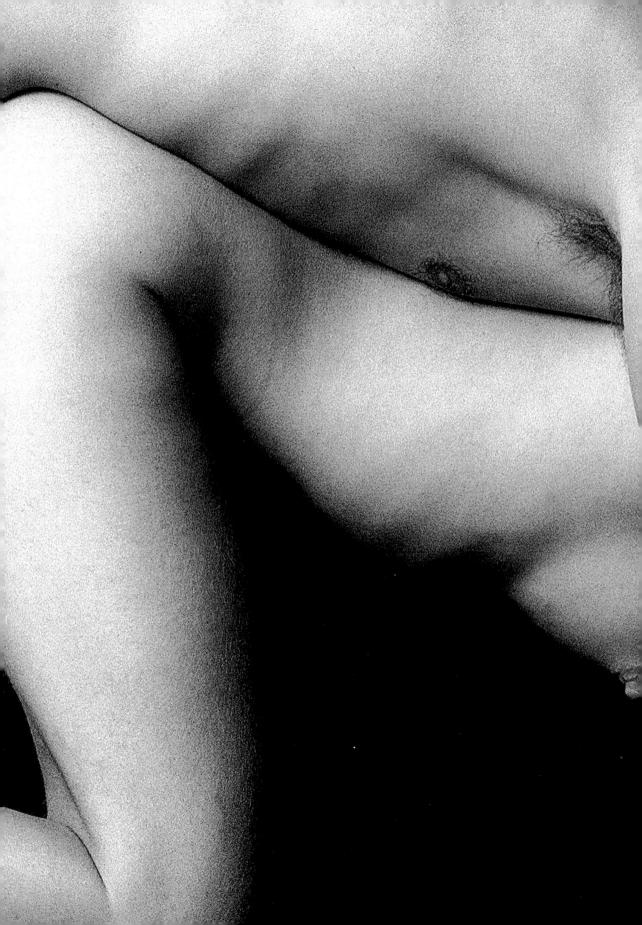

'Show me those fleshy principalities; thy thighs,
Show me those fleshy principalities;
Show me that hill where smiling love doth sit,
having a living fountain under it;
Show me thy waist, then let me therewithal,
By the assentation of thy lawn, see all.'

SHOW ME THY FEET Robert Herrick

The Body

4

Shifting Erogenous Zones
The way of all flesh

Lizzie Speller

ABOUT THE TIME THAT DR ALEX COMFORT was first promulgating the science of hydraulic woman – one whose elaborate system of knobs and levers, would, if pressed, pushed and fondled in the right sequence, cause her to open up like a Lawrentian fig – my own ventures into sexuality had got as far as the knob on a biro. In the barrel, a miniature Claudia Cardinale lookalike posed, hips akimbo, the continent of her bust compressed into a swimsuit. Click the pen and down went the costume – or rather, curiously, up; and she was revealed pinkly, her slightly under-defined private parts made public at the flick of a button twenty times a day.

No flesh-and-blood woman was ever so obliging, no sexual revelation so smoothly accomplished. But although risqué – she would certainly have been confiscated – the *déshabillement* of Biro-woman carried no electric charge. In other circumstances, the neck, shoulders, nipples, umbilicus, the shadowy triangle between the thighs, the knees and tiny ankles might all have been so, but what was lacking was any associated sense of quest, any thrill of uncertainty. The erogenous zones, the unpredictable geography of the sexual body, are discovered only with difficulty – and by implication, only by the *cognoscenti*, the powerful, the experienced. At different times and in different cultures the focus of eroticism may shift, but the sense that there exists a secret alchemy of sex, which through exposure or manipulation will turn the dross of rude coupling to gold of the most sublime and consensual of erotic experiences is constant.

The stripper was a pervasive sexual image of the mid-twentieth century, although one much parodied, hence Claudia's intrusion into my adolescent pencil case. The stripper is all false promise as she struts her

OPPOSITE: A Woman Before a Mirror (*1841*) by the Danish Neo-Classical painter, C.W. Eckersberg. The most erotic parts of a woman's body are not always the obviously sexual ones.

OPPOSITE: La Comparaison *by Jean Frédéric Schall. This amusing composition focuses on a light-hearted comparison between the statue of Venus Callipyge and the two bathers. These are thought to be portraits of young but worldly 'Janettes', so called after the two-headed god Janus, because of their supposed predilection for both vaginal and anal sex.*

stuff and as spectator and performer know that sexual resolution is impossible, the tension is infinitely extended. Salome, sensually energetic, oriental belly-dancers and hard-body lap-dancers, plaiting titillation and male humiliation, have used the incremental exposure of erogenous zones as currency. Now for the cyber-potato, the stripper at your fingertips has a new incarnation: the lap-top dancer; at virtual-girl.com is an elfin stripper who struts her stuff in a one-inch square on your computer screen.

In the 1970s Comfort may have been a pioneer in mapping tactile erogenous zones, but it was horribly clear when you fell into the clutches of a man who had done his research. The previous decade had placed the clitoris at the centre of the erogenous map, but post-Comfort came the hopeful ear-probing tongue and the endless nipple-sucking, both of which, it was alleged, could bring the obliging woman to orgasm. There have always been, from Ovid's manual *Ars Amatoria* (*c.*1BC) onwards, erogenous zone guidebooks; volumes of optimism proffering sexual salvation. With a fair wind, the right chart and a good sextant, the most impregnable woman could be conquered like the mysteries and territories of old. She would not merely succumb, she would melt into deliquescent longing.

The erogenous zone is invariably a threshold; a hint at greater liberties to come or a mimic of less readily accessible female parts. The glance and the moment lingers at the fissures and folds of the ear, the glistening mouth, the soft skin of the inner arm; any cleft; behind the knee, between the toes and the indirect caress. The skin of the areola so similar to the texture and hue of the *labia minora*, the creamy fissure of the breasts a precursor of the buttocks. But to the eye and to the sensual, as opposed to campaigning, touch, it is the liminal areas of the body which excite most. The strange shore between hair and smooth flesh, between dry and moist skin; the neck, the innermost, uppermost thigh; the velvety softness of earlobes, the umbilical whorl, the webs between the fingers.

Erogenous zones are both visual and strategic; tempting and facilitating. They thrive in the distance between desire and gratification; too easily seen or reached and their compelling charm disappears. Perhaps this accounts for the reality that the vulva – although it may be replete with promise or terror – is not truly an erogenous zone; it is too ultimate, smacks too much of arrival rather than hopeful travelling. Pubic hair may be, if only because it confuses the topography at the moment of triumph. But an unexpected sight of flesh, whether teasing or inadvertent, creates a rapid, lurching closure of intimate distance. Hence the current popularity of web-cams purporting to spy on girls' dorms, in lavatories, up skirts, through a long-distance lens. With all human body-parts accessible, at least in photograph and on Internet, we are straining for the salvation of erogenous zones by replacing them out of bounds. The voluntarily displayed body is erotically surpassed by the carelessly exposed one.

Fashion too expands and contracts around the human form, ingeniously re-creating novelty in the face of a human propensity to weary of the familiar. From the Empire-line gown and its nipple-revealing, dampened muslin transparency to the constraints of corsetry and the distortions of the bustle, from hotpants to topless dresses, the fashion industry has always been engaged in an elaborate power game, destroying the erotic simply by delivering it, only to reinvigorate it by shrouding it again.

It is a marker of all the major erogenous zones that since the Garden of Eden they have been at the centre of attempts to confine and civilise them. Paradoxically, the very attempt at control – at helping men to resist their allure – has only emphasised their charms further. Hair has almost always been visually erotic, from the plucked brows of milk-white medieval ladies to the coiffed nun and the flame-haired penitent Magdalene. In the nineteenth century, the formality of hair elaborately pinned and arranged not only contained sexuality but permitted the possibility that as it was unloosed by a lover so was the delicious licence of the woman's body. The fallen or about-to-be-toppled woman is the woman letting her hair down. Hair which smells both of natural hormonal cycles and of the dressings and perfumes of the sophisticated dressing table reminds the sensualist that under the trappings of social woman is the animal. The apparently casual raising of the arms to reveal tufts of hair, which instantly convey the information that the woman is sexually mature, is still the antithesis of erotic to Americans and many British men, but to Continental cultures, the broad hint that the same wiry hirsutism is more privately accessible elsewhere and the sweet, strange

OPPOSITE: *Jean August Dominique Ingres*, Female Nude *(1807). Delacroix said of Ingres that his art was 'the complete expression of an incomplete intelligence'. The chilly perfection of his voluptuous nudes is, however, the most complete expression of Neo-Classical eroticism.*

OVERLEAF: *Chinese School, c.1900. A detail from a watercolour titled* The Visitor.

OPPOSITE: *Erogenous zones are both visual and strategic, tempting and facilitating. The model is offering herself in the position of* venus aversa.

smell of female sweat are deeply arousing. But to the connoisseur, the softest finest hairs on the forearm, which rise to the faintest of stimuli, can be as sensual as the more deliberately arranged head of curls.

> *Oh! My God! The down*
> *The soft young down of her, the brown,*
> *The brown of her – her eye, her hair, her hair.*
>
> Charlotte Mew, 'The Farmer's Bride' (1916)

For the Japanese, famously, the back of the neck, accentuated by the boundaries of silken hair and collar, is where allure traditionally resides. The neck is undoubtedly the subtlest of erogenous zones. While canvassing female friends, the back of the neck was the area of erotic delight most consistently mentioned. Women love being guided, stroked, their hair lifted in handfuls to free the skin for kissing or biting. With no direct connection to sexual penetration either visually or functionally, the neck has powerful connotations of vulnerability. At its nape is the soft, hidden, white undulation between hair and flesh, dewy with sweat in response to fear, exertion or arousal.

> *I remember the neckcurls, limp and damp as tendrils*
> *And her quick look, a sidelong pickerel smile.*
>
> Theodore Roethke, 'Elegy for Jane' (1953)

Through the neck, blood pounds and between two hands, life can be extinguished. No wonder Caligula asserted his power and Lady Jane Grey her powerlessness by attention to this slender and defenceless piece of anatomy. W. B. Yeats made the otherwise unimaginable myth of the rape of a woman by a swan intensely erotic by focusing on the neck grasp as an icon of sexual subjugation:

> *…her thighs caressed*
> *by the dark webs, her nape caught in his bill*
> *he holds her helpless breast upon his breast.*
>
> W. B. Yeats, 'Leda and the Swan' (1928)

Breasts have always been the most ubiquitous of erogenous zones. Covered, naked, accentuated, hidden, they are perhaps the earliest target of young male fantasy, yet Samuel Johnson was not alone in seeing the profundities of a woman's cleavage as being a place where a rational man might come to grief: 'I'll come no more behind the scenes, David; for the silk stockings and white bosoms of your actresses excite my amorous propensities.'

Perhaps again because they are symbols both of maternity and of youth and sexual arousal, they occupy an ambiguous spot in the panorama of desire, ambiguous even to women; nipples and breasts are amazingly sensitive but to a baby's mouth as much as to a lover's hand or tongue. The pale-skinned, rose-tipped breast of Victorian erotica still enchants; the browner, tanned breast of modern woman demonstrates that her breasts are no longer her own. Yet sexual drive is pleasingly inventive; the same breasts that are wholesome with an infant nuzzling at them and interesting on a Greek beach, ignite a sexual flare when glimpsed down an inadequate neckline in the office. The versatility of breasts has meant they are so enduringly popular that they have their own merchandising; sweeping corsets and bras, lacing, surgery, tassels and piercing all find their place in the erotic consciousness.

The eighteenth- or nineteenth-century ankle revealed as a lady crossed from the protection of her carriage (and man) to the possession of a house (and man) has currently declined in response to contemporary fashions and social desiderata. So too has the fecund, ample belly. But long, coltish legs and the curve of an otherwise firm stomach, defined by piercings and cropped tops, are back in vogue; proclaiming the young, fit, childless – and historically available – woman. In real life, it is often the unexpected, even flawed, quirk of anatomy that individuals find irresistible. Breasts and earlobes are well signposted but many an experienced gynophile has been erotically surprised by the little roll of flesh above the waistline, the Rubenesque dimpled thigh, even the shadow of a stubbly armpit, or fabric drawn too tightly over the belly.

Finally, there are what might be regarded as the erogenous garnishes. These may be highly idiosyncratic but some are so familiar as to be a shorthand for sexual promise. Louis MacNeice's train passenger in *Autumn Journal* (1939) recognises what is at stake when 'a woman gets in painted

BELOW: *High heels enhance sexuality because their flashy redundancy suggests an enticing willingness to make practical sacrifices in the pursuit of pleasure.*

with dyed hair but a ladder in her stocking and eyes patient beneath the calculated lashes'.

The stocking – the laddered stocking, like the tangled tresses of the nineteenth-century heroine on the slide – is the twentieth-century gauge of recent sexual abandon and the public application of lipstick, once the marker of an adept fellatrice, still draws attention to a dominant erogenous zone and exposes private vanities as it slips glossily over the loose and open mouth of, by association, a loose and open woman. High heels may enhance the onlooker's pleasure in a taut calf, or the swaying awkwardness of the wearer's gait. A double helix of carefully rising smoke, which anticipates seduction, is echoed in post-coital figures, narrow-eyed as they draw on their cigarettes sheeted to the armpits like sculptures on a medieval tomb. Smoking may be antisocial but by God it is sexy.

But where to draw the line between the fetishist and his object of desire and the sensualist and his catalytic experience of flesh? It must surely be that an erogenous zone is part of a journey, even if it is only a journey of the imagination, whereas the fetishist can obtain complete satisfaction in the contemplation or possession of the arch of a foot or a lock of hair. It is the difference between the seventeenth-century fixations of Robert Herrick and the delicious contemporary explorations of John Fuller:

Fain would I kiss my Julia's dainty leg
Which is as white and hairless as an egg

Robert Herrick, 'On Julia's Legs' (1648)

Herrick's statue-like vision is an end in itself, a rather curious and unsensual prospect to any other than a man obsessed, whereas Fuller's contemplations are of a man delightedly in transit. His inventory of erogenous zones is simultaneously intimate and commonplace and as erotic as it gets.

I like each softly moulded kneecap.
I like the little crease behind them.
I'd always know, without a recap,
Where to find them.

John Fuller (1937)

OPPOSITE: *1930s commercial pornography,* Two Friends. *Body types, as well as fashions in underwear, come and go with the 'spirit of the age'.*

Dual Controls
The place of the bosom in the erotic landscape

Stephen Bayley

'NO ONE', AS GERSHON LEGMAN SAID in his classic *Rationale of the Dirty Joke* (1969), 'needs to be told that the female breast has become…the principal fetich [*sic*] of male attraction.' Appended to the ventral area between the bottom of the rib cage and neck, are to be found on mature women a pair of fleshy sacs that in observation, touch, feel and (perhaps mostly) imagination are the compelling landmarks of the greater part of a man's erotic landscape. In the male's endless and arduous search for sexual gratification, the breasts are beacons.

This sexual rôle is doubly charged, semantically enriched and oedipally muddied by an unavoidable relationship to motherhood and to matters so deeply buried in the id that surgical, rather than psychoanalytical techniques might be required to locate them. A *fetich* indeed, these breasts. They are a means of enchantment. They possess magical powers. They are reverenced beyond rationality.

All of this is magnificently resolved in that curious word 'bosom' whose suggestions of agreeable homeliness and intimacy are nicely complicated by a surreal sort of onomatopoeia. 'Bosom', with the symmetry of those double Os and the generosity of its sound, is perfectly suggestive of the warmth and weight and, indeed, symmetry of the breasts. Yet it is also revealing of the hilarious irrationality of human desire. Men may enjoy them – 'fun bags' is one current vulgarism – but unlike the primary sexual organ, for much of the woman's life the breasts are redundant fatty tissue with little practical function. More, really of an encumbrance which has created a huge international industry of support garments, not to mention erotic props. Humans are the only female mammals to sport permanent breasts: their place in culture and in comment is disproportionate to their temporary usefulness.

OPPOSITE: *Jean-Jacques Lequeu. The secret sex life of nuns is a staple of erotic speculation, as Diderot knew. The title of this astonishing image* – Et nous aussi nous serons des mères: car…! – *evokes an essential ambiguity. A woman showing you her breasts is making a maternal or a sexual gesture.*

Breasts, as anthropologist Lionel Tiger observed, generate social as well as erotic power. This is perhaps a modern reflection of a universal primitive understanding about the benefits to survival of the tribe of having fruitful women around. This first found expression in the bare-breasted mother-goddess, which is the subject of the oldest art we have. Later, the many-breasted Diana of Ephesos was, if you like, a multi-cylindered Ferrari to the caveman's single-cylinder Benz, expressive of the advances in civilisation. The positive associations of the breast were, of course, also later assimilated into the Christian cult of the Virgin. The bosom suggests not just the potential for erotic riches, but the existence of material wealth as well.

Poets, as it were, make great play with the ambiguities of the breasts. Robert Herrick noted 'That brave vibration each way free' as his lover ran towards him, enthusiastic for her assignation in a bower, or wherever. Algernon Swinburne wrote mesmerisingly of the deep division of prodigious breasts. James Joyce's Molly brought stream-of-consciousness to the matter when she 'put my arms around him yes and drew him down to me so he could feel my breasts all perfume yes and his heart was going like mad'. Gavin Ewart caught the bosom's delicious tension between cosiness and naughtiness when he wrote:

> Miss Twye was soaping her breasts in the bath
> When she heard behind her a meaning laugh
> And to her amazement she discovered
> A wicked man in the bathroom cupboard

And Adrian Henri, in his marvellously bathetic 'Song of the East Lancs Road', said 'I wanted your soft verges but you gave me the hard shoulder.'

Freud is the source for the belief that there is substantial oedipal complexity in organs which simultaneously signal motherhood and, when revealed outside the context of lactation, suggest sexual availability. Psychologists believe that the link between motherhood and sexual gratification (to both parties) has its source in the sense of touch common to both breast-feeding and to fondling. They were keen to demonstrate this by experimenting with the physiological and neural links between the

OPPOSITE: *Gerald Leslie Brockhurst*, Adolescence, *(1932). The sultry possibilities of erotic life in suburbia are captured in this dark image. Dorette Woodward was the artist's fifteen-year-old mistress who was living with Brockhurst and his wife at the time. This image became one of the most important erotic icons of the 1930s yet few admirers knew the true identity of the model.*

OVERLEAF: *René Magritte,* Le Viol, *1934. The master Belgian surrealist paints a visual pun.*

One Million Years BC, *1967. A masterpiece of Hollywood kitsch: coarse troglodyte reality brightened and tightened into Raquel Welch.*

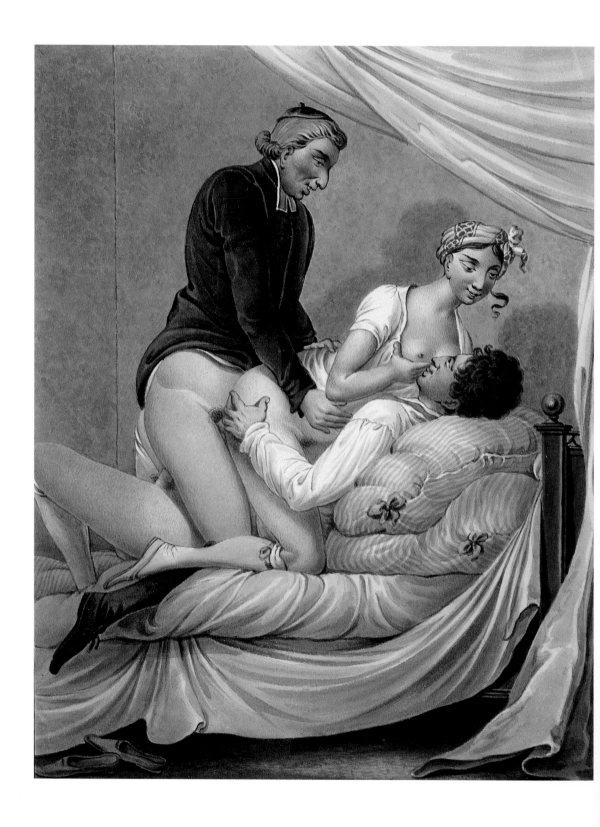

OPPOSITE: *Georg Emmanuel Opitz,* Sacred and Profane Love, *c.1820. There are physiological and neural links between the breasts and the primary sexual organ: hence, to enhance her pleasure, she offers her nipples to the supine lover.*

breasts and the primary sexual organs. In the late nineteenth and early twentieth centuries, the glory years of experimental sexology, mad German scientists attached electrodes to the nipples of volunteers and, on the passage of a current, measured the consequential contraction of the uterus to prove that the act of suckling produces in most women a voluptuous sexual response.

The bosom may be stuffed with only secondary sexual characteristics, but it has a primary role in both genders' preoccupations with sex and style. The basis of the attraction was understood by Johann Friedrich Blumenbach who, in his study of London prostitutes published in his *Anthropological Treatises* (1865), declared that 'precocious venery', what we would describe as 'putting it about a lot', enlarged the breasts. This is an association that appears to be as old as time.

To appreciate the curiosity of the breast, the French example offers an instructive comparison. As if to prove they are more at ease with hedonism and sex, the French have a huge literature on the subject. An early authority, was Mercier de Compiègne, author of *L'Eloge du sein des femmes* (*c.*1795), but the leading modern authority on mammary matters technical, artistic and sexual was G. J. Witowski, author of, among others, *Anecdotes historiques et religieuses sur le sein et l'allaitement* (1898); *Curiosités medicales littéraires et artistiques sur les seins et l'allaitement* (1898); *Les seins dans l'histoire* (1903); *Les seins à l'église* (1907) and a synthetic English-language volume called *Tetoniana – medical, literary and artistic curiosities of breasts and breast-feeding* (1898).

In Britain, we have no native studies of such depth or authority. Moreover, the cultural differences – perhaps even an inferred inferiority – between bosom and *poitrine* are reflected in the slang annexed by the bust. While the French have bizarre *ropolopots*; magnificent *nichons*; feminine *miches*; exciting *tétons*; and seductive *doudounes*, we are more likely to have tits. Again, the association is comic rather than sexual. There's a 1714 usage for tit meaning a 'pleasant fellow' and, according to lexicographer Eric Partridge, its use as a blokish word for breasts can be traced back to 'Australian low colloquial' usage. These same Australians have supplied us with an agreeable alternative to 'tit', more amiable and less abusive. Etymologists argue about its origin, but it seems likely that the wonderful term 'norks' was inspired by Norco, a brand of butter popular in New South Wales whose wrapping shows a cow with an ample udder.

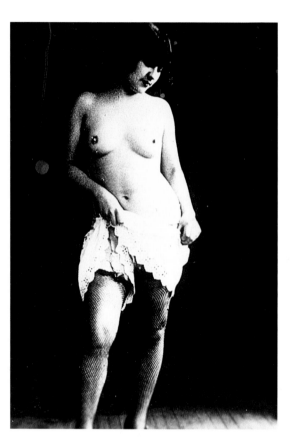

OPPOSITE: *Commercial French pornography, early twentieth century. Some connoisseurs claim to be able to date dirty photographs by the style of the breasts.*

The Americans are, if anything, even more mixed-up about breasts than the British. An internal 1993 memorandum from Fox Television was picked up by the satirical *Spy* magazine. The memo concerned a forthcoming programme about women with notably large breasts and the author was concerned with the station's 'Standards and Practices' lest any lapse might affect viewers and advertisers. His pronouncement was Solomonic in its wisdom. This Prince of Political Correctness said that while the words 'tits' and 'knockers' were not allowable, no exception would be taken to the use of boobs, bazongas, jugs, hooters and snack trays.

Just as lascivious humour is the male's defence against the woman's powerful and disturbing combined arsenal of sex and motherhood, so it is equally revealing of something profound in Anglophone culture and its observations of taboo that underwear has to be disguised in a foreign language. And that language is, one is tempted to say 'naturally', French. We have no proper English word for the *brassière*, nor for *lingerie*. And as philologists might insist, a language which has no words of its own to describe something has no natural understanding of the concepts in hand. Thus, in the same way as *liaison, affaire, enceinte* and *petite amie* have entered our vocabulary of erotic discourse, so *brassière* and *lingerie* conveniently combine evasive sophistication with wince-inducing coyness.

There is a big human history of concern about underwear and about gender relations with certain types of clothes. The Bible tells us that 'a man who putteth on a woman's garment becometh an abomination.' Indeed, with the image in mind of Federico Fellini (by no means a conventional heterosexual) who enjoyed making love while wearing a bra, we might agree. But underwear can be put to all manner of imaginative uses in man's battle to understand and consume the bosom. Literature's best description of the powerful erotic associations of underwear is Philip Roth's. In his 1969 tale of adolescence, *Portnoy's Complaint*, the hero uses one of his sister's bras to secure the bathroom door while he masturbates. Disturbed in his act by a knocking on the door, Herrick's consequential brave vibrations set up in the tensed bra only increase his manual frenzy.

But the reality of underwear is really rather dire. Exposed bra straps are near the top of a list of motifs that have a powerful counter-erotic character. There is not a woman, nor perhaps a fat Italian film-maker, on the planet whose attractiveness is enhanced by the exposure of these joyless elasticated belts. They do not imply suspension of a gorgeous, firm bosom, rather the brute depressing mechanics of flesh and gravity. These prosthetics of *lingerie* are grim – and often grubby – bookmarks of the humdrum. Careless exposure is not titillating, but depressing evidence of incipient and unpromising slatternliness. And thus we are back to the question of an ample bosom and its relationship to precocious venery.

Perhaps only in Britain with its specially complex attitude to the bosom could the recent Wonderbra poster campaign have become a national phenomenon. Britain is still, after all, home to millions of men who stand and gawp on foreign beaches at what Continental men ignore. I know I do. It was in Britain that an extremely pretty, but in fact rather skinny, Czech model was translated through an adman's fetish into a symbolic figure as resonant of the bosom as Diana of Ephesos. With hair and make-up, pouting lips and the extraordinary mechanical advantage of the Wonderbra which gives vectored thrust and powerful cantilevers to otherwise unremarkable lunchtrays, the 'Hello Boys' advertisement was very revealing in its use of the masculine diminutive. This was an invitation both enticingly erotic and, of course, utterly maternal.

This copyline caught the ambiguity of the bosom perfectly; for a man, the sight of naked breasts means two contradictory things. A perhaps unconscious memory of Mother mingles with the suggestion of sexual availability. It is enough to turn you to drink. And as someone once said, a dry martini is like a woman's breasts. One is not enough, but three is too many.

OPPOSITE: '...*redundant fatty tissue with little practical function*'?

Does Size Matter?
African and Afro-American super-sexuality

Ronald Hyam

JOHN OGILBY'S COMPILATION of travellers' tales, *Africa* (1670), recorded that Negro men sported 'large Propagators'. From at least the fifteenth century, it was widely put about in Europe that Africans were exceptionally well-equipped sexually. Coupled with this belief in the larger black penis was an apprehension that African sexual prowess and staying-power were also greater than white men could sustain. By the eighteenth century these propositions were probably commonplace in educated circles, and it was assumed that the 'noble savage' had an impressive 'propagator'. However, the notion of a black 'super penis' only began to assume widespread and obsessional significance in the 1860s, as a result of the deterioration of race relations throughout the Anglo-Saxon world. These processes were especially notable in the increasing segregation, negrophobia and sexual paranoia of the American South following the end of slavery, and they persisted well into the twentieth century. The Afro-American novelist James Baldwin once remarked that white Southerners were obsessed with the black man's organ, and whenever a black man was lynched the first thing done 'was to cut his penis off'.

Many commentators dismiss these propositions as myths, as no more than part of the racist paraphernalia and thus automatically discredited. They argue that there is no essential difference between penis size in blacks and whites, and that blacks were stigmatised as 'sexually depraved' as part of the battery of justification for European influence in Africa and domination in the New World. They suggest that the image of the black super-stud was invented in order to deter white women from seeking inter-racial liaisons. Had not Shakespeare himself identified the danger when he wrote that 'it is an old saying that black men are pearls in beauteous ladies'

OPPOSITE: *Aubrey Beardsley's* The Examination of the Herald, *1896, from* Lysistrata. *Aristophanes' bawdy play about the women of Greece's successful campaign to end the Peloponnesian War by denying their men sexual favours was a perfect vehicle for Beardsley's pen. The exquisite economy of line of these drawings represents the pinnacle of Beardsley's achievements. The hilariously distended phallus is a potent diagram of male vanity.*

eyes'? (*Two Gentlemen of Verona*, V, ii, 10–13, published around 1589–93). These sexual worries were in the opinion of many historians of race, 'the ultimate basis of racial antagonism' (J. S. Walvin), since all racism derives from fear of competition. Assumptions about an aggressive black sexuality were certainly deeply ingrained in Britain and throughout the American and colonial world.

One of the first historians to challenge the 'myth' – if that is what it was – was the Portuguese writer Gilberto Freyre in his celebrated book translated as *The Masters and the Slaves: a Study of the Development of Brazilian Civilisation* (1946). Freyre argued that Negro sexuality was in fact characterised by a greater moderation than European sexuality, and was in constant need of sharp stimulation, hence the need for such aids as 'aphrodisiac dances'. He pointed out that appearances could be deceptive, with many a giant-framed Negro having the 'penis of a small boy'; moreover, he declared, the sexual organs of 'primitive people' were comparatively under-developed.

On the other hand, the alternative picture has never lacked its advocates. Professor J. Philippe Rushton, professor of psychology at the University of Western Ontario in Canada, as the twentieth century drew to its close, attempted to demonstrate statistically in *Race, Evolution and Behaviour* that blacks have larger genitals and smaller brains than whites or Asians, and that there was an inverse correlation between penis size and brain power. He summed up his thesis thus: 'It's a trade-off. More brain or more penis. You can't have both.'

Whatever the facts, of course, the important thing is what people think is the case. Thus the notion of the black 'super penis' remains a 'classic instance of the influence of sexual insecurity upon perception'. As W. D. Jordan writes of the American South:

> Whatever the objective facts, the belief blended flawlessly with the white man's image of the Negro. If a perceptible anatomical difference did in fact exist, it fortuitously coincided with the already firmly established idea of the Negro's special sexuality; it could only have served as a striking confirmation of that idea, as salt in the wounds of the white man's envy.
>
> *White Over Black: American Attitudes Towards the Negro, 1550–1812* (1968)

OPPOSITE: *Thomas Rowlandson.* The Jester. *This aquatint of an unlikely juggling act was a work of the imagination rather than of observation, but nicely articulates a male longing for a prehensile phallus.*

So what are the 'objective facts'? Men vary in their sexual drive and capacity, in the intensity of their need for sexual satisfaction, and in the dynamic power of their ejaculatory force, just as they vary in every other attribute and characteristic. Best ejaculatory performance, for example, can vary in individuals between expulsion to three inches or less, to three feet or more. And, whether white or black, manifestly they vary – dramatically – in penis size. These differences, whether of size or capacity, are genetically determined in the sense that they depend on whether particular features are inherited from the mother's or the father's genes. Thus it is perfectly possible within one family for two brothers to exhibit the extreme range of penile variation, with the younger boy possessing from birth a penis twice the size of his brother's. Or one may see cases where a son inherits most physical

ABOVE: The Phenomenal Phallus *by Baron Vivant Denon, from his oeuvre* Priapic, *1793. Vivant Denon was, in fact, the first director of the Louvre and accompanied Napoleon on his Nile campaign. This print was a spoof of a seventeenth-century etching of a beached whale. It was executed during a period before Freud offered the world his insights into sexual symbolism.*

attributes, including a large and stocky frame, from his father, paradoxically combining it with a small penis from his mother's side.

Scientific penis measurement is known as phalloplethysmography, literally an assessment of volume. Linear estimation is made upon the erect upper surface from the urethral opening to the junction with the stomach. Flaccid size is not indicative. A long flaccid penis does not increase proportionately in erection: smaller penises increase from the flaccid state more than larger ones do.

Adult erections normally range from 4.5 inches to 9 inches: that is to say, some men have erections which are twice as long as others. Almost all, however, are between 5 inches and 7 inches, though 8 inches is not uncommon; 6 inches, plus or minus, may be regarded as standard, a

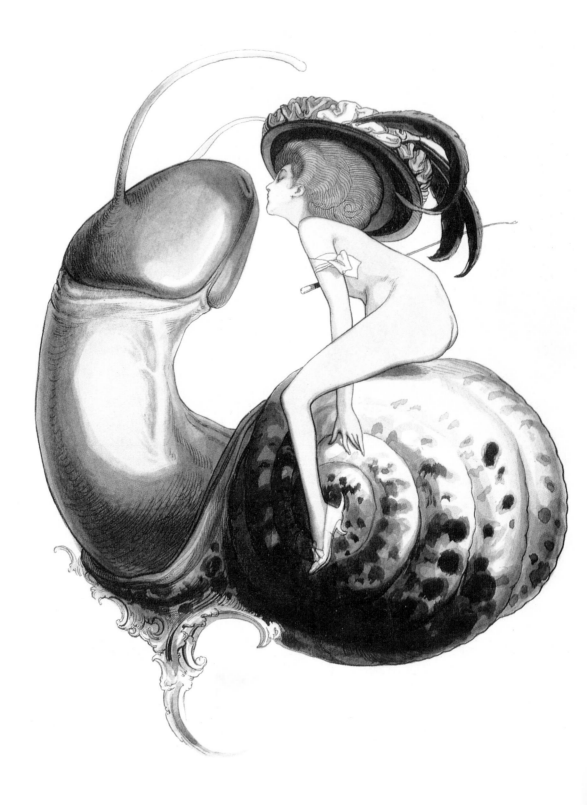

OPPOSITE: *Franz von Bayros, Sweet Snail. Bayros made his living designing bookplates and illustrations for the 'amorous' book market. A whole series of his bookplates, including this one, were published in 1909. This plays on the observation that the form of the penis is often found in nature.*

RIGHT: *A French print, c.1830, illustrating an episode from Voltaire's* La Pucelle d'Orléans. *Hydraulic pressures in the urino-genitary system overnight often contribute to impressive erections in the morning.*

OPPOSITE: *On average, the black man's penis is a little larger than the white man's, but not to the extent established by folklore.*

respectable average. There is an inherent improbability about anything genuinely and verifiably in excess of 9.5 inches, although there has never been any shortage of claimants. In 1890 a French doctor, A. Charpy, documented an erection of 14.5 inches, and this is frequently cited as the record length in man. Unfortunately, virtually all the subjects available for scientific measurement appear to have been Caucasian. Even the great Kinsey himself was dissatisfied with his 'black' sample (mostly of the lower social level) and encountered problems in getting the confidence of Afro-American groups. Although the data was routinely collected, his *Sexual Behavior in the Human Male* (1948) is therefore silent on the whole issue. Privately, Kinsey said he dared not publish his findings because they confirmed the racial stereotype that blacks did indeed have larger penises, higher frequencies of sexual activity, and rose to orgasm more slowly than quick-firing whites; he feared that American neo-Nazis would say 'we told you so'. Perhaps not entirely incidentally he found that black women were more likely than white women to have clitorises which stood out more than one inch. The longest penises reported were, however, white.

Nevertheless, Kinsey was probably right, and there is a marginal correlation between blackness and penis size, a black penis on average being a little larger that the white man's, but exactly the same variations in size can be observed in black as well as white. There are documented cases of Africans with smaller-than-average appendages, most famously the warrior-leader Shaka, ruler of Zululand between about 1818 and 1828. Shaka was taunted by other boys when he was eleven: 'Look at his cock: it is just like a little earthworm'; whether puberty brought any significant improvement is not known, but Shaka took his revenge later by impaling his boyhood tormentors.

Anyone who has seen ethnographic photographs or television pictures of the Masai of Kenya, or the Nuer and Nubians of the Sudan, will probably agree that their men do appear mainly to be well-endowed. But as pointed out earlier, a goodly flaccid length should not be assumed to extend proportionately into its erect state. The appearance, or actuality, of impressive penises in Africans may derive not so much from genetic determination as from lifestyle. Going routinely nude in hot climates would certainly seem to help, while regular sexual usage would seem to be an essential concomitant. An under-used penis will tend to retreat inwards towards its buried root – a factor which may explain recent claims that (supposedly promiscuous) homosexuals have significantly longer propagators than (supposedly apathetic) heterosexuals. Some African peoples may also have resorted to artificial devices for lengthening the penis. And circumcision, though not practised by all Africans, may provide a 'value added' increment by exposing the glans to a subtle degree of continuous stimulation.

Many men wish they had larger penises, even though they know perfectly well it is not necessary for giving a good sexual performance. All claims that a long penis improves sexual efficiency are fallacious; the reverse may even to some extent be true, for, as a general rule, the longer the phallus the lower the angle of erection, and the poorer the consistency or hardness. Excessive length may be counter-productive, and girth may signify more than length – certainly in anal penetration, where it is the extent of lateral stretching which causes the greatest difficulty or produces the best effect.

As far as sexual desire, capacity and performance are concerned, any special African reputation would seem to rest on even shakier foundations than that of significantly superior penis size. There is nothing instinctive about the capacity to provide sophisticated sexual performance. It has to be learned, and it takes time and patience. Although it is perfectly possible that Africans cultivated their sexuality more than many Europeans, and were less inhibited about it, there is little evidence that they evolved an art of sexuality in any way comparable to that of the Indians or the Chinese, or even the Japanese; still less can such an evolution have happened among Afro-Americans in the unpropitious circumstances of a slave plantation. Indeed, if by 'sexual capacity' we mean maintenance of continuous erection over the space of many hours or a whole night, the world champions would undoubtedly be the Taoist masters of sex. The *Kama Sutra* may reflect a culture that was adept at strategies of arousal and the variation of positions for sexual intercourse, but only the Tao philosophers of sex concentrated on techniques for improving erectile function (or curing dysfunction and combating old-age deterioration), for developing sexual energy, multiplying and controlling male orgasm, and practising semen retention, or any of the other arts which alone can maximise male sexual performance as such.

OPPOSITE: The Erotic Crop, *an etching by Pipifax, c.1910. Predatory, feral penis-like vegetables playfully surround a waking girl: a metaphor of sexual arousal.*

ABOVE: *Félicien Rops,* L'Idole, *1870s. Rops' libertine lifestyle and the scandalously erotic subjects he chose to illustrate made him infamous during his own lifetime.*

Le Con
The vagina uncovered

Stephen Bayley

IT (ALMOST) GOES WITHOUT SAYING that men are fascinated with woman's sex. But it is not a simple fascination, instead a rather more complex one in which lust and disgust are mixed. The lexicon of swearing is evidence of this ambiguity. Nothing else can explain the most hostile expletive in the English language. Men think about sex all the time, but their focus is not always the obvious one. Pubic hair is, for instance, treated amiably in jokes, the vagina less so. Hence, the extraordinary charge of word and image in this area. We even had to disguise the subject of this chapter with the pseudo-elegant French term: English would be too explicit. Yet even the French struggle in the delta of Venus, perplexingly giving this defining feminine feature a masculine gender.

'A crack with hair on it' is what we are discussing, at least according, somewhat charmlessly, to Henry Miller who gave nearly forty pages to the subject in *The Tropic of Cancer* (1934). The closing pages of Joyce's *Ulysses* (1922) offer another literary tribute to that congruence of flesh and fur, of slippery mucous and crackling bush, that so bewilders us with mixed desire and revulsion that no sensible name exists for it. Even the Romans, frank in their pleasures and passionate readers of Ovid's *Ars Amatoria* (*c*.1 BC), used the expression 'pudendum'. This means something to be ashamed of.

So what to call it? Classical Latin will not do: degradation should be optional. And scholarly medico-Latin – derived from Ali Ibn Sina (known as Avicenna) – is too clinical, not the language of passion. No one has ever – no one could ever – purr, 'You have the most beautiful vagina.' Other gentle classical terms, such as clitoris (for 'little hill', although the French, in deference to their gastronomic interests, insist on 'praline') and labia have been replaced in the vulgar tongue with 'spasm chasm', 'love button' and

OPPOSITE: *A German watercolour, c.1910, whose title translates as* The Entrance of the Ruler. *With Teutonic formality and affection for uniforms and efficiency, liveried footmen pull apart the outer labia for the ceremonially approaching crowned penis.*

'pissflaps'. It is evident that sex does not always stimulate the language of love, or even of affection. Kingsley Amis once said we are looking at something like an obscure exotic fruit, not even much prized by the natives. The imagery of the pet shop takes us little farther. Beavers may inhabit wetlands, but they are creatures more charming than erotic. Pussy is twee, although also used by the French who sometimes say '*chat*', other times '*lapin*', more raunchily '*le con*' (which seems to be etymologically related to the Sanskrit word for trench). Still, we can't be thinking of all that as we swive towards the *moment critique*. A dignified reticence and a mumbled obfuscation are called for, unless, of course, you are actually prepared to say 'cunt'.

Cunt. Why is its use so inevitably indecorous? Here's a fine old word whose reverberations of love and disgust mirror the loathing and longing generated from 'down there'. Pre-Christian civilisations used a lozenge symbol ambivalently: the sexual invocation had – dependent on

circumstance and context – the optional characteristics of being a blessing or a curse, thus mirroring the frivolous gravity and grave frivolity of love in action. (This same lozenge shape, known in Italian as a *mandorla* – or almond – often surrounds the Virgin in Renaissance art.) The ambivalence remains. Odon of Cluny gloomily wrote that 'inter faeces et urinam nascimur'.

Well, yes. Oh dear. I see what you mean. Burgundy must have been dull in the twelfth century and poor Odon did not have access to psychoanalytic insights, but the odd trick of nature that put the target of lust, the inspiration of art, the source of life, the object of fantasy, the stuff of pornography, the stimulus of poetry, mother, sister, wife, whore…the fact that nature put the honeypot between two exhausts has left us with this crippling ambiguity that gives the word 'cunt' such power. Its currency in polite society, *The Oxford English Dictionary* says with much refinement and taste, 'is restricted in the manner of other taboo-words'…which all have four letters.

The cult of Venus, which (but for a keystroke error would have been much funnier) flourished throughout the Latin world, then migrated to Phoenicia in the form of Astarte and then became the Jewish Esther. Despite this multicultural presence, the goddess of love's dominant sexual feature has rarely been an explicit subject of art. The synonyms Aristophanes uses for the female sex are eloquent of a need to camouflage reality with poetic description. He searches for arboreal, animal and vegetable metaphors: so you get box, piggie, pomegranate, rose, garden, delphinium, meadow, thicket, plain, celery, mint, fuzz, gate, circle, pit, gulf, vent hole, sea urchin, hearth, brazier, hot coals, boiled sausage, barleycake, pancake, thrush, mouse hole, bird's nest, gravy boat. In classical Greek there is no pussy, but instead, the words for 'sow' and pudenda are the same: *xoipos*. This, it has to be admitted, given the negative associations of the word pudendum, is eloquent of the status of pigs in antiquity. As if to confirm, in the collection of Roman agricultural writings *De Re Rustica* (first published 1514), pudenda are called 'porcus'. Thus it is tempting to infer that pinkness is a shared characteristic of the sexual and porcine associations of this 'nook of lechery'.

But revulsion and reticence may be historically specific. It was not always so. The urban geographer can provide the evidence: in thirteenth-century London there was a city passage called Gropecuntelane. What went on there we do not actually know, but discounting even the high level of ambient

OPPOSITE: La Chasse
c.*1800 by Philibert-Louis Deboucourt.*

bawdy of the late Middle Ages, the existence of so graphic a denomination suggests a level of acceptability rather than of taboo. But the status of the word 'cunt' has rapidly changed. In his epic study, *Swearing – a social history of foul language, oaths and profanity in English* (1991), Geoffrey Hughes makes the interesting point that the Norman French title 'Count' had to be abandoned in England (and replaced by the Anglo-Saxon 'eorl', which became 'Earl') because of its phonic similarity to what in 1598 John Florio, Montaigne's translator, pleasantly called a woman's 'privities', or, as we would say, cunt.

In the nineteenth century science and art were magnificently at odds in understanding sex. The case of the Hottentot Venus shows the mixture of fascination and revulsion excited in men by the female genitalia. Since the first regular European contacts with Africans in the seventeenth century, travellers had been obsessed with native sexuality. It may be noteworthy that Rousseau, champion of the noble savage, was much given to systematic solitary masturbation. Whatever, this European fascination with African sex life speaks of repression at home: by the early nineteenth century it had reached the proportions of a vast collective fantasy. Scientists, of varying degrees of professionalism, were fascinated by the enlarged labia minora of the Hottentots, the nomadic pastoral people of south-west Africa.

So, in 1810 a ship's surgeon kidnapped a Hottentot woman of about twenty years old. Given the Dutch name Saartje Baartman, she was brought to England as part of a freak show. As the unfortunate woman – who spoke three languages – stood on a plinth two feet high, visitors specially enjoyed poking the elastic and quivering mass of her buttocks. Removed to Paris, rebranded Sarah Bartman, the Hottentot Venus went on show in the Rue Neuve des Petits Champs. Formal scientific investigation now began: this being an age of pre-Darwinian social anthropology, the search was on for the 'missing link'. Accordingly, from 1815 in the Jardin du Roi a small group of prominent scientists and anatomists attempted to assign the precedence between poor Sarah, of the 'lowliest race of humans', and the orang-utan. Most particularly, the scientists wanted the most thoroughgoing study of her genitals. Understandably reluctant, despite various torments Sarah retained a form of modesty – at least until her death nine months later from an 'inflammatory and disruptive sickness', presumably syphilis. Georges Cuvier (1769–1832) revealed the mystery of the 'Hottentot Apron': the 'two wrinkled fleshy petals'

RIGHT: The Hottentot
Venus, c.*1810. Saartje
Baartman's extraordinary rump
and massively enlarged labia
were the subject of a popular
collective fantasy in the
nineteenth-century scientific
community, obsessed with
native sexuality.*

of her labia minora were distended to about four inches. Sarah Bartman's
genitals were until recently preserved in a bell jar in the Musée de l'Homme in
Paris. Of the sixteen pages devoted to her in Cuvier's contribution to the
Mémoires du Muséum d'Histoire Naturelle (*c.*1816), nine were devoted to her
genitalia, breasts, buttocks and pelvis. One paragraph was devoted to her brain.

Mid-nineteenth-century art was better able than mid-nineteenth-century science to articulate the greater part of man's interest in the most significant part of woman. Thus, Gustave Courbet's scandalous 1866 painting *L'Origine du Monde*. Let us not beat around the bush: this is the first picture of its sort by a major artist, an astonishingly explicit depiction of what in artistic custom had hitherto been veiled, symbolised, blurred, obscured or disguised by mythological reference. Of course, private portfolios of drawn erotica were often to be found in painters' studios, but the presentation in oil on canvas shows that Courbet and his patron attached a particular – and more lofty – status to this picture. *L'Origine* was painted for the bathroom of Khalil-Bey, a Turkish pasha-collector resident in Paris, who also owned Ingres' erotic *Bain Turc* (1859–62). Courbet's unforgettable image is both shocking and allusive. A politically inspired realist, but more combative than Daumier and Millet, he shows the woman's headless fleshy midriff with magnificent bush and an almost unbearable suggestion of damp, pink inflammation beneath. It is at once dehumanising and intensely humane. Here, as the canvas' title states, is nothing less than the origin of the world, the source of life itself. At a time when photographic pornography was becoming familiar in Paris, a masterpiece by a great painter became the perfect expression of male desire, balanced in its delicate position between mother and lover. Somehow, *L'Origine du Monde* equivocates between birth and sex.

And this, of course, is what loads the word 'cunt' with so much meaning. The preoccupation in early psychoanalytical literature of man's castration fears was directly linked to the eternal mystery of the female genitalia, Miller's 'crack with hair on it', which Freud believed excited anxiety simply because it so evidently and tragically lacked a penis. This opinion, of course, says more about Freud than it does about male motivation beyond the analyst's consulting rooms. No one thinks any more about Freud's 'Oedipus complex', his term for the incest taboo, the young boy's unrecognised sexual longing for his mother. Yet even here at lust's ground zero, some fears remain. The majority of jokes about women's genitalia concern the size of the vagina, a sort of mirror-image projection of the wishful fantasy about a large penis. Again, the mythic *vagina dentata* projects onto the woman the responsibility for man's fretful inadequacies. Nothing is more illustrative of the ambiguities in the erotic impulse than a cleft that entices, but then bites.

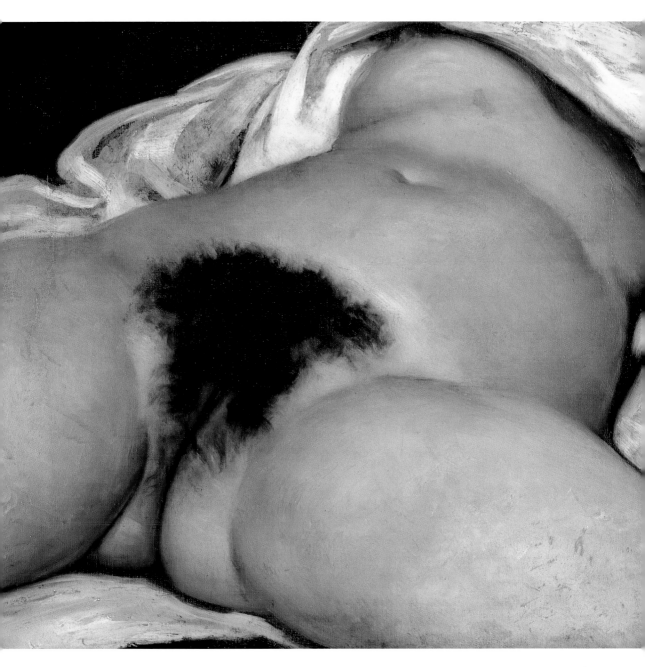

ABOVE: *Gustave Courbet,* L'Origine du Monde, *1866. This painting was commissioned as part of two works. The first, a landscape, was painted on a hinged board with a button which, when depressed, sprang aside to reveal this image behind it. It disappeared in the twentieth century but reappeared in the 1990s to be bought by the Musée d'Orsay. It remains a striking symbol of male desire.*

OPPOSITE: *Thomas Rowlandson*, The Swing, *c. 1810. The complete abandon of the clothes and the spreading of the legs is a graphic realisation of male voyeurism.*

And nothing could be more illustrative of the distinction between French culture and British than the different styles of two erotomaniac contemporaries. *My Secret Life* was published by the pseudonymous Walter (now convincingly shown by Ian Gibson to be the *nom-de-plume* of Henry Spencer Ashbee) in 1888–94, exactly the same time as Pierre Louÿs published his own masterpiece, *Aphrodite* (1896). Walter was a dirty-mac stalker who writes of being sickened with desire, pining for unseen, unknown cunts. Exhausted by his erotic depletions, Walter finds new strength in the cheery formula 'fresh cunt, fresh courage'. Pierre Louÿs prefers suggestive imagery, as purple as it is pink: 'It is like a flower of crimson, full of honey and perfumes. It is like a hydra of the sea, living and soft, open at night. It is the humid grotto, the shelter always warm, the Asylum where man rests from his march toward death.'

After Freud, the Modernists felt more comfortable. The year 1928 was an *annus mirabilis* of erotic publishing. In *Lady Chatterley's Lover* D. H. Lawrence refers to a 'bit o' cunt', an earthy familiarity with the vernacular that kept the book out of print for nearly forty years. But in a contrast of sophistication reminiscent of that between Walter's dirty old man and Pierre Louÿs' pan-sexual poetaster, the same year also saw publication of Georges Bataille's sickly surrealist masterpiece *Histoire de l'Oeil* as well as Louis Aragon's even more bizarre *Le Con d'Irene*, described by Albert Camus as the finest of all erotic works. This was not a Lawrentian 'bit o' cunt', it was the complete thing. Aragon, originally anonymously, tells the story of a man obsessed to the point of depravity with the parts of an imaginary woman. Engaging in a surrealist vortex of flesh and fantasy he captures the enormous curiosities of sex, birth, life, death that animate erotica. The Earl of Rochester, however, had been there before (in about 1680):

> *Oh, that I now cou'd by some Chymick Art*
> *To Sperm convert my Vitals and my Heart,*
> *That at one Thrust I might my soul translate,*
> *And in the Womb myself regenerate:*
> *There steep'd in Lust, nine Months I wou'd remain*
> *Then boldly fuck my Passage out again.*

Le Con: *l'origine du monde*, indeed. A resting place on the march towards death.

Yes!
The mysteries of the orgasm

Stephen Bayley

I T IS NOT A PRETTY WORD, nor perhaps a pretty idea, although it exerts ineluctable appeal. 'The deepest and most volcanic of human impulses', according to pioneering nineteenth-century sexologist Havelock Ellis. From the Greek 'to swell with moisture' we get the word orgasm. Its sense is not purely sexual, but has suggestions of anger, excitement and rage: 'When there appears an Orgasm of the Humours, we rather fly to bleeding as more safe' someone wrote in 1684. Technically, an orgasm occurs at the acme of the sexual embrace when vascular turgescence leads to the unitary and involuntary contraction and expansion of mind and body in a neural explosion with fluid side-effects. If you are lucky, you also get biting and screaming.

The mysteries of the orgasm confound attempts at elegant description. To the physician G. V. Hamilton in his book *A Research on Marriage* (1929) it is 'the spasmodic, highly pleasurable feeling with which the sex act ends for both men and women'. The Victorians used the words 'spend' or 'spent', rather as we do the word 'come'. The nineteenth-century metaphor is as revealing of the Victorian obsession with commerce as it is of the ideas of transaction and donation and depletion which define sex. And when you think of it, 'come' is revealing of the peremptory style of our culture and our own obsession with transport arrangements. On the other hand, the Taoist preference for deferring the male's climax might be cited as an oriental expression of the old truth that it is better to travel than arrive.

Described by medieval physicians as a 'certain tremor', orgasm was advocated as a relief from unhealthful congestion. Of which, one imagines, there was a great deal. The nature of orgasm divides the sexes. Gore Vidal helpfully explained the gender distinctions: men just want to squirt and

OPPOSITE: *Attributed to Hokusai (1760–1849)*, A Farmer Making Love in a Field. *The explosive ecstasy of orgasm produces grimaces and solace. The theme of an aristocratic woman being pleasured by a rough man of the lower orders is common to many* shunga *images.*

women just want to have babies. The issue, as it were, separates us. The combination of pleasurable frivolity and the mystical gravity of natural forces which this most exquisite pleasure possesses are captured by the French expression *jouissance* (for coming) and *petit-mort* for the moment of blissful nervous release.

Taoists aside, healthy men always squirt. Orgasm is more subtle and elusive in women. 'The evidence remains hazy, if not outright dubious,' says Lionel Tiger, Charles Darwin Professor of Anthropology at Rutgers University in his book *The Pursuit of Pleasure* (1992) 'regarding the existence of female orgasm during heterosexual intercourse among non-human primates.' Tiger goes on to describe laboratory experiments which show that, while a male rhesus monkey can pleasurably climax within fifteen seconds of take-off, the female of the species needs to administer and control her own pleasure, requiring up to half an hour to achieve orgasm and then not through penetration by the simian intromittant organ, but more likely by systematic erotic rubbing against a piece of furniture. So, Tiger concludes, advocates of letting the animal in you take over in the interests of fabulously gratifying sex have certainly not been observing monkeys and their furniture very closely. Sex for them is poor, nasty, brutish: a rude and evanescent spasm in the groin for the male, an unsatisfying act of submission for the female.

Orgasm has preoccupied erotic thinkers, not to mention erotic doers, since the ancient days. While, for the male, the pleasure of orgasm is so obviously and visibly linked with the decongesting physical ejaculation which is, equally obviously, a fundamental part of the reproductive process, the female orgasm seems to have no proven link with conception. When the man, as he occasionally does, inquires 'Was it good for you?', he actually wants to know whether his mate experienced a climactic sexual event accompanied by involuntary rhythmic contractions of the vagina, possibly some of that same biting and screaming, with complementary contractions of the urethral and rectal sphincters in symphony with the bombs-away of vasocongestion and muscular tension.

Vidal's squirting has not inspired much poetry: the simplicity of the male orgasm has left literature and science to ponder the more subtle characteristics of the female. Because men almost always achieve orgasm

ABOVE: *An untitled image by Count Mihaly von Zichy from his series* Liebe c.*1870. Zichy's drawings, with their exquisitely observed anatomy and wonderful evocation of atmosphere, still have the power to arouse and inspire.*

OVERLEAF: *Egon Schiele.* The Embrace, *1917. Schiele's idiosyncratic eroticism had a dark side: in the hectic pursuit of pleasure these lovers are attempting to outrun the epidemic of Spanish influenza that killed the artist.*

in intercourse, they are closer to the primates. The woman's graph of orgasm is less predictable, although spontaneous orgasm is, one gathers, more familiar among women than men: Schrenk-Notzing, another pioneer sexologist, had female patients who could reach sexual climax on contemplating seaviews, although his example of a lesbian trick cyclist in the music halls who was excited by colleagues in tights is perhaps more typical.

There is a genuinely mystical sense to orgasm since it unites body and mind in a single event. Flaubert's 'complex convergence of lust and bitterness, such a frenzy of muscle and sound of gold' is better than Victorian 'spending'. On the way to orgasm, all the senses are muted: a rush of information between the sexual organs and the brain, bits rushing

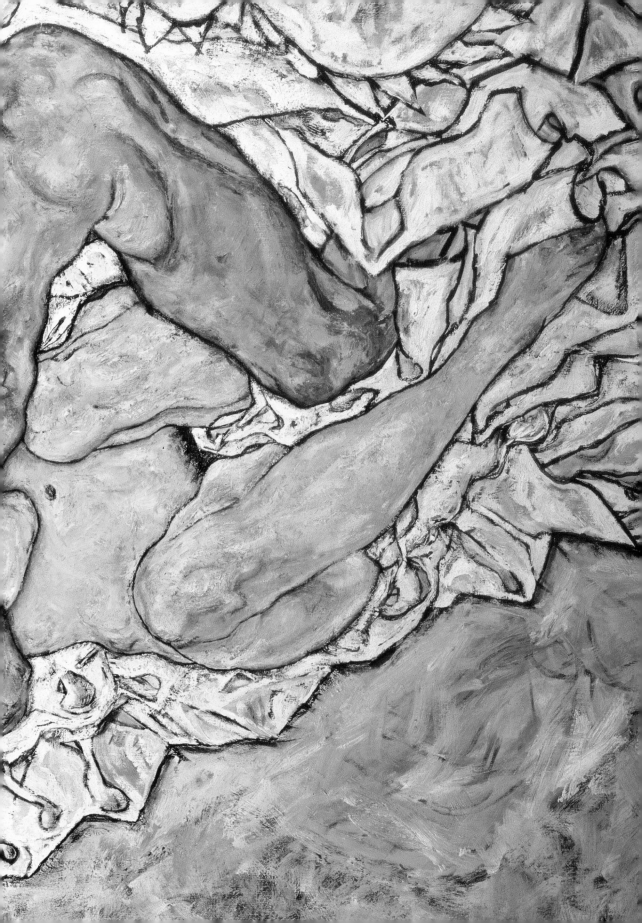

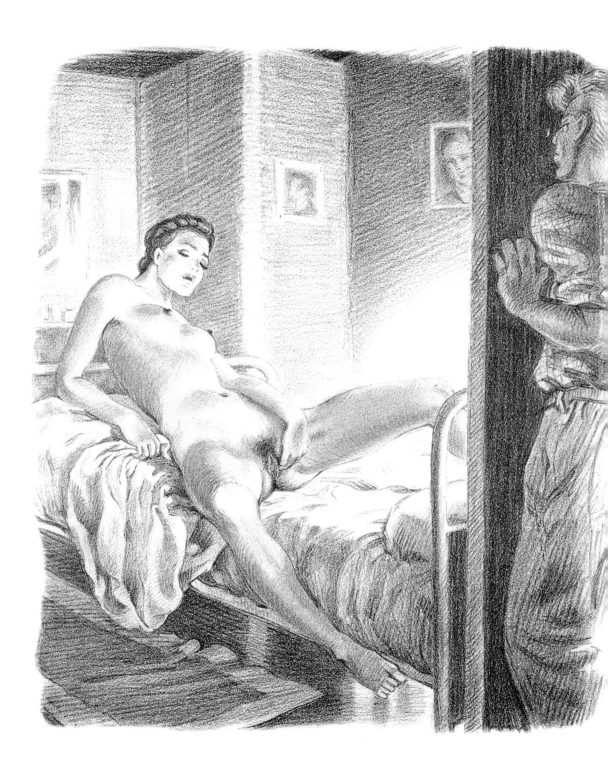

OPPOSITE: Clayton's College *is a classic of 1950s French erotica. Unobserved, Job is watching Consuela bring herself to a climax.*

up the spinal column, the hormonal channels and through the finger tips. It is what Simone de Beauvoir described as the 'piercing sensation of imminence' to be enjoyed by both man and woman. In general, orgasm has four parts:

1. Overwhelming desire for penetration.
2. As intercourse begins, a rising precipitousness,
   felt in the guts, behind the ears and in the obvious places.
3. An enlarging sense of 'no turning back'.
4. At climax, a sense of relief and a return to the senses,
   refreshing or depressing, depending on the circumstances.

Perhaps it is because of the brain overload involved in all this neural activity that accurate observation of orgasm is rare, at least by participants. Geographical metaphors have been useful. Freud's poetic insights into the sexual nature of falling and climbing may have been inspired by some of the vertiginous sensations experienced during orgasm, that sense of struggling up a peak just to fall off again. The complementary notion of pressure relief may have its origins in Freud's conviction that travelling on trains, with their regular vibratory motions and long wave rhythms may lead to sexual arousal. Others have compared it to bursting, an explosive event followed by dreamy rapture or morbid *tristesse* depending, perhaps on your literary inclination.

In classical mythology, Jupiter and Juno debated whether the male or female got more pleasure from sex. They consulted the priest, Tiresias, an expert in the matter since he had been turned into a woman as a penalty for seven years. That this was an unusual, but not cruel, punishment was shown by his response:

If the sum of loves pleasure adds up to ten, nine parts go to women, only one to men.

Come together does not mean equal opportunities. For this insight, Juno struck Tiresias blind.

Fetishism
Bound to obey

Stephen Bayley

A FETISH, FROM THE LATIN *factitius*, meaning 'artificial', was the name given by Portuguese navigators to Guinea-Coast amulets claimed by the natives to possess special, magical characteristics. Most 'primitive' societies acknowledge fetishes, when possession of a physical property gives privileged access to the services of a divinity. Although entirely conventional sexual practitioners may enjoy a 'fetish' for bosoms, bottoms or other bulges, the expression is more commonly used by psycho-pathologists to describe minority sexual practices when the erotic focus is less on the conventional mechanics of the body than on other objects without which sexual gratification may not always be achieved. The classic novel of sadism, whose author gave his name to a psychiatric category, was Leopold von Sacher-Masoch's *Venus in Furs* (1870): here the gentleman hero becomes the woman's slave, cheerfully receiving ritual floggings. When beaten by his inamorata's lover, our hero kisses his feet in gratitude.

Feet are more typical than fur. Foot and shoe fetishism has been a consistent behavioural pattern in civilisation: Ovid knew the erotic power of the foot. In medieval Europe shoes *à la poulaine* (in the form of a beak or a claw or sometimes even in the form of a penis) advertised the wearer as a scandalous libertine. Casanova, a generalist in erotic matters, remarked that all men tend to be attracted by feet. The eighteenth-century French novelist Restif de la Bretonne used shoes as an aid to masturbation. Pre-Maoist Chinese women would not expose their feet to any but their lovers, believing they had a specific sexual character. It was an article of 1898 published in the *Archives d'Anthropologie Criminelle* that explained to the British pioneer sexologist Henry Havelock Ellis the erotic character of the Chinese foot. To hold a foot is, it was said, a superior erotic sensation to the 'palpation of a

OPPOSITE: *Stitched-up from Trevor Watson's* Girls Behaving Badly, *1997. Certain forms of fetishism, once rare or even taboo, are now entering, first, the mainstream of polite erotica and, second, the mass-market of fashion.*

young and firm bosom'. Taking the penis between small feet 'produces in the male an indescribable degree of voluptuous feeling'.

Contemporary shoe fetishism takes a rather different form. While anthropologists reported that the Chinese erotic reverence for feet extended even unto chaste Siberia, where women would be happily seen in the fields with shamelessly exposed breasts, but would insist on keeping their boots on in the interests of modesty, the conventions of contemporary erotic photography reverse this. In pictures by Trevor Watson or Helmut Newton, women are often naked except for extravagant, and usually vertiginous and shiny footwear. In this sense the shoe performs what might be called a dually supportive role: the implication of wearing dressy shoes while naked implies a sexually stimulating form of body consciousness. At the same time, the stress put upon the tendons of the leg in the wearing of high heels tends to create a posture which, anthropologists might venture, invites sexual inspection. More straightforwardly, a nude woman wearing shoes does not so much disguise her feet as emphasise the nakedness and availability of the rest of her body.

Other familiar fetishes are leather, hair, boots, tattoos, rubber and piercing. The *locus classicus* of this last is Pauline Réage's *Histoire d'O* (1954), where the central character has her labia pierced the better to allow her lover and tormentor, Sir Stephen, to dominate her (with the help of a chain). Male erotic piercing has a different character. In a paper in the *Archives of Sexual Behaviour* (1983) a direct association between piercing and homosexuality was established. Japanese *yakuza*, or gangsters, on the other hand, occasionally have a pearl inserted beneath the skin of the glans of the penis in order to gratify the prostitutes maintained in their employment.

The majority of fetishistic practices and preferences fall into the clammy category of sado-masochism. The Kinsey survey of 1953 found that only three per cent of females and one per cent of males had any interest in erotic pain, although the ready availability of all the S&M paraphernalia of studded jockstraps, cone-bras, whips, thongs, ligatures, hooks, riding crops, masks, spike-heel boots, truncheons, racks and so on hints at a more widespread interest fifty years on. Nowadays, a conventional listings magazine, such as London's *Time Out*, can print a description of the social and entertainment opportunities offered by an entirely legal London club:

OPPOSITE: Anticipation, *1999. Julian Murphy invests everyday objects with a sexual character and at the same time makes irreverent and witty references to fetishistic practices, including body piercing and bondage.*

Russian Dolls, *1995, by Julian Murphy. With the removal of successive layers, a matronly babushka becomes a bound and gartered temptress, although by the time she is completely naked, she has disappeared…*

OVERLEAF: *Trevor Watson's image, from his book* Cheek, *2000, combines a number of fetishistic motifs: the quadruped gesture is already powerfully erotic, but significantly enhanced by the salacious quality of the footwear. The hard, dark, shiny materials contrast magically with the soft, pale flesh.*

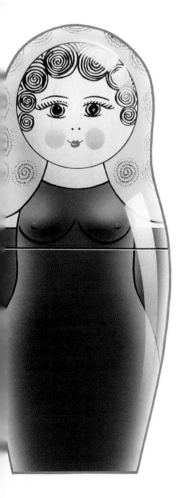

OPPOSITE: *Allen Jones was a founder of British Pop Art, although his style has continuously evolved into a body of work that is uniquely his own. Central to Jones' iconography are the spike heels and tight-laced bustier of the S&M business, but raised by him to the status of art.*

Rubber, leather, bondage, or latex…all ages and sexes, looks and sizes, corseted, chained, bound or spiked in a variety of shiny, slippery, garments. There's a girl up against the far bar; she wears a nippleless white rubber bra and a short, flared miniskirt…At her feet kneels a man wearing jeans, sweatshirt and unzipped leather rapist's mask; his head is up her skirt. Behind him stands a young woman dressed in black rubber, complete with thigh-high boots. She is alternately teasing and cracking a riding crop across his buttocks.

The link between masochistic practices and sexual gratification is ancient: the Talmud says that a little light whipping may cause the involuntary discharge of semen. In *Sexual Anomalies and Perversions* (1944) Magnus Hirschfeld describes the old British interest in flagellant brothels. In 1828, Theresa Berkley, an enterprising madame, created the Berkley horse or chevalet, a sort of adjustable ladder or rack to which the customer was tied. While thus trussed, it also allowed exposure of sexual parts. The operating madam would whip the happy customer with a thong or a cat-o'-nine-tails, a supple switch or a leather strap studded with nails, sometimes with holly or gorse, while an assistant massaged his testicles.

This flagellant fetish was the famous 'English Vice', but Pauline Réage lent it a French character too. At night, O has her hands bound and her vulva and anus exposed for all comers to enjoy as they please:

The corset which held her upright, the chains which maintained her in subjection…. The awareness of her own body…soiled by saliva and sperm, by sweat mingled with her own sweat, she sensed herself to be, literally, the vessel of impurity, the gutter whereof Scripture makes mention. And yet in all, those parts of her body which were most continually offended, having become more sensitive, seemed to her to have become, at the same time, more lovely, and as though ennobled.

Réage says, from being prostituted O's dignity increased. That's the perversity of fetishism. Graham Greene said the *Histoire d'O* was 'without a trace of obscenity'. Perhaps the one certain thing about the erotic is its irrationality.

MADAM GABRIELLA

WORSHIP
AND
OBEY

LUXURY
CITY
APT.

7916

OPPOSITE: *A disciplinarian card found in a London phone booth. This graphic form of soliciting has become a minor, but vigorous, folk art.*

RIGHT: The Mistress, c.*1997, by Lynn Paula Russell. Erotic flagellation is the classic English vice, although the link between sadistic or masochistic practices and sexual gratification is an ancient one.*

ABOVE: The Corsetière
who came in from the
Cold. *David Holland is an
illustrator who plays with the
humorous side of sexual
obsession. Wearing women's
underwear is a keen stimulus to
men of certain tastes, but rarely
on the outside of a dark suit.*

OPPOSITE AND OVERLEAF:
*In his photographs, Trevor
Watson exploits the fetishistic
repertoire of the sado-
masochistic wardrobe as items
of style. The effect is both
ludicrous and unsettling.*

ABOVE: La Clystère de Madame la Vicomtesse, c.*1930*.
This early twentieth-century photograph shows a reenactment of a
composition popular in eighteenth-century erotic prints. The condition
where people get sexually excited by an enema is known as
klismaphilia. *As a specialised fetish there is usually an element of*
privacy required, although pornography can exploit this necessary
discretion to amusing effect.

'I wouldn't recommend sex, drugs
or insanity for everyone, but
they've always worked for me.'

Hunter S. Thompson

Sex, Drugs and Virtual Reality

5

In Ecstasy
Sex, drugs and self abuse

Will Self in conversation with Stephen Bayley

WILL SELF WAS BORN IN LONDON in 1961 and educated at Oxford. And that's the end of the conventional stuff. Self, who is six feet six inches tall, is one of the most extraordinary figures in contemporary British life: he is a journalist of entertaining genius, a novelist who violates conventions, but remains readable, a popular media figure who sustains invigorating irreverence. Self had a privileged, if complicated, childhood: he once made a pilgrimage to see Anthony Storr, the distinguished Cambridge psychiatrist who, some years earlier, had dissuaded his mother from aborting the foetus that became himself. Self, who specialises in baroque visions and S&M insights into human frailty, is sometimes compared to Hunter S. Thompson, William Burroughs, J. G. Ballard and even Jonathan Swift, but is in fact an authentic original. A famous history of drug and alcohol abuse, on which he is characteristically frank and funny, may have stimulated his surreal world-view: people become monkeys, a man finds a vagina growing behind his knee, the dead are alive. His real life is as odd as his fiction: Self was sacked from a job on the *Observer* in London when discovered snorting heroin while on assignment aboard the Prime Minister's plane. He said this was hypocritical because 'I'm a hack who gets hired because I do drugs.'

'Know thy self' is a maxim that unites Judaism and Freud: it is marvellously appropriate that this unique talent has a surname so suggestive of personal revelation. Will Self has memorably combined low-life with high-concept; there are few people who know more about sex and drugs in both theory and practice. I met him in a Kennington, south London restaurant, near where we both live, to ask him about self, love and abuse.

SB I'm interested in how science – mind-altering drugs and reality-altering technology – might enhance or, perhaps, diminish sex.

OPPOSITE: *Hans Bellmer,* Après la fermeture hebdomadaire, *c.1963. Bellmer's etching creates a surreal mood similar to the trance-like state induced by some drugs.*

PREVIOUS PAGE: *Jane Fonda in Roger Vadim's fetishistic film* Barbarella, *1968.*

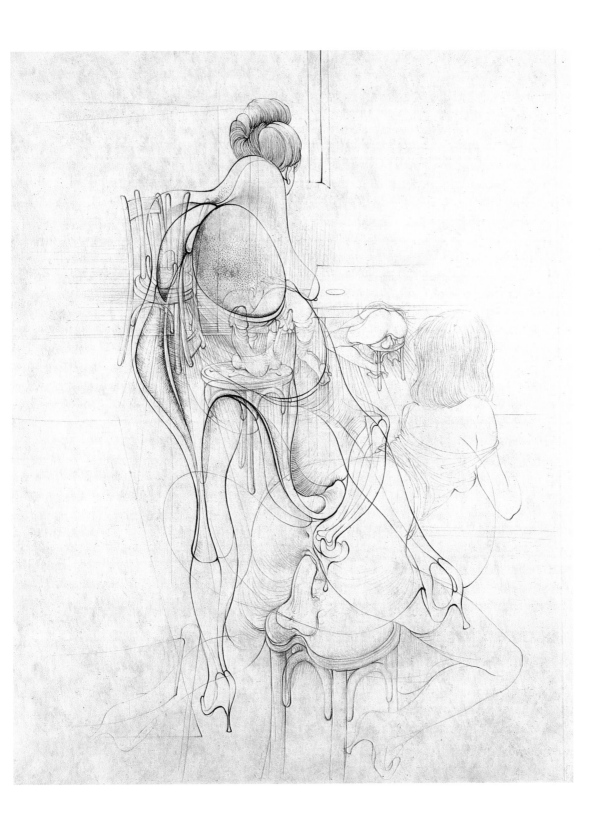

WS Wanking with some slapper over the internet doesn't sound quite as enticing as 'virtual sex'. Drugs do enhance sex, but as [Thomas] de Quincey said of literary endeavours in respect of opiates, 'opium eventually defeats the steady power of exertion'. The same can be said for all drugs and sex.

SB Like [Oliver] Goldsmith saying 'and toiling pleasure sickens into pain'?

WS Hmmmm. The different categories of drugs all have markedly different physiological and psychological effects. Hallucinogens are very good for the surfaces. They are good for the perceptions. Whether you are looking at sex as an aesthetic exercise or not, you know the colours and whether you are looking at that and relating it to an emotional frame of reference as well. You can say that what hallucinogens do in the sexual arena is to make everything much more microscopically visible. The play of emotions on your partner's face and the colours those emotions represent: there is a kind of efflorescence in all those characteristics.

SB Rather like [Bob] Dylan said 'the ghosts of electricity howl in the bones of her face'? In my view, his best ever line.

WS Hmmmm. I rather prefer 'On the back of the fish truck which loads while my conscience explodes'. That, I would say, is an acid sex observation.

SB OK. What about narcotics?

WS Ah. Narcotics. The great virtue of the narcotic influence on sexual behaviour is that for a man they desensitise you to the point that you are likely to maintain an erection, but unlikely to achieve orgasm.

SB Is that a good thing? Is it pleasurable?

WS It can be because it gratifies the male instinct to give pleasure and induce orgasm without being milked of your natural body fluids. It gives you that sense of being contained and being powerful while being able to engage in humping the while. There is also a kind of infantile sex that happens when you are into an addiction to opiates. If you have two heroin addicts having sex, and neither party is in it for orgasm, then there comes a kind of regress to pre-pubescent sexual games so that it becomes touchy-feely, cuddly sex.

SB So what in this case is the purpose of penetration?

WS Well, penetration may not occur because at the point of being a committed addict, most men cannot maintain an erection.

SB So. Amphetamines and sex?

WS Let's say amphetamines and cocaine. If you are young, they are fine. You can maintain an erection and you don't come too quickly. You hammer away, mildly desensitised. Cocaine also has some hallucinogenic characteristics, including an increased sense of touch. Very good! But with age – which defeats the steady power of exertion – you begin to suffer from the inability to get an erection.

Of course, women find cocaine enormously stimulating. I have seen women smoke crack cocaine and spontaneously orgasm. A large rush of cocaine is incredibly close to orgasm. In fact, I think that it is probably hitting a lot of the same receptors. For a man, the sensation of smoking crack cocaine or mainlining it is of the redundancy of orgasm. For women it is tantamount to orgasm.

SB I'm beginning to think sex and drugs may not be compatible.

WS The thing is, some drugs knock orgasm out of the equation. And you can say that just as people in the 1960s thought that the experience of an acid trip was a short-cut to Nirvana, by the same token, as far as sex is concerned, drugs can be a short cut too. On drugs, sex is still very intimate, but depersonalised. In other words, not connected to your masculinity or your femininity. And the drug that is particularly noted for that is ecstasy, which dominates the drugscape in this country. Ecstasy seems to enact not on people, but on the interstices between them. I mean it is a very interesting phenomenon. I used to do a lot of ecstasy.

SB But you surely didn't go to clubs?

WS My dear boy, I used to get enormously loved-up and went to the Reform Club and the Athenaeum. No! I was too old for that.

SB But I thought ecstasy was a social thing.

WS Well, if you took it alone, I mean completely alone, it would register almost no effect at all. Perhaps a lifted heart rate, a little distorted peripheral vision, not much more. But take it with another and you notice an enormous sense of attraction to the other person. In fact, almost anybody. I mastered the rather different art of getting angry on ecstasy which is almost the Zen end. To be angry when you are on E is compellingly difficult. It is not for nothing known as the Love Drug.

SB But hasn't it been around for more than fifty years?

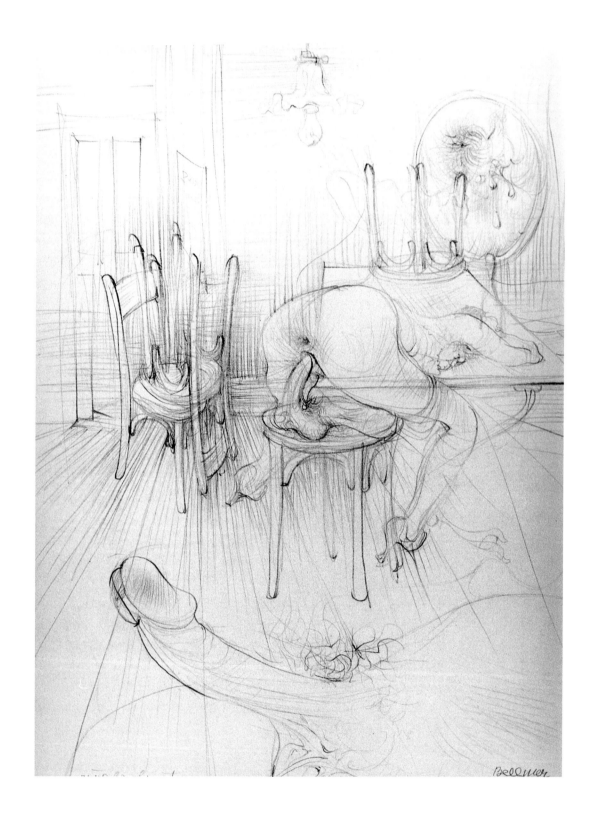

OPPOSITE: *Hans Bellmer,* Après la fermeture hebdomadaire, c.*1963. The private world depicted here is one of narcoleptic excess.*

WS Well, it is a form of speed. Anyway, to be with another person when you are on E is to feel acutely that the interpersonal relationship is an almost reified thing. Like on speed or cocaine, everything is interesting. It creates interest, it is very touchy-feely. It gives you an almost unquenchable urge to touch other people. It has a sexual, erotic, character. Again, orgasm is out of the window: it's like heroin sex. We live in a society which is over-sexualised in its imagery, but under-sexualised in its activities. Ecstasy in an interesting way acts to fill that gap. It is the kind of infill of eroticism. Orgasm is not achieved, but it is advertised.

SB So what about alcohol, the most popular drug of all?

WS Well, alcohol is a fantastic sex drug, isn't it? It disinhibits, it makes you extrovert, it makes you horny. It just kind of works.

SB Rather as [William] James said: 'it is the great votary of the "yes" function in man'?

WS I have a favourite from [Jean] Cocteau: 'Charm is the ability to solicit the answer "yes" before the question is asked.' Alcohol is the great charmer here.

SB Can dance replicate the effect of drugs?

WS My wife is a good dancer. She loves to dance. So we do dance. It is something that has to be relearned when you give up all of these drugs. (I have a line in the novel I'm writing: 'They form a conga line of buggery.')

SB I sense you are not much interested in virtual sex.

WS We have that already. It is called pornography. A form, particularly for men, of autoerotic stimulation effected by visual imagery is virtual sex. Real sex is personalised and intimate and, in a sense, you have to use a friend. And you have to be somebody in relation to the body you are fucking to abandon yourself.

SB So you feel it is necessary to have a fondness for your partner?

WS Well, no. I think it's fine to have sex with people you hate. Hate is a strong emotion as well. But I think it is very important that people have sex with people. I think that anonymous sexual encounters are only fine up to a point.

SB Had many anonymous encounters?

WS I have been extraordinarily promiscuous. But not as promiscuous as….

SB I now realise you are a romantic. The idea of depersonalised disembodied gratification does not appeal?

WS I think it is corrupting.

Cybersex
The dark side of the Net

Nathan McLaughlin

A DARKENED ROOM IN AN ORDINARY HOUSE, in an unremarkable street. The guy strains his eyes to see the keyboard in the dim, half-light of the computer monitor. After several minutes of general conversation in the public chatroom, a window pops up on the screen, the Holy Grail of cybersex, the private 'whisper' window, inviting him to get up close and personal with a perfect stranger…

> **A**: A/S/L?
> **B**: 32/M/NYC
> **A**: cool, wanna cyber?
> **B**: u first, what u wearing?
> **A**: hardly anything…it's real hot here 2night. u?
> **B**: mmm…sounds good. me: boxers and t-shirt, but it's starting 2 get hot here too, i might be persuaded 2 take them off…
> **A**: i reckon i could persuade u, big boy…

…and so begins another foray into the soft, white underbelly of the Internet – a place where strangers meet online to exchange explicit fantasies and pornography; where people can throw off their inhibitions and obtain sexual gratification, either alone or with others, in complete anonymity. Welcome to the world of online sex.

When the World Wide Web was first being developed, its creators envisaged a user-friendly interface to the Internet. By making it more intuitive and graphical, they planned to open up the Internet and, by extension, the information revolution to the masses, instead of it remaining the exclusive domain of a select few academics and computer whizz kids.

OPPOSITE: *Lara Croft, the first pixellated sex symbol. Quaintly, the new technology had to rely on the old motif of an ample bust to achieve erotic effect. It is now cyberworld folklore that Lara's impressive cup size was caused by the slip of the designer's mouse at the crucial moment.*

Back

Forward

Reload

Home

Search

Netscape

Images

Print

Security

Stop

Netsite : http://home.

ENT

10K read

e.com

 What's Related

TER

What they could never have imagined is that, whilst providing easily accessible information on demand and a huge increase in convenience in all areas of life, from shopping to academic research, the Internet has also adapted to cater to our less intellectual, more basic needs. Sex, in its many forms, now accounts for over a third of all Internet usage. Be it cybersex in chatrooms, or pornographic photos and videos, electronic sex is huge business and is here to stay.

So why has the Internet become such a popular tool in the continuing sexual revolution? Perhaps this is the wrong question to ask. Maybe we'd be better off asking why pornography and other forms of casual sexual gratification were only ever indulged in by a minority of people prior to the emergence of the Internet. It's not really a case of the Internet spawning a new generation of cyber-perverts or in any way stimulating our need for easy sex. What is more than likely the case is that humans are sexual creatures and always have been, but often don't express this as fully as they'd like because of the inconvenience and social stigma attached to porn and casual sex. With the Internet comes a new level of convenience and an unprecedented level of anonymity and protection. While the man walking through the red-light district is visible, restricted in his choice and must deal with staff if he is to purchase material in a sex shop, the cyber-smut connoisseur is invisible, alone and can span the globe in his search for people or material to satisfy his needs; his options are limitless and the world his oyster...

> **B**: ...yeah, reckon you could hotstuff, I'm getting hard just thinking about what you're gonna do to me.
> **A**: tell me what you look like, then I'll tell you what I'm going 2 do 2 u.
> **B**: 6'1", blue eyes, slim, athletic, 8"/uncut...

... and that's where the beauty of cybersex lies. By removing visual and audio cues from the encounter, you are left only with your imagination to guide you through the experience. While reality can rarely come up to our idealistic standards and our fantasies are often limited by unwanted stimuli, the nature of the Internet makes it far easier to become lost in the fantasy and to recreate ourselves, physically and mentally to suit the person with whom we're engaging. When a man says he's 6'1" with blue eyes and a slim, athletic build, is he telling the truth? What about a woman who claims to be tall, curvaceous, blonde and wildly attractive? Is she telling the truth? Well, who knows and, frankly, does anyone really care? Whilst the primary goal of anyone involved with cybersex is personal gratification, there is also a huge element of role-playing. The thrill of making someone believe you are someone you're not and getting them to open up and share their most intimate fantasies with you can be as great as the thrill of cybersex itself.

> **A**: …got an email address? I could send u a picture of me right now…
> **B**: yeah, send it 2 ******@*****.com…can't wait to see yur hot body…

But with this anonymity and seeming unaccountability comes a (perceived) dark side. Stories abound of paedophiles peddling kiddie-porn across the globe, serial rapists picking people up in chatrooms and young children stumbling across shocking pornography. This is sometimes true, but is no more prevalent proportionally than 'real-world' sex-crime. The Internet is merely a tool, and one which is open to abuse. During hundreds of hours spent cheerfully downloading the latest sweaty hardcore action from the farthest corners of the globe and gazing at the monitor intently while someone on the other side of the world describes in minute detail what they're doing to themselves at that very moment, this author has never come across anything other than consensual, adult fun. It is virtually unheard of to 'stumble' across porn sites accidentally. If a thirteen-year-old boy types all manner of filth into a search engine, it is highly likely that several porn sites will pop up in the results. However, since the thirteen-year-old knows what to type in the first place, it is probably fair to assume that the damage has already been done and the parents need to take a long, hard look at their child-rearing skills rather than try to offload blame onto the Internet.

Things are rarely as bad as they seem. The vast majority of folks surfing the 'information super-smutway' are average, everyday people who simply enjoy the ease with which they can access erotica and connect with other, like-minded people. As safe sex goes, this has to be one of the safest kinds, not to mention one of the most satisfying – on so many different and often unexpected levels.

PLAYBOY

ENTERTAINMENT FOR **MEN**

50c

FIRST TIME
in any magazine

FULL COLOR

the famous

MARILYN

MONROE

NUDE

VIP ON SEX

'Sexual intercourse began
In nineteen sixty-three
(Which was rather late for me) –
Between the end of the Chatterley ban
And the Beatles' first LP.'

'ANNUS MIRABILIS', Philip Larkin

Chronology of Sex

compiled by Jonathon Green

6

The Venus of Willendorf c.*25,000 BC*

c.25,000 BC The *Venus of Willendorf* – lacking a face but with large breasts, a podgy belly and an unmistakable vagina – was created probably as a primitive fertility goddess. More than sixty similar statues have been discovered in Europe.

c.1850 BC The Egyptian Kahun Papyrus cites a variety of contraceptive methods, notably a tampon-like plug composed of crocodile dung inserted into the vagina, which has been smeared with honey and natron ('a kind of Salt drawn from the Water of the River Nile').

c.594 BC Solon, the Athenian judge, established state-licensed brothels. Further sex-related legislation empowered a cuckolded husband to kill his adulterous rival, set the price of rape at a one-hundred-drachmas fine and ordered any man married to an heiress to have sex with her at least three times a month.

c.500 BC Miletus, a city in Ionia, established itself as the dildo-manufacturing capital of the (known) world.

c.200 BC Chinese Pillow Books were introduced for newlyweds. They offered details on forty-eight sexual positions plus the need for foreplay. Anal and oral sex were also suggested.

c.1 BC Ovid's *Ars Amatoria* was published.

14 AD Tiberius became the emperor of Rome. He forbade the execution of virgins so that when such women were condemned to death, they would have to suffer the extra humiliation of being publicly deflowered by the executioner just before the sentence was carried out.

33 The cult of Jesus of Nazareth, Christianity, was launched with his crucifixion, bringing with it, *inter alia*, two millennia of sexual repression with its attendant persecutions, censorship, 'morality', hypocrisy and guilt.

130 The word gonorrhoea was coined by the noted Greek physician Galen. Erroneously describing one of the symptoms, it literally means 'a flow of seed'.

138 Soranus, a Greek physician, died. His *Gynaecology* gives his foolproof method of contraception: '...the woman ought, in the moment during coitus when the man ejaculates his sperm, to hold her breath, draw her body back a little so that the semen cannot penetrate into the *os uteri*, then immediately get up and sit down with bent knees, and in this position, provoke sneezes.'

c.200 The *Kama Sutra* of the Indian guru Vatsayana appeared.

309 The Council of Elvira (now Granada, Spain) promulgated a number of canons aimed to govern sexual behaviour. All non-procreative sex was outlawed, as was homosexuality. Adulterous women and whores were to be punished. The clergy were to be strictly celibate.

500 The Frankish Salic Law enforced the death sentence on adulterous wives. Husbands could philander unrestrained, although there were various cash penalties for groping women who would prefer otherwise.

c.600 The penitential, a manual of fixed penalties for confessed sins, was adopted by the Church. The severity of the punishments depended on whether the sin in question was a one-off or habitual and whether one was active or passive. Sins could be expiated by dieting, fasting, prayer, attending mass, displaying contrition in public, and charitable donations. Adultery was punished by seven years' penance, anal or oral sex required between three and fifteen years, bestiality from one to ten, fornication three and coitus interruptus between two and ten. A spontaneous wet dream could be cancelled out with a week's fasting. Sex had to be in the missionary position; the admission of any alternatives required penance. 'Habitual' homosexual fellatio brought seven years' penitence; inter-femoral sex (between the thighs) two. The punishment for lesbian sex or female masturbation was three years.

c.743 Walid II instituted the harem and its attendant eunuchs. Muslims could not become eunuchs, but Jewish and Christian candidates were available at a price.

875 The Scottish King Ewen III established the rights of 'the First Night' (*'jus primae noctis'*). According to a chronicle: 'Another law he made, that wives of common men shall be free to the nobles; and the Lord of the ground shall have the maiden-heads of all the virgins dwelling in the same'. This popular sport may have continued up to the beginning of the Middle Ages.

1072 Pietro Damiani, an Italian reformer, died. Totally obsessed by the idea that virginity should be pre-served, he spent his whole life trying to convince girls to abstain from sex. He also spent much time attempting to stamp out prostitution by preach-ing inside brothels. His zeal was undoubtedly fired by the fact that he was the son of a prostitute.

1161 State-sanctioned brothels were legitimised in England; this tolerance only ended in 1545.

1191 At the start of his first crusade against the infidels, King Richard

Chinese pillow books c.200 BC

the Lion-Heart arrived at Marseilles and was horrified to discover that his advance party of trusty knights had spent all the campaign funds on prostitutes.

1174 Saint Thomas Aquinas, whose theories and writings have become the cornerstone of the Roman Catholic Church, died. His fundamental opinions on sex (which he called 'lust' – women being no more than men perverted) are significant. Any sexual activity other than that intended for procreation was a sin against nature. His four offending categories were, in descending order: (1) bestiality; (2) homosexuality; (3) using any position other than face to face with the woman on her back; and (4) masturbation, which he considered effeminate in men.

1275 Angela de Labarthe of Toulouse became the first woman to be burned at the stake for having sexual intercourse with the Devil. Her crime was discovered after she reportedly gave birth to a child with a wolf's head and a snake's tail.

1300 The Lothardi sect flourished in Russia. Their belief was that while above ground, men should lead moral lives, but once they were at least twenty-seven inches below ground, everything changed. Hence, all their meetings were held in subterranean caves and were riotous orgies.

1382 The word sex made its first appearance in English in Wycliffe's translation of the Bible: 'Of alle things havynge sowle of ony flesh, two thow shalt brynge into the ark, that maal sex and femaal lyven with thee.'

1415 Antipope John XXIII was deposed for 'notorious incest, adultery, defilement, homicide, and atheism'. Earlier, while still a chamberlain, he quite openly kept his brother's wife as a mistress. In an effort to squash the scandal, his superiors promoted him to cardinal and sent him to Bologna, where 'two hundred maids, matrons, and widows, including a few nuns fell victim to his brutal lust.'

1484 Pope Innocent VIII was elected. He was nicknamed 'the Honest' because he was the first pope to acknowledge his illegitimate children publicly.

1490s Syphilis made its premier appearance in the Old World. While some physicians theorise that Columbus carried the disease back from America, others have suggested that venereal organisms had long been in Europe but in a far less potent form. In any event, an epidemic swept Europe beginning in the mid-1490s, sparked by the French assault on Naples. Thousands of warring French and Neapolitans were stricken with what became widely known as the French disease, to the chagrin of the French monarch, Charles VIII. The French christened it the 'Neapolitan disease'. The scourge hit Germany in the summer of 1495, Holland and England by 1496, India and the Middle East by 1498 and China by 1505.

c.1500 *The Perfumed Garden* by the Tunisian Shaykh Nefzawi was published.

1521 First use of the term 'syphilis', coined by the Italian physician

Hieronymus Fracastor in his poem *Syphilis Sive Morbi Gallicus*, a medical tract on the still novel disease. The term may have been derived from Greek words meaning either 'lover of swine' or 'companion in love'.

c.1524 Pietro Aretino wrote sonnets to accompany erotic drawings made by the architect Giulio Romano. These were subsequently engraved by Marcantonio Raimondi. The collection of erotic poses was called *I Modi* and known in English as *Aretine's Postures*.

1527 The term 'venereal disease' was coined by Jacques de Bethercourt.

1529 During Cardinal Wolsey's trial for treason, he was accused of giving Henry VIII syphilis by persistently whispering in the King's ear.

1530 The German doctor Paracelsus initiated the mercury treatment for syphilis.

1535 An ecclesiastical tribunal in Toledo, Spain, found a Catholic priest named Valdelmar guilty of rape, blasphemy, consorting with prostitutes and extorting the favours of a young woman in exchange for absolution and sentenced him to a mere thirty-day house arrest and a fine of two ducats. Such leniency for debauchery was said to be commonplace in the early sixteenth century.

1542 Andrew Boorde, in his *A Dyetary of Helth…the boke for a good husbande to lerne*, solemnly warned that eating lettuce killed sexual desire: 'Lettyse doth extynct veneryous actes'. He offered an

The Perfumed Garden *published c.1500*

antidote, saying that figs 'stere a man to veneryous actes, for they doth urge and increase the sede of generacyon.' Boorde later became Bishop of Chichester, where he was publicly defrocked for keeping three prostitutes in his chambers.

1546 Martin Luther died. According to his *Table Talk*, 'women ought to stay at home; the way they were created indicates this, for they have broad hips and a wide fundament to sit upon to keep house and bear and raise children.'

1555 Pope Paul IV ordered the removal of Michelangelo's paintings from the Sistine Chapel on the grounds that they were obscene. After a storm of protest, a compromise was agreed upon and the Pope ordered the naked figures (including all the angels and the Virgin Mary) in 'The Last Judgment' to have clothes painted on them. Michelangelo's pupil Daniele da Volterra executed the task and afterwards was commonly known as 'the Breeches Maker'.

1559 Pope Paul IV began compiling the *Index Librorum Prohibitorum*, a list of books deemed off-limits to Catholics due to blasphemous or profane content. To date, over four thousand titles have been thus listed, including the total output of Balzac, Dumas, Stendhal and Alberto Moravia. In 1962 Pope John XXIII decreed that new authors would be given a chance to justify the content of their books before being added to the list. The Church stopped publishing the *Index* in 1966.

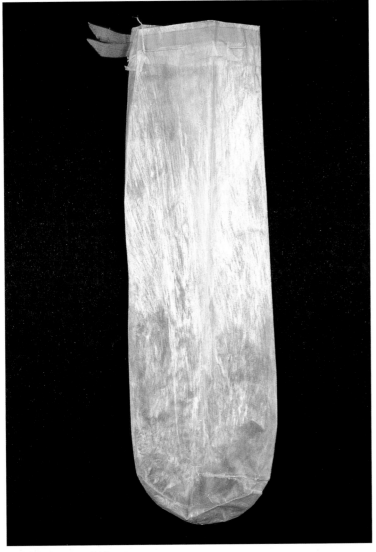

Condom invented 1560

1560 In the wake of history's first recorded syphilis epidemic, Gabriel Fallopius invented the condom, a linen sheath which Madame de Sévigné was later to describe as 'gossamer against infection, steel against love'. It fitted over the glans and beneath the foreskin. Fallopius was also the author of *De Morbo Gallico* ('The French Disease') in which he recommended postcoital cleansing of the genitals to prevent infection. Fallopius also gave his name to the female 'fallopian tube'.

1560 France outlawed prostitution.

1565 An epidemic of erotic convulsions swept the Convent of Nazareth in Cologne. According to the German doctor De Weier, who investigated the phenomenon, the nuns would throw themselves on their backs, shut their eyes, raise their abdomens erotically, and thrust forward their pudenda. Other such cases were documented by De Weier in his book *De Praestigiis Daemonum*.

1585 Mary Magdalene de Pazzi endured one of history's first documented masochistic obsessions. She would run madly about the convent grounds, rolling around on thorns and burrs, whip herself savagely, and beg the other nuns to bind her tightly to posts and hurl hot wax at her. She was entrusted with the guidance of her convent's novices and was once found forcing one of her charges to thrash her. Saint Mary was canonised in 1671.

1588 All whores were expelled from Paris. Those who defied this ordinance had their heads shaved and were confined to an iron cage. In Toulouse the whores were stripped, tied up and plunged three times into the river. Any who survived were imprisoned for life.

1611 Two unmarried women who were discovered to be pregnant on arrival in Virginia were immediately returned to England. In the next years, many such girls were returned in an attempt to stamp out the risk of promiscuity in the colony.

1634 In Loudon, France, Jeanne des Anges, a nun, suffered nightmarish erotic hallucinations and convulsions and ultimately a false pregnancy after being spurned by the Curé Grandier. For his part in Jeanne's misfortunes, the curé was burned at the stake; the nun herself was widely venerated. The incident was the basis for Aldous Huxley's 1952 novel, *The Devils of Loudon* and Ken Russell's 1970 film *The Devils*.

1638 The first woman forced to wear a distinctive mark on her clothing for a sex offence resided in Plymouth, Massachusetts. Mary Mandame was charged with 'dallyance diverse tymes with Tinsin, an Indian' and 'committing the act of uncleanse with him'. She was sentenced to be whipped through the town's streets and at all times to wear a badge of shame on her left sleeve under penalty of being burned in the face with a hot iron if she neglected to do so. Tinsin was whipped at the pillory for 'allurement & enticement'.

1640 Philippe, Duc d'Orléans, was born. He was raised as a girl so that he would not be a rival to his brother, the future Louis XIV. He played the part well, leading his soldiers into battle while wearing high heels, a long black perfumed wig and elaborate jewellery, but no hat, because he didn't want to spoil his hairdo. His wife commented, 'He was more afraid of the sun, or the black smoke of gunpowder, than he was of musket bullets.'

1649 The earliest lesbian trial in America took place in Plymouth when Goodwife Norman and Mary Hammon were charged with 'lude behavior uppon a bed, with divers lascivious speeches allso spoken'. Goodwife Norman was found guilty and sentenced 'to make publick acknowledgment…of her unchaste behaviour'; the charges against Mary Hammon were dropped.

1655 *L'Ecole des Femmes* was published. This anonymously penned guide to the joys of sex, for women only, included practical tips on methods of contraception and how to choose a proper merkin (pubic wig).

1655 The Frankish Diet, a Protestant body, legalised bigamy as a means of replenishing the population of Europe, badly decimated by the recent Thirty Years' War.

1656 Found guilty of 'lewd and unseemly behavior', Captain Kemble of Boston was placed in the public stocks for two hours. His crime: kissing his wife in public on the Sabbath after three years' sojourn at sea.

1658 Puritans in Plymouth, Massachusetts passed the infamous adultery law, which required a female offender not only to be whipped, but to wear for the remainder of her life the letter A on her breast. Failure to comply at all times meant she was liable to have the letter A branded on her face with a red-hot iron. The horror of this disgusting righteousness was brilliantly portrayed by Nathaniel Hawthorne in his 1850 novel, *The Scarlet Letter*.

1664 Richard Cornish became the first man to be convicted of a homosexual offence in America. Despite extremely flimsy evidence, he was hanged for forcing a young man into unnatural sexual relations. Two men were later pilloried and had their ears sliced off for protesting that Cornish 'was put to death through a scurvie boys meanes & no other came against him'.

1665 The word condom first appeared in print in *A Panegyric upon Cundum* by the notorious rake John Wilmot, Earl of Rochester. The word was not derived from the legendary but mythical Dr Condom, but more likely from the Latin *cunnus* (for the female pudenda) and *dum* (implying an inability to function).

1677 While peering though a microscope at a specimen of his semen, Anton van Leeuwenhoek, a Dutch microscopist, discovered sperm. They were 'little animalcules that moved forward with a snaillike motion of the tail', Leeuwenhoek and his co-discoverer Stephen Hamm reported. Leeuwenhoek noted: 'What I here describe was not obtained by any sinful contrivance …but the observations were made upon the excess with which Nature provided me in my conjugal relations.' Nevertheless, few scientists recognised the connection between the wriggling creatures and conception. Many deemed them to be parasites. Others theorised that miniature likenesses of the organisms in question were concealed in the tip of the spermatozoa and that they slowly expanded upon entering the female. One biologist claimed he had observed perfectly formed microscopic roosters in the seed of roosters and tiny horses in semen of that animal.

1684 The first sensible printed sex manual was published in London under the title *Aristotle's Masterpiece, or the Secrets of Generation Displayed in All Parts Thereof*. A deserved bestseller, it advised extensive sexual foreplay and emphasised the value of clitoral massage, saying 'blowing the coals of these amorous fires' pleased women.

1688 Sir Charles Sedley, who 'excrementiz'd' on the crowds beneath the Covent Garden tavern where he was drinking, was fined for obscene libel, the precursor of modern obscenity laws.

1695 The world's first lonely hearts advertisement was published in John Houghton's *Collection for the Improvement of Husbandry and Trade*. It read: 'A Gentleman about 30 years of age that says he has a Very Good Estate, would willingly Match Himself to some young Gentlewoman that has a fortune of 3000 or thereabouts, And he will make settlement to content'.

1702 A transvestite, Lord Cornbury, became Governor of New York and New Jersey. He performed most of his official duties in women's clothes. He was recalled in 1708 after landing in jail for debt.

1707 Read, an English publisher, was arrested and tried for printing *Fifteen Plagues of a Maidenhead*, deemed obscene but not punishably so by the Queen's Bench Court. It was the first trial prompted by the publication of allegedly obscene literature.

c.1710 The first bidets came into use in France.

1714 The Roman Catholic Church banned the confessional requirement that men name their partners in fornication when it was discovered that priests were making carnal use of the information.

1723 French police in Montpellier raided a meeting of the Multiplicants, a sect devoted to orgies. (Their members married, but for only twenty-four hours; the marriage was consummated publicly on the altar.) The leaders were hanged, the remaining men were sentenced to life in the galleys, and the women, after having their heads shaved, were placed in nunneries.

1724 Daniel Defoe wrote an essay entitled 'Conjugal Lewdness, A Treatise concerning the Use and Abuse of the Marriage Bed, and Marital Whoredom'. In it he outlined a popular custom amongst cads of the day of kidnapping likely heiresses and forcing them into marriage, thereby enjoying the fruits of the nuptial bed and not infrequently securing a large dowry. Defoe wrote: 'It seemed a little hard that a gentleman might have the satisfaction of hanging a thief that stole an old horse from him, but could have no justice against a rogue for stealing his daughter.' Just after the essay's publication, 'stealing ladies' was made a capital offence.

1725 The publisher/bookseller Edmund Curll was successfully prosecuted under the Common Law for selling *Venus in the Cloister, or the Nun in her Smock*, a blasphemous tale of lesbian nuns, first published in France in 1682. This was the first such case in the UK.

1727 Helen Morrison, a lonely spinster from Manchester, England, became the first woman to place a lonely hearts advertisement. It appeared in the *Manchester Weekly Journal*. The mayor promptly committed her to a lunatic asylum for four weeks.

1749 John Cleland's erotic novel *Fanny Hill, or the Memoirs of a Woman of Pleasure* was published.

1750 The practice of 'bundling' – a man and a woman lying in the same bed with their clothes on – began in the US. Clothes were often removed and bastards conceived, though the practice was mainly permitted to courting couples.

1752 The Hellfire Club was founded by Sir Francis Dashwood and sundry other rakes.

1757 The Society for the Reformation of Manners was founded in the UK.

1767 John Hunter, a brilliant English surgeon, began an experiment attempting to prove that gonorrhoea was only a manifestation of syphilis and that in fact they were one and the same disease. He dipped a lancet into some pus previously taken from the sores of a venereal patient, then inoculated the foreskin and head of his own penis. If his theory was correct, the pus taken from the patient suffering from gonorrhoea would give him syphilis. According to his diary, by Sunday there was 'a teasing itching in those parts'. This lasted until Tuesday, when 'the parts of the prepuce where the puncture had been made were redder, thickened, and had formed a speck.' A week later 'the speck was increased.' This perfect description of the symptoms of syphilis seemed to prove his theory correct. Unfortunately, Hunter was wrong in his assumption that the original donor of the pus was suffering from gonorrhoea. Actually he had the far

1788 Police raid a brothel in Paris. The whores were sent forcibly to populate America.

more deadly disease syphilis. But, Hunter's reputation was so great that his theory was automatically accepted, and this classic error retarded the investigation of venereal disease for fifty years. Even sadder was the fact that Hunter eventually died from the effects of his experiment.

1768 The *Encyclopaedia Britannica* was first issued, in instalments. The entry for 'Woman' stated, 'The female of man. See *Homo*.'

1770 Pope Clement XIV outlawed the two-hundred-year-old practice of using *castrati* in papal choirs. These

were men deliberately castrated when young to preserve their 'soprano' singing voices. Persons performing such operations on young boys were excommunicated, though the boys were made very welcome into the choirs thereafter.

1772 The Marquis de Sade was sentenced to death for overdosing a number of prostitutes with the supposed aphrodisiac Spanish Fly (*cantharides*). He had also tortured another girl, who managed to escape and inform the authorities. The death penalty was commuted, after appeals from his family; de Sade then fled to Italy.

1775 The Italian biologist Lazzaro Spallanzani first proved the procreative powers of sperm by mating a female frog with a male frog cloaked in a pair of tight-fitting contraceptive trousers fashioned from waxed cloth. When the eggs failed to fertilize, Spallanzani scraped some of the semen from the inside of the trousers and with it successfully inseminated the eggs. However, he attributed the fertilisation not to the sperm, but to some other agent in the semen.

1775 Lords Moray and Aboyne quit London's Wig Club, taking with them that which gave the club its singular name – a wig reputedly made entirely of the pubic hair of the mistresses of King Charles II. All would-be members had to produce a lock of their own mistress' pubic hair, which would then be woven into a wig.

1777 After a career of sodomy, rape, mutilation, and sundry other perversions, the Marquis de Sade was imprisoned, at his mother's behest, in the Bastille, where he composed most of his astoundingly obscene literary output. De Sade argued that because women could sham sexual pleasure but not pain, pain must be the higher form of sexual activity. He also said that out-lawing pederasty and lesbianism was unfair because no 'abnormality of taste' can justifiably be considered a crime. Seeking understanding, he said that his real crime was loving women too much. He died at the lunatic asylum at Charenton in 1814.

1780 Harris's *List of Covent Garden Ladies*, a popular guide to London whores, was published.

1782–9 Jean Jacques Rousseau's *Confessions* was published. After admitting to a natural reluctance to reveal his personal sex life, he over-came this aversion and 'frankly and sincerely' told all. Addicted to masturbation, he confessed to doing it while fantasising over the spankings meted out by his foster mother. He also stated that his first heterosexual encounter left him feeling he had committed incest, and that thereafter he always had difficulty having inter-course with women.

1782 The first child of artificial insemination was born. A London

1814 Death of the Marquis de Sade

draper and his wife consulted the English surgeon John Hunter about their childlessness. Hunter diagnosed 'hypospadias', a condition where the urethra opens upon the undersurface of the penis, making it impossible for sperm to exit from the glans during intercourse. Hunter got the draper to masturbate, then took the semen in a warm syringe and injected it into the posterior part of the wife's vagina. The result was a bouncing success.

1782 Choderlos de Laclos scandalised France with *Les Liaisons Dangereuse*s, his novel of seduction and adultery among the aristocracy. Attacked as a 'work of revolting immorality', the novel was banned in France in 1824.

1783 During one of his popular London 'sanitary lectures' in his Temple of Health, Dr James Graham, a Scot, introduced his 'medico-magnetico-musico-electrical bed', designed both to 'insure the

removal of barrenness' and to 'improve, exalt, and invigorate the body and through them, the mental faculties of the human species'. The twelve-foot-by-nine-foot wonder rested on twenty-eight glass pillars, was equipped with a mattress stuffed exclusively with hair from the tails of the finest English stallions, and was topped by a mirrored dome. Most important, one thousand five hundred pounds of lodestones were arranged about the bed, so as to be 'continually pouring forth in an ever-flowing circle inconceivable and irresistibly powerful tides of the magnetic effluxion, which is well known to have a very strong affinity with the electric fire'. It was said to be guaranteed to produce 'strong, beautiful, brilliant, nay, double distilled children'. Supplementing Dr Graham's bed as a sexual stimulant was beautiful sixteen-year-old Emma Lyon, later the renowned Lady Hamilton and mistress of Horatio, Lord Nelson, who performed erotic dances around it in the nude.

1785 M. Thouret, head of the medical faculty at the University of Paris, announced the discovery of artificial insemination. He impregnated his wife, using a tin syringe to insert his own semen. The first insemination with 'third-party' semen was performed in Philadelphia in 1884.

1788 Mary Wollstonecraft's *Mary, a Fiction*, the first lesbian novel written by a woman, was published. It was based on Mary's real-life passion for Fanny Blood, an emotion Mary's husband once described as 'so fervent [that it] constituted the ruling passion in her mind'.

1792 Mary Wollstonecraft published *Vindication of the Rights of Women*, the first – and much-denounced – feminist treatise.

1797 A manual, *The Duties of the Female Sex*, by Thomas Gisborne set these out as: submission, honesty, and providing pleasure for men. The book bespoke a widespread reversion to medieval notions of women's responsibilities at this time.

1798 The Bishop of Durham warned Britain's House of Lords that France had given up on the idea of conquering England militarily and was instead attempting to destroy the moral underpinnings of English society by smuggling in hordes of ballet dancers.

1821 A Massachusetts court found printer Peter Holmes, the American publisher of *Fanny Hill*, guilty of smut-peddling, in the nation's first obscenity trial. Massachusetts was not to pass a specific law defining and outlawing obscenity until 1824.

1822 A statue of Achilles representing the invincibility of the Duke of Wellington was unveiled in Hyde Park (where it still stands). A gasp of horror swept the crowd of spectators as they realised they were witnessing the unveiling of London's first nude statue, especially since it had been commissioned and paid for by the women of England. Within a few days Achilles miraculously grew a fig leaf.

1824 Mary Wilson, London's most successful brothel owner, outlined her ambitious plans to open a luxurious brothel for women only in an essay titled 'Adultery on the Part of Married Women, and Fornication on the Part of Old Maids and Widows, defended by Mary Wilson, Spinster. With Plans for Promoting the Same, Addressed to the Ladies of the Metropolis and Its Environs'. Her salon was to be stocked with 'the finest men of their species I can procure…all kept in a high state of excitement by good living and idleness', and there 'any lady of rank and fortune' could 'have one or a dozen men as she pleases'. Subscription was to be 100 guineas per annum. Sadly, Mary failed to get her plans off the drawing board.

1828 The 'Berkley horse' was invented by the well-known madam, Theresa Berkley. The horse catered for those of Berkley's large clientele whose tastes ran to flagellation. It consisted of a padded device, resembling a ladder, with spaces through which the face and genitals were accessible. Whips of choice included a cat-o'nine-tails, leather straps studded with nails, and birch rods kept in water, thus providing a more exquisite agony.

1829 The British government banned the Hindu practice of *suttee* in India and elsewhere throughout the Empire, although it continued until at least 1905. *Suttee* was the enforced immolation of a widow on her husband's funeral pyre. In 1803 there were 275 recorded instances of it within 30 miles of Calcutta.

1830 Invention of the cervical cap.

1832 Dr Charles Knowlton wrote *The Fruits of Philosophy*. In the book he explained the importance of the postcoital douche, which he claimed to have invented. The liquid for the douche was a solution of alum mixed with any astringent vegetation, such as green tea or raspberry leaves. The following year, Dr Knowlton was arrested in Cambridge, Massachusetts, and jailed for three months for trying to sell his book.

1834 'A Lecture to Young Men on Chastity, Intended Also for the Serious Consideration of Parents and Guardians' was written by Sylvester Graham. Probably the most hilarious condemnation of sex ever published, it gave bountiful advice and declared that excessive sexual desire heightened by 'high seasoned food, rich dishes, the free use of flesh' led to insanity. Graham also warned that married couples overdoing it sexually would be struck down with 'languor, lassitude, muscular relaxation, general debility and heaviness, depression of spirits, loss of appetite, indigestion, faintness and sinking at the pit of the stomach, increased susceptibilities of the skin and lungs to all the atmospheric changes, feebleness of circulation, chilliness, headache, melancholy, hypochondria, hysterics, feebleness of all the senses, impaired vision, loss of sight, weakness of the lungs, nervous cough, pulmonary consumption, disorders of the liver and kidneys, urinary difficulties, disorders of the genital organs, spinal diseases, weakness of the brain, loss of memory, epilepsy, insanity, apoplexy, abortions, premature births, and extreme feebleness, morbid predispositions, and an early death of offspring'. If that dire warning wasn't sufficient, Graham later announced that every ejaculation lowered a male's life expectancy.

1843 Joseph Smith, founder of Mormonism, first exhorted his followers to practise polygamy.

1844 With the invention by Goodyear of vulcanised rubber, a new and improved condom went on the market.

1846 The Oneida Society New England was founded by J. H. Noyes, who urged members to practise free love and birth control.

1847 A British physician named Simpson angered churchmen when he administered the newly discovered chloroform to a woman in childbirth. The Church claimed that to shield a woman from the natural agony of delivery was a blatant violation of the Bible's commandment that women should bring forth their children in sorrow.

1850 Sir Richard Burton's sixteen-volume translation of *The Arabian Nights* – generously footnoted with his comments on clitoral surgery, homosexuality, and bestiality – was published. In later years Burton began an English rendering of *The Scented Garden Men's Hearts to Gladden*, which, he predicted, would be 'a marvelous repository of Eastern wisdom: how eunuchs are made and married...female circumcision, the fellahs copulating with crocodiles'. Following Burton's death, it was destroyed by his prudish wife.

1857 A court for divorce and matrimonial cases was established in England. Men were permitted a divorce on the grounds of adultery alone; women had to prove not only adultery but also additional abuses such as sodomy, rape, bestiality or incest.

1857 Britain passed the Obscene Publications Act, the country's first anti-obscenity legislation; it remained in place, widely abused by the authorities and a tool for philistine 'moralists', until its similarly named replacement of 1959.

1857 Publication of William Acton's *The Functions and Disorders of the Reproductive Organ*. It concentrated primarily on the 'evils' of 'self-abuse'. It also noted that in general, other than mistresses and whores, women 'are not very much troubled with sexual feelings of any kind'.

1864 The *Lancet*, Britain's leading medical journal, warned of the sex traps involved in hypnotising women (hypnotism was then known as animal magnetism): 'The magnetizer – independently of making the passes and of fixing his eye upon her – often takes her hands between his and then draws his fingers over various parts of her body, now over her face, and then over her body and legs, pressing, perhaps, his knees against hers, and sometimes applying (we have seen this done) his lips to her stomach, and making insufflations upon it. Have we said enough to show that in some cases at least the use of animal magnetism is morally dangerous? We have heard it acknowledged by a most zealous practitioner of the art, that he has, more than once, witnessed all the excitement of action coition thus produced in a woman.'

1866 *Sexual Physiology* by Dr Russell Thacker Trall was published in the US. The author of this sensational bestseller claimed that during his travels in the Friendly Islands and Iceland, he had noticed that 'some women have that flexibility and vigour of the whole muscular system that they can, by effort of will, prevent conception.' Based on these observations, Trall told the women of America, '...sometimes coughing or sneezing will have the same effect. Running, jumping, lifting and dancing are often resorted to successfully.'

1867 The British parliament approved the Contagious Diseases Act, which mandated that prostitutes working near military encampments or naval bases receive periodic medical examinations and, if necessary, treatment for venereal infections.

1867 'The Influence of the Sewing Machine on Female Health' was published in the *New Orleans Medical Society Journal*. The article strongly advised the use of bromide to prevent seamstresses from becoming too sexually excited by the erotic rhythms of the foot treadle.

1869 The term 'homosexuality' was coined by Dr Benkert, a Hungarian physician.

1872 The first scientifically observed female orgasm in the United States occurred when Dr Joseph R. Beck of Fort Wayne, Indiana, was fitting a pessary in a woman who had asked him to take great care since she was of such a passionate nature she might have an orgasm. Overcome by scientific curiosity, Beck deliberately induced the orgasm by sweeping his 'right forefinger quickly three or four

WHAT ARE THE CONTAGIOUS DISEASES ACTS?

THE Contagious Diseases Acts are laws in force, at the present time, in many towns in the South of England and Ireland, under which policemen in disguise are employed, as spies, to watch the women of those towns, and to force all those whom they suspect of immorality to undergo, every fortnight, a revolting personal examination, to see whether they are, in the opinion of the official who makes the examination, fit for vicious men to consort with. If any woman, pursued by these spies, refuses to submit to this treatment, she is punished with imprisonment with hard labor. If the official who makes the examination considers his unhappy victim not fit for vicious men, she is sent to a hospital-prison, where she may be kept for many months, and where she is compelled to submit to whatever doctoring, &c., the officials there choose to inflict upon her. If she make her escape from this hospital-prison, she is an outlaw, and may be arrested by any policeman, in any part of the United Kingdom without a warrant.

ENGLISHMEN!! IRISHMEN!!
ELECTORS OF NEWCASTLE!!!

Are you prepared to submit to such "horrible" laws in this borough? Are you prepared to have those dearest to you always under the eyes of degraded spies, subject to the secret accusations of dastardly or designing informers, exposed to the most infamous insults? Are you prepared to withdraw the shield of our ancient constitutional laws from every helpless unprotected female, and to abandon large numbers of your countrywomen as a prey to calculating vice, and heartless cruelty? If you are NOT prepared to do this,

VOTE FOR
COWEN AND HEADLAM
AND
IMMEDIATE, GENUINE REPEAL
OF SUCH INFAMOUS ATROCIOUS LAWS.

1867 Parliament approves the Contagious Diseases Act

---

times across the space between the cervix and the pubic arch, when almost immediately the orgasm occurred'. Dr Beck later published a full account of the experiment.

1872 Sexologist Richard von Krafft-Ebing coined the term 'sadism'.

1872 A London confectioner named Samuel Parkinson was jailed for selling sweets emblazoned with 'the figures of men and women in the most disgusting positions'.

1873 The US Congress passed the Comstock Act, banning obscene materials – including rubber prophylactics – from the mail. Anthony Comstock himself, the legendary anti-vice crusader, was named special agent for the post office to help enforce the new law.

1877 More than forty years after the publication of *The Fruits of Philosophy*, Charles Knowlton's pioneering work on birth control, Charles Bradlaugh and Annie Besant

were tried at the Old Bailey, London, for republishing it. The prosecution declared that '…this is a dirty, filthy book, and the test of it is that no human being would allow that book to lie on his table; no decently educated English husband would allow even his wife to have it…' Although the jury declared the book was 'calculated to deprave public morals', it exonerated the defendants, who had been charged with having 'corrupt motives'. On appeal, Besant and Bradlaugh won the right to publish.

1878 Pope Leo XIII banned the use of *castrati* in the papal choir of the Sistine Chapel; their employment had begun *c*.1550.

1882 Aletta Jacobs opened the world's first birth-control clinic, in Holland. She popularised the diaphragm, which was known as the 'Dutch cap'.

1885 The British campaigning journalist W. T. Stead, editor of the *Pall Mall Gazette*, published a series of pieces, entitled 'The Maiden Tribute', decrying the rampant state of prostitution in London. The climax of his campaign came when he bought a thirteen-year-old girl from her parents, ostensibly to make her into a whore. In fact he turned her over to the Salvation Army. Her parents, encouraged by an embarrassed police force, sued Stead for abducting their daughter and the campaigner served six months in jail.

1886 Richard von Krafft-Ebing published *Psychopathia Sexualis*, which linked, *inter alia*, masturbation to criminality.

1887 J. L. Milton published *Spermatorrhea*, a tract against masturbation in which he advocated spiked rings that would prevent erections, and electrical bells that could be attached to the penis and would ring in the parents' bedroom whenever their sleeping son had an erection.

1895 Arrested for 'gross acts of indecency committed with persons of the masculine sex', Oscar Wilde was sentenced to two years' hard labour. At the time, one of the few people to say anything fair about him was the journalist W. T. Stead (famed for his exposure of child prostitution in London), who wrote, 'If all the persons guilty of Oscar Wilde's offences were to be clapped into jail, there would be a very surprising exodus from Eton and Harrow, Rugby and Winchester.'

1895 Striptease shows began in Paris. The first, called *Le Coucher d'Yvette*, showed a girl gradually taking off all her clothes as she vainly searched for a flea.

1895 Sigmund Freud published *Studies in Hysteria*.

1897 The first legalised surgical sterilisations were performed in the US.

1897 British sex psychologist Henry Havelock Ellis published *Sexual Inversion*.

1900 Sigmund Freud wrote *The Interpretation of Dreams*, in which he underscored the importance of repressed sexual desires in human behaviour.

1907 The British Parliament repealed a longstanding law making it illegal for a widower to marry his wife's sister.

1907 Clarence Richwood patented the first hand-held vibrator. Powered by water pressure rather than electricity it required that the user be near a convenient tap.

1912 Dr Paul Ehrlich discovered Salvarsan, a treatment for syphilis.

1913 The world's first nude calendar was published. It reproduced a prize-winning painting called *September Morn* by the French artist Paul Chabas. When the great anti-pornography crusader Anthony Comstock saw it on sale, he said, 'There's too little morn and too much maid.'

1916 In the US, Margaret Sanger opened the first 'birth-control clinic' (a phrase she coined) at 46 Amboy Street, Brooklyn, New York. To make sure that the poor were aware of its operation, she had circulars printed in three languages – English, Italian and Yiddish. After a police-woman posed as a patient, the establishment was closed.

1919 Tubal ligation was introduced as a means of birth control.

1920 The League of Nations organised a thirty-five-nation conference on 'The Suppression of International Traffic in Obscene Materials'. Unable to agree on a single working definition of 'obscene', the council nonetheless discussed many methods of purging obscenity from the world.

1921 Roscoe 'Fatty' Arbuckle was tried for the rape (and consequent death) of starlet Virginia Rappe.

1922 The Hays Office was set up in Hollywood to censor American film.

1922 *Ulysses* by James Joyce, was published by Shakespeare and Co, in Paris. It was immediately banned in the US and UK.

1922 In a Sheffield, England, court-room, accused bigamist Theresa Vaughn admitted under oath that in the past five years she had acquired sixty-one husbands in fifty cities across England, Germany and South Africa, averaging a marriage a month.

1923 Adultery became grounds for divorce in the UK.

1924 French writer André Gide, in his autobiographical novel *If It Die*, became the first important modern public figure to declare publicly that he was a homosexual.

1927 K-Y Jelly was patented for medical use; it was not sold to the public until 1980.

1928 The first IUD (intra-uterine device) was created by Ernst Gröfenberg.

1928 The first volume of the encyclopaedic *Bilder-Lexikon der Erotik*, embracing every imaginable aspect of sex and lavishly illustrated, was printed in Germany.

1928 D. H. Lawrence's *Lady Chatterley's Lover* was published. Promptly barred from his native Britain, it would not be published there legally until 1961.

1929 Radclyffe Hall's allegedly lesbian novel *The Well of Loneliness* was tried for obscenity.

1930 An underground amusement called *le cirque erotique* flourished in Paris. Nude women bicycled speedily around an indoor track while spectators bet on which cyclist would reach orgasm first from the rubbing of clitoris against bicycle seat.

1934 Henry Miller brought out *The Tropic of Cancer* in Paris. 'At last,' said poet Ezra Pound, 'an unprintable book that is fit to read.'

1936 The first use of sulphonamide drugs for the treatment of gonorrhoea.

1938 The Roman Catholic-oriented National Organization for Decent Literature was founded. In the years to come it would condemn such works as C. S. Forester's *The African Queen* (1935), Ernest Hemingway's *A Farewell to Arms* (1930), James Michener's *Tales of the South Pacific* (1951) and Christopher Morley's *Kitty Foyle* (1940).

1944 Ernst Gröfenberg discovered the female 'G-spot', situated inside the front wall of the vagina behind the pubic bone and along the urethra.

1945 The French government created the Commission of Control, a Ministry of Information subdivision empowered not only to censor all movies shown in France, but also to review the scripts of all films prior to shooting.

1946 Mahatma Gandhi, Indian leader, publicly confessed that he had been taking naked girls to bed

Barred when first published in 1928, Lady Chatterly's Lover was only legal in 1961

with him for many years to test his mastery of celibacy.

1946 Charging Kathleen Winsor's *Forever Amber* with being obscene, the state of Massachusetts made an attempt to ban its sale. Attorney General George Rowell supported his request for the ban by charging that the novel contained the following: seventy references to sexual intercourse; thirty-nine illegitimate pregnancies; seven abortions; ten descriptions of women dressing, undressing, or bathing in the presence of gentlemen; five references to

incest; thirteen references ridiculing marriage; '49 miscellaneous indefensible passages'. Afterwards, one radio comedian was censored for suggesting that Miss Winsor should have called her book *Forever Under*.

1947 The first screen kiss was shown in Japan. Up until then kissing was considered a shockingly private and erotic activity.

1948 Dr Alfred Kinsey and associates published *Sexual Behaviour in the Human Male*, to be followed

1957 Roger Vadim's film And God Created Woman *with sex kitten Brigitte Bardot.*

five years later by *Sexual Behaviour in the Human Female*.

1952 Sex-change surgery was performed in Denmark on ex-GI George Jorgensen, later to win fame and stardom as entertainer Christine Jorgensen. Surgeon Christian Hamburger was subsequently so swamped with applications for the operation that the Danish government restricted it to Danish patients only.

1953 *Playboy* magazine first appeared on American newsstands. The first issue was undated, because publisher Hugh Hefner didn't know whether there would be a second. The first playmate was Marilyn Monroe in a Tom Kelley photograph supposedly taken in the same session as the famous nude calendar pinup. According to the first anniversary issue, *Playboy* was aimed at 'that select group of urbane fellows who were less concerned with hunting, fishing,

and climbing mountains than with good food, drink, proper dress and the pleasure of female company'.

1954 Pauline Réage's novel of sexual abuse and enslavement, *The Story of O*, was published in Paris by the Olympia Press.

1955 An English newspaper asked mothers to come forward who had been virgins at the time they gave birth to their children. Nineteen women sent details. Upon investigation eleven of the women were instantly dismissed, because although their hymens were still intact, the women had all conceived through sexual intercourse. After a six-month detailed medical study, however, the *Sunday Pictorial* announced that Mrs E. Jones had been delivered of a baby daughter while still a virgin.

1957 In Roth v. US, the Supreme Court ruled that purveyors of obscene materials were not protected by the First Amendment and might legally be arrested and prosecuted, but only if the materials were utterly without redeeming social value. This and other Roth restrictions soon led to the end of prosecutions of literary works and 'softcore pornography'.

1958 The Mississippi State legislature categorised voyeurism as an exclusively male crime, thereby exempting women from prosecution as Peeping Toms. A Peeping Tom, the lawmakers decreed, was 'any male person who enters upon real property…and thereafter pries or peeps through a window…for the lewd, licentious, and indecent

purpose of spying upon the occupants thereof.'

1961 The world's first contraceptive pill went on sale in the US; it appeared in Britain a year later.

1962 Helen Gurley Brown published *Sex and the Single Girl*.

1963 In Britain, the Profumo Affair occurred. Tory Minister of Defence John Profumo allegedly shocked the nation, and certainly contributed to the end of the Macmillan government, when he was found, 'despite lying to the House of Commons', to have been sharing a call-girl, Christine Keeler, with a Russian diplomat.

1963 Scabrous 'sick' comedian Lenny Bruce was barred from entering Britain by the Home Secretary.

1965 *Penthouse* magazine was introduced in London. An American *Penthouse*, the first US magazine to show pubic hair, would not be published until 1968.

1966 The International Modern Kissing School, in Schagen, Holland, was closed by orders of the tutor's new bride. Tom Zwagg, alias Johnnie van der Laan, had been offering one-minute lessons for a dollar, including kissing from three angles: vertical, at forty-five degrees and horizontal.

1966 William H. Masters and Virginia F. Johnson published *Human Sexual Response*, the first detailed description and analysis of the physiological aspects of sexual excitation and orgasm.

1967 The UK passed the Homo-sexual Law Reform Act, permitting homosexual acts in private between consenting adults (over twenty-one).

1967 *I Am Curious Yellow*, one of the first popularly distributed movies in the US to portray sex explicitly, was produced in Sweden. In an attempt to gain further distribution – which was widely banned – a heavily cut version, *I Am Curious Blue*, was released the following year.

1968 US sex researchers, Drs Phyllis and Eberhard Kronhausen, organised the world's first interna-tional exhibition of erotic art, shown in Sweden and Denmark.

1968 The UK legalised abortion on demand.

1969 The Danish government legalised the sale and distribution of all forms of sexually explicit materials. The revolutionary action failed to prompt the outbreak of sex crimes many had predicted.

1969 Drag queens fought the police when they raided the Stonewall Bar on New York's Christopher Street. The upshot of this landmark refusal to accept what had become institu-tionalised homophobia was the founding of the Gay Liberation Front.

1970 In the US the President's Commission on Obscenity and Pornography urged restraint in governmental attempts to 'interfere with the rights of adults who wish to read, obtain, or view explicit sexual materials'. Senate leaders denounced the commission's report and President Nixon called it 'morally bankrupt'.

1963 Christine Keeler, the call-girl blamed for the downfall of the British government.

1970 The *British Journal of Hospital Medicine* estimated that one out of every forty-five British women was a lesbian.

1970 Germaine Greer published *The Female Eunuch*.

1971 Lord Longford, one of Britain's best-known (and widely ridiculed) anti-pornography campaigners, published his report on pornography.

1971 The world's first commercial sperm bank was opened in New York.

1971 The trial of the 'underground' magazine *Oz* for its 'Schoolkids' issue – bringing together, among other things, the children's comic character Rupert Bear and the more scabrous inventions of American cartoonist Robert Crumb – was the longest obscenity trial ever held in the UK.

1973 Sexologist David Reuben published *All You Ever wanted to Know About Sex…* The guide sold heavily, but promoted a number of popular sexual myths and was notably homophobic.

1973 The Lambton Affair: British government minister Lord Lambton was forced to resign when the *News of the World* printed pictures of him with a prostitute, Norma Levy.

1977 A female University of Missouri student underwent the first female-to-male transsexual operation in history. She was provided with a penis that could have an erection. The *New York Times* reported: 'The doctors said the penis contained a tiny hydraulic system that permitted a fluid to be pumped from a reservoir in the abdomen into the penis to cause erection. Investigation shows that the penis erection device has been used in more than 200 operations in the country to date, most performed by the device's inventor, Dr F. Brantley Scott, a urologist affiliated with the Baylor College of Medicine in Houston.'

1977 A French boss known only as 'Mr D.' unexpectedly returned home to find his wife in bed with one of his employees, identified as 'Robert C.'. The employee was immediately fired, but a local arbitration board in Laon, north of Paris, held that the employee was owed $800 because he hadn't been given proper notice and $500 in severance pay. Mr D. took the case to an appeals court which reversed the decision and ruled that Robert C. was justly fired and should collect nothing because he 'was fooling around on company time'. The favourable ruling for the French boss was in part due to the fact that when Mr D. surprised the amorous couple he was not alone, but was accompanied by the mayor of Laon.

1977 On 13 December the New Jersey Supreme Court, in a 5–2 vote,

1971 *The* Oz *magazine obscenity trial was the longest ever in UK legal history.*

overturned a state law that forbade sexual intercourse between any man and an unmarried woman. According to the judges, the law violated 'the zone of privacy protecting individuals from an unwarranted governmental intrusion into matters of intimate personal and family concern'. Those who wanted to keep the law contended that the statute was needed as a protection against venereal disease, but the court rejected that argument.

1981 The first cases of a fatal illness, known as GRID (gay-related immune deficiency) are reported in the US gay community. The disease was renamed AIDS (Acquired Immune Deficiency Syndrome) in 1982.

1984 Death of Gaetan Dugas, one of the very first gay men to be diagnosed with AIDS and thus known as 'Patient Zero'.

1985 The pro-censorship Parents Music Resource Center was founded in the US. Terrified by the lyrics their children were hearing via rock and, more particularly, rap music, they successfully campaigned for the labelling of supposedly 'dangerous' CDs and tapes with a label reading 'Parental Guidance: Explicit Lyrics'. Sales were unaffected.

1990 Militant homosexuals began promoting 'outing', the publicising of the homosexuality of a number of public figures, often politicians and rock or movie stars, who had chosen to hide their sexual preferences to advance their careers.

1992 Elaine Lerner, a New England Sunday School teacher, patented a system of straps and loops that would allow one partner to exercise control of the movements of the hips of the other partner during lovemaking. Supporters at the Sex Institute in New York argued that in-flight intercourse (using this system) would help relieve astronauts of the enormous amount of stress they undergo during missions.

1992 Rock star Madonna's book *Sex*, featuring the singer in a variety of pastiche poses based on hard- and soft-core pornography, sold out its 375,000 UK print run in three hours.

1993 The female condom, essentially a large polyurethane tube inserted into the vagina, went on sale. Considered expensive, unsafe (more than a quarter failed), and off-putting (during intercourse it produced a distracting squeaky sound), it remained less than universally popular.

1994 The Wonderbra, originally created by British lingerie firm Gossard in 1969, was relaunched. Comprising fifty-four individual bits of latex, wire and fabric, it claimed to give even the least 'well-endowed' woman a movie-star cleavage. The ad campaign, featuring a pneumatic model, was suitably controversial, and sales of the bra boomed.

1998 Viagra, the first oral medication designed to overcome impotency, was launched. It was the most successful new drug in history: 120,000 prescriptions were written in the first week (at $10 a pill).

1998 Despite a variety of contacts which included fellatio, mutual masturbation, substantial fondling, and the use of a cigar as a sex aid, President Clinton denied that his relationship with White House intern Monica Lewinsky was in any way 'sexual'. Oral sex, in particular, he claimed, was not a 'sexual act'.

2001 The appositely named Good Vibrations Association in the US organised a Masturbate-A-Thon as part of National Masturbation Month, with all proceeds going to sexual health charities. Participants were called on to ask friends to sponsor them per minute of masturbation. The association's aim is to create a 'clearer masturbation conscience' for all.

2001 Tring, a Dutch telephone dealership, caused a stir by giving away free vibrators with its mobile phones. The firm, based in The Hague, gave out a free Nokia handset plus a sex toy when customers connected to the KPN network. Both KPN and phone-maker Nokia urged Tring to drop the deal.

2001 Gary Kremen, the rightful owner of the web domain 'sex.com' was awarded $65 million in a US court. His victory followed a fifteen-year suit against Stephen Cohen, who had attempted to 'hijack' the site name. Given porn's hold over the Net, the domain name is estimated to be worth as much as $100 million.

2001 The world's first two babies conceived from both frozen eggs and frozen sperm were born in Singapore. The doctor who pioneered the technique, Cheng Li Chang, said it gave hope to couples where both partners had fertility problems.

2001 Following the lead of countries such as the Netherlands and Sweden, Germany began legalising gay marriages. The new legislation would allow gay couples to exchange vows at partnership ceremonies and receive some heterosexual marriage rights.

2001 According to research, women who emulate Mrs Robinson from *The Graduate* and seduce younger men leave them with lasting emotional damage. A survey of two thousand five hundred men showed that those who had had sex with an older woman were up to three times more likely to suffer psychiatric problems, and up to four times more likely to harm themselves in adulthood.

2001 The 'reality TV' programme *Temptation Island* arrived on US screens. A group of attractive young men and women, all of whom had partners 'in the outside world', were thrown together with only the cameras for company. Voyeurs waited to see how long all that fidelity could last.

2001 The latest edition of Britain's *Policing Diversity Handbook* instructed police officers not to refer to gays and lesbians as homosexual because it 'criminalises' them. The manual states that 'Homosexual [is] a medical term used to criminalise lesbians, gay men and bisexuals in the nineteenth century. The term should generally be avoided, although some older LGB people may describe themselves in this way.'

Contributors' biographies

Yasmin Alibhai-Brown is a very serious person. She writes very serious weekly columns in the *Independent* and is the author of several equally serious books, including *Who Do we Think We Are? Imagining the New Britain* (2001), *Mixed Feelings: The Complex Lives of Mixed Race Britons* (2001) and *After Multiculturalism* (2000). She describes herself (to the irritation of many) as female, Muslim (not a very good one), black, Asian, British and a Londoner. Married to a delightful Englishman, she is currently confusing the population by being nice to the English.

Stephen Bayley is a well-known authority on design and popular culture, the creator of London's Design Museum and the author of many books, including *Taste* (1991), *Harley Earl and the Dream Machine* (1983), *The Albert Memorial* (1981) and *Labour Camp* (1998), as well as countless articles and broadcasts. In 1989 he was made a Chevalier de l'Ordre des Arts et des Lettres by the French Minister of Culture.

Trevor Beattie was born in Birmingham a very long time ago. Since then, he's moved to London, where his advertising campaigns have provoked a series of unsightly media kerfuffles and a marked increase in product sales. Wonderbra, Nissan Micra, Pretty Polly, FCUK, PlayStation and the Labour Party have kept Beattie in work, and tabloid editors in punning-headline heaven for over a decade.

He occasionally writes for *The Guardian*, *GQ*, *Esquire* and *Campaign magazine*. His chief pastime is writing adverts.

Rabbi Schmuley Boteach is the author of ten books, including the international best-seller *Kosher Sex*. His weekly essays and columns are read by a vast following. An internationally acclaimed speaker, Rabbi Boteach won *The Times* Preacher of the Year Competition in London. He lives in New Jersey with his wife and their seven children.

Kate Copstick has been a lawyer, copywriter, actress, stand-up, singer, television presenter, director, producer and writer. She is a theatre critic and feature writer for the *Scotsman*, writes regularly for *The Erotic Review*, is the author of *The Illustrated Book of Sapphic Sex* and is presently completing *Pleasure/Pain: The Art of BDSM*.

Lesley Downer went to Japan twenty years ago and has been trying to escape ever since. Her books on Japan include *On the Narrow Road of the Deep North* and *Geisha: The Secret History of a Vanishing World* (2000), published in the US as *Women of the Pleasure Quarters: The Secret History of the Geisha* (2001). She has also presented television programmes on Japan and writes for the *Wall Street Journal* and the *Financial Times*.

Dr David Gaimster FSA, AMA, MIFA is an Assistant Keeper in

the Department of Medieval and Modern Europe at the British Museum, London, responsible for post-medieval archaeology and social history, including the museum's nineteenth-century Secretum collection. He has written about the collection in *History Today* (September 2000) and compiled a biography of the Victorian antique erotica collector, George Witt, for the *New Dictionary of National Biography*.

Jonathon Green began his sexual career as letters editor of *Fiesta* magazine and climaxed with the novel *Diary of a Masseuse* (1976). The oral history: *It: Sex since the Sixties* (1992) side-stepped vulgar interest en route to the remainder shops. He is now 'dirty words' columnist for *The Erotic Review* and pursues linguistic voyeurism as a lexicographer of slang.

Christopher Hart is the author of two highly acclaimed novels, *The Harvest* (2000) and *Rescue Me* (2001). His third, *Julia*, was published in September 2001. His journalism includes travel articles and book reviews, as well as more gruelling assignments, such as attending a suburban orgy in Hertfordshire and interviewing Lord Archer. He is Literary Editor of *The Erotic Review*. His parents do not approve.

Philip Hensher was born in London in 1965 where he still lives. His novels include *Kitchen Venom*, 1996, which won the Somerset Maugham award, and *Pleasured*,

1998. His new novel, *The Mulberry Empire*, is published by Harper Collins in 2002.

Dr Ronald Hyam is Emeritus Reader in British Imperial History at the University of Cambridge. His book *Empire and Sexuality: the British Experience* was first published in 1990, and he is a recognised authority on the history of sexuality.

Catherine Johns has been a curator at the British Museum for over 30 years and is an authority on Roman art and material culture, in particular jewellery and silver plate. She is the author of eight books, including *Sex or Symbol: Erotic Images of Greece and Rome* (1982), and of over a hundred articles in scholarly journals.

Rowley Leigh was brought up in various areas of England and Ireland and read English at Christ's College, Cambridge. He failed his degree, pretended to write a novel, then farmed for a few years before coming to London. He got a job as a grill chef at the Joe Allen Restaurant and then worked for the Roux brothers for several years. He became head chef of Kensington Place in 1987. He is still there and is the cookery writer of the *Sunday Telegraph* and the author of *No Place Like Home*, a prize-winning cookery book.

Nathan McLaughlin – the original one-handed typist – discovered the dark side of the Internet in 1998. He has since been on a singular mission with the apparent goal of registering himself blind. A true connoisseur of pornography, Nathan is the Cyrano de Bergerac of cybersex and the most dedicated compiler of

pixellated filth never to have been inside a maximum security prison.

James Maclean was educated at Eton and Edinburgh. He formed the Victorian Paintings Department at Sotheby's, worked for Wildenstein's, then opened his own gallery specialising in Modern British art. Later he helped found The Erotic Print Society and *The Erotic Review*. His father was Fitzroy Maclean, author of *Eastern Approaches* (1991) and allegedly role model for James Bond.

John Pawson returned to England, after teaching in Japan and travelling extensively, to study at the AA in London. He set up his own practice in 1981. To date, his varied architectural career has ranged from a compact apartment for the writer Bruce Chatwin to Calvin Klein's flagship store in Manhattan. Current projects include a new Cistercian monastery & his most recent book, *Living & Eating* (2001), explores how the philosophy of simplicity, which informs all of his architecture, may be applied in the kitchen.

Christopher Peachment was Film Editor for *Time Out* magazine in the 1980s, and later Deputy Literary and Arts Editor for *The Times*. His first novel, based on the life of Caravaggio, is published by Picador in February 2002. He is currently writing a novel about Andrew Marvell and the Earl of Rochester.

Will Self is the author of three short-story collections, *The Quantity Theory of Insanity*, *Grey Area*, and *Tough Tough Toys for Tough Tough Boys*; novellas *Cock & Bull* and *The Sweet Smell of Psychosis*; and three novels *My*

Idea of Fun, *Great Apes* and *How the Dead Live*. He has written for countless publications is a regular broadcaster on television and radio. Self was sacked from a job on the *Observer* in London for taking heroin while on assignment aboard the Prime Minister's plane.

Lizzie Speller is a freelance writer, poet and librettist, who has contributed to publications as diverse as the *Observer*, *The Erotic Review*, *Woman's Journal* and the *Big Issue*, as well as to features for BBC Radio 4. Since reading Classics at Cambridge she has been discovering 101 things to do with a dead emperor and is currently completing her own book on Hadrian, due for publication by Headline in 2002.

Dave Tomlinson is vicar of St Luke's Church in Holloway, North London, and founder of 'Holy Joes', an unconventional Christian group that meets in a London pub. He is a widely travelled speaker and the author of *The Post-Evangelical* (1995). Dave and his wife Pat have three grown-up children and two grandchildren.

Evelyn Welch is Reader in History of Art at the University of Sussex and author of *Art in Renaissance Italy* (2000) and *Art and Authority in Renaissance Milan* (1995). She is currently working on a book on Renaissance shopping.

Xiao Jiao has contributed her thoughts on sex life in ancient China to a variety of specialist publications. She is ninety-five years old and lives in the Lake District with her athletic jazz musician boyfriend.

Index

Acknowledgements and credits

PICTURE CREDITS

The publishers and the Erotic Print Society would like to thank the following for permission to reproduce the illustrations listed below. Every care has been taken to trace copyright holders. However, if there are any omissions we will be happy to rectify them in future editions.

Advertising Archives: *224–5*

Akehurst Bureau: *1, 268, 281, 295, 304, 327, 332–3, 339, 340* (Trevor Watson); *244* (Richard Sandon-Smith); *245, 278* (Ian Sanderson); *247* (Walter Hirsch); *373* (Lewis Morley)

Allen Jones: *334*

Antonia Mulas/Archaeological Museum of Naples: *29*

Arena Images: *254* (Berg Días), *255* (Anna León)

Anthony Blake Photo Library: *239* (Amanda Heywood)

Trevor Beattie: *226–7, 228–9, 230–231*

Bridgeman Art Library: *2–3 (National Gallery, London), 10 (Private Collection © DACS 2001), 14 (Bibliotheque Nationale, Paris), 20–21 (Louvre), 23 (Stapleton Collection, UK), 30 (Staatliche Antikensammlung und Glyptothek, Munich), 37 (Ashmolean Museum), 48–9 (Victoria & Albert Museum), 58 (Rubenshuis, Antwerp), 61 (Hamburg Kunsthalle), 64 (Private Collection © ADAGP, Paris and DACS, London 2001), 92–3 (Kunsthistorisches Museum, Vienna), 109 (Private Collection © DACS 2001), 120–21 (Musee des Beaux-Arts, Bordeaux), 122 (Fitzwilliam Museum), 186–7 (Phillips, The International Fine Art Auctioneers), 192–3 (Private Collection), 194 (Private Collection © Succession Picasso/DACS 2001), 201 (Stapleton Collection, UK), 211 (Private Collection), 212–13 (Gemaldegalerie, Dresden), 214–15 (Galleria degli Uffizi), 242–3 (Musée d'Orsay, Paris, France), 250 (Stapleton Collection, UK), 251 (Zuloaga Collection, Zumaya, Guipuzcoa, Spain © DACS 2001), 275 (Musée Bonnat, Bayonne), 288 (Private Collection © ADAGP, Paris and DACS, London 2001), 313 (Private Collection), 315 (Musée d'Orsay), 322–3 (Osterreichisches Galerie, Vienna), 358 (Naturhistorisches Museum, Vienna)*

British Museum: *33, 34, 127, 130, 131, 133, 135, 136, 138, 139, 204–5, 219, 221, 362*

Corbis: *9, 24, 25, 73, 257*

Eric Gill Estate: *55, 148*

Erotic Print Society: *13, 17, 18, 22, 38, 41, 42, 45, 46, 51, 52, 53, 74, 79, 81, 82–3, 88, 91, 94, 97, 98, 100, 104, 106, 110, 113, 115, 116, 117, 125, 141, 142, 145, 147, 151, 152, 153, 154, 155, 156, 159, 160, 161, 162, 165, 166, 169, 170 (© ADAGP, Paris & DACS, London 2001), 171, 172, 174–5, 177, 179, 180, 181, 182–3, 185, 189, 190–91, 198, 202–3, 208–9, 218, 249, 272, 276–7, 281, 283, 287, 290, 292, 297, 299, 300–1, 303, 306, 307, 310, 316, 319, 321, 324, 337, 338, 341, 345, 348*

Hirschsprung Collection: *271*

Hulton Getty: *363, 371*

Illustration Ltd: *384* (Gray Jolliffe)

Images of India/Link: *69*

Interflora: *6*

Kobal Collection: *70, 258, 261* top and bottom, *265, 289, 372*

Mary Evans Picture Library: *366, 369*

Julian Murphy: *329, 330–1*

Tsuzen Nakajima: *206, 207*

John Pawson/*Minimum*, by Phaidon Press *233, 234, 235, 236–7*

Ronald Grant Archive: *260, 261* middle, *262–3, 264, 266, 267*

Scala: *63*

Sergio Rossi: *223*

Tony Stone: *103*

Tate Gallery: *87*

Vin Mag Archive: *356, 374*

Werner Forman Archive: *26*

www.tombraider.org/pictures (Eidos): *351*

PAGES 1: *Trevor Watson*

PAGES 2–3: *Agnolo Bronzino* An Allegory with Venus and Cupid *(c.1540–50)*

THE EROTIC PRINT SOCIETY

This book is published in conjunction with the Erotic Print Society and the publishers would like to thank the Society for providing the majority of the images in this book. Started in 1994, the EPS is now firmly established as the leading source of collectible erotica worldwide – from pocket-sized paperbacks to cased limited editions. www.eroticprints.org, or catalogue £5 from EPS, PO Box 10, Sevenoaks, Kent TN14 5FG UK

THE EROTIC REVIEW

Founded in 1995 as the EPS newsletter, *The Erotic Review* has fast become a national institution under Rowan Pelling's highly individual editorship. It now attracts a unique group of professional writers and illustrators who can at last explore human sexuality without the editorial constraints of more orthodox magazines. www.eroticreview.org.

First published in the United Kingdon in 2001 by Cassell & Co

Text copyright 'The Lotus Foot' © 1999 Xiao Jiao; 'Asian Sensuality' © 2001 Yasmin Alibhai-Brown; 'The Nooks of Lechery'; 'Taboo'; 'SXE' (with Trevor Beattie); 'Sexual Spaces' (with John Pawson); 'Dirty Pictures'; 'Dual Controls'; 'Le Con' 'Yes!'; 'Fetishism'; 'In Ecstasy' © 2001 Stephen Bayley; 'The Sin of Virginity' 2001 © Rabbi Schmuley Boteach; 'A Good Lay' © 2001 Kate Copstick; 'The Geisha' © 2001 Lesley Downer; 'Under Lock and Key' © 2001 Dr David Gaimster; 'Chronology of Sex' © 2001 Jonathon Green; 'Ancient Sex Manuals'; 'The Professionals' © 2001 Christopher Hart; 'Rhythm is a Dancer' © 2001 Philip Hensher; 'Does Size Matter?' © 2001 Dr Ronald Hyam; 'Eros and the Classical World' © 2001 Catherine Johns; 'Food and Sex' © Rowley Leigh 2001; 'Cybersex' © 2001 Nathan McLaughlin; 'Orgies' © 2001 James Maclean; 'A Story of Adultery' © 2001 Christopher Peachment; 'Shifting Erogenous Zones' © 2001 Lizzie Speller; 'The Divine Joke' © 2001 Reverend Dave Tomlinson; 'Facing Flesh' © Evelyn Welch 2001.

The moral rights of all the authors in the book have been asserted in accordance with the Copyright, Designs and Patents Act of 1988.

Design and layout copyright © Cassell & Co, 2001 All rights reserved. No part of this publication may be reproduced in any material form (including photocopying or storing it in any medium by electronic means and whether or not transiently or incidentally to some other use of this publication) without the written permission of the copyright owner, except in accordance with the provision of the Copyright, Designs and Patents Act, 1988, or under the terms of a licence issued by the Copyright Licensing Agency, 90 Tottenham Court Road, London WIP 9HE.

Permission to quote from Philip Larkin's 'Annus Mirabilis', published in *Collected Poems*, granted by Faber and Faber and Farrar, Straus & Giroux.

Applications for the copyright owner's written permission to reproduce any part of this publication should be addressed to the publisher.

The photographic acknowledgments on page 382 constitute an extension to this copyright page.

Distributed in the United States of America by Sterling Publishing Co., Inc. 387 Park Avenue South New York NY 10016-8810

A CIP catalogue record for this book is available from the British Library.

ISBN 030435 9467

Design Director David Rowley Designer Nigel Soper Copy Editor Anderley Moore Indexer Derek Copson

Printed and bound in Italy

Cassell & Co Orion House 5 Upper St Martin's Lane London WC2H 9EA